Apprising AI Driverless Cars

Practical Advances in
Artificial Intelligence and Machine Learning

Dr. Lance B. Eliot, MBA, PhD

Disclaimer: This book is presented solely for educational and entertainment purposes. The author and publisher are not offering it as legal, accounting, or other professional services advice. The author and publisher make no representations or warranties of any kind and assume no liabilities of any kind with respect to the accuracy or completeness of the contents and specifically disclaim any implied warranties of merchantability or fitness of use for a particular purpose. Neither the author nor the publisher shall be held liable or responsible to any person or entity with respect to any loss or incidental or consequential damages caused, or alleged to have been caused, directly or indirectly, by the information or programs contained herein. Every company is different and the advice and strategies contained herein may not be suitable for your situation.

 First Edition.

ISBN: 978-1-73-630317-7

DEDICATION

To my incredible daughter, Lauren, and my incredible son, Michael.

Forest fortuna adiuvat (from the Latin; good fortune favors the brave).

CONTENTS

Acknowledgments iii

Introduction 1

Chapters

1 Eliot Framework for AI Self-Driving Cars 13
2 Move Over and Self-Driving Cars 23
3 Crossing Chicken and Self-Driving Cars 33
4 Code Breaches and Self-Driving Cars 43
5 Car Paint Colors and Self-Driving Cars 53
6 Bait Cars and Self-Driving Cars 63
7 Jinxes and Self-Driving Cars 73
8 Bouldering and Self-Driving Cars 83
9 Drivers Speeding and Self-Driving Cars 93
10 Snitch On Drivers and Self-Driving Cars 105
11 Reprogramming Pedestrians and Self-Driving Cars 117
12 Points Of Failure and Self-Driving Cars 127
13 Minecraft and Self-Driving Cars 137
14 Add-on Options and Self-Driving Cars 147
15 Car Pile-Ups and Self-Driving Cars 159
16 Crossing Guards and Self-Driving Cars 171
17 Driving Robots and Self-Driving Cars 183
18 Rain Driving and Self-Driving Cars 193
19 Stop Signs and Self-Driving Cars 203
20 Cloud and Autonomous Vehicles 215
21 Opposition to Self-Driving Cars 225
22 Neophyte Testimonials and Self-Driving Cars 239
23 Verbal Commands and Self-Driving Cars 251
24 Computer Chip Shortages and Self-Driving Cars 263
25 Chasing Dogs and Self-Driving Cars 273
26 Rolling House and Self-Driving Cars 283
27 Multi-Clouds and Autonomous Vehicles 293
28 Steep Hills and Self-Driving Cars 303
29 Bootstrapping and Self-Driving Cars 313
30 Teenage Drivers and Self-Driving Cars 321

Appendix A: Teaching with this Material 333
Other Self-Driving Car Books by This Author 340
About the Author 389
Addendum 390

ACKNOWLEDGMENTS

I have been the beneficiary of advice and counsel by many friends, colleagues, family, investors, and many others. I want to thank everyone that has aided me throughout my career. I write from the heart and the head, having experienced first-hand what it means to have others around you that support you during the good times and the tough times.

To Warren Bennis, one of my doctoral advisors and ultimately a colleague, I offer my deepest thanks and appreciation, especially for his calm and insightful wisdom and support.

To Mark Stevens and his generous efforts toward funding and supporting the USC Stevens Center for Innovation.

To Lloyd Greif and the USC Lloyd Greif Center for Entrepreneurial Studies for their ongoing encouragement of founders and entrepreneurs.

To Peter Drucker, William Wang, Aaron Levie, Peter Kim, Jon Kraft, Cindy Crawford, Jenny Ming, Steve Milligan, Chis Underwood, Frank Gehry, Buzz Aldrin, Steve Forbes, Bill Thompson, Dave Dillon, Alan Fuerstman, Larry Ellison, Jim Sinegal, John Sperling, Mark Stevenson, Anand Nallathambi, Thomas Barrack, Jr., and many other innovators and leaders that I have met and gained mightily from doing so.

Thanks to Ed Trainor, Kevin Anderson, James Hickey, Wendell Jones, Ken Harris, DuWayne Peterson, Mike Brown, Jim Thornton, Abhi Beniwal, Al Biland, John Nomura, Eliot Weinman, John Desmond, and many others for their unwavering support during my career.

And most of all thanks as always to Lauren and Michael, for their ongoing support and for having seen me writing and heard much of this material during the many months involved in writing it. To their patience and willingness to listen.

INTRODUCTION

This is a book that provides the newest innovations and the latest Artificial Intelligence (AI) advances about the emerging nature of AI-based autonomous self-driving driverless cars. Via recent advances in Artificial Intelligence (AI) and Machine Learning (ML), we are nearing the day when vehicles can control themselves and will not require and nor rely upon human intervention to perform their driving tasks (or, that allow for human intervention, but only *require* human intervention in very limited ways).

Similar to my other related books, which I describe in a moment and list the chapters in the Appendix A of this book, I am particularly focused on those advances that pertain to self-driving cars. The phrase "autonomous vehicles" is often used to refer to any kind of vehicle, whether it is ground-based or in the air or sea, and whether it is a cargo hauling trailer truck or a conventional passenger car. Though the aspects described in this book are certainly applicable to all kinds of autonomous vehicles, I am focused more so here on cars.

For this book, I am going to borrow my introduction from those companion books, since it does a good job of laying out the landscape of self-driving cars and my overall viewpoints on the topic.

INTRODUCTION TO SELF-DRIVING CARS

This is a book about self-driving cars. Someday in the future, we'll all have self-driving cars and this book will perhaps seem antiquated, but right now, we are at the forefront of the self-driving car wave. Daily news bombards us with flashes of new announcements by one car maker or another and leaves the impression that within the next few weeks or maybe months that the self-driving car will be here. A casual non-technical reader would assume from these news flashes that in we must be on the cusp of a true self-driving car.

We are still quite a distance from having a true self-driving car. A true self-driving car is akin to a moonshot. In the same manner that getting us to the moon was an incredible feat, likewise, is achieving a true self-driving car. Anybody that suggests or even brashly states that the true self-driving car is nearly here should be viewed with great skepticism. Indeed, you'll see that I often tend to use the word "hogwash" or "crock" when I assess much of the decidedly ***fake news*** about self-driving cars.

Indeed, I've been writing a popular blog post about self-driving cars and hitting hard on those that try to wave their hands and pretend that we are on the imminent verge of true self-driving cars. For many years, I've been known as the AI Insider. Besides writing about AI, I also develop AI software. I do what I describe. It also gives me insights into what others that are doing AI are really doing versus what it is said they are doing.

Many faithful readers had asked me to pull together my insightful short essays and put them into another book, which you are now holding.

For those of you that have been reading my essays over the years, this collection not only puts them together into one handy package, I also updated the essays and added new material. For those of you that are new to the topic of self-driving cars and AI, I hope you find these essays approachable and informative. I also tend to have a writing style with a bit of a voice, and so you'll see that I am times have a wry sense of humor and poke at conformity.

As a former professor and founder of an AI research lab, I for many years wrote in the formal language of academic writing. I published in referred journals and served as an editor for several AI journals. This writing here is not of the nature, and I have adopted a different and more informal style for these essays. That being said, I also do mention from time-to-time more rigorous material on AI and encourage you all to dig into those deeper and more formal materials if so interested.

For those of you that are reading this book and have a penchant for writing code, you might consider taking a look at the open-source code available for self-driving cars. This is a handy place to start learning how to develop AI for self-driving cars. There are also many new educational courses spring forth. There is a growing body of those wanting to learn about and develop self-driving cars, and a growing body of colleges, labs, and other avenues by which you can learn about self-driving cars.

This book will provide a foundation of aspects that I think will get you ready for those kinds of more advanced training opportunities. If you've already taken those classes, you'll likely find these essays especially interesting as they offer a perspective that I am betting few other instructors or faculty offered to you. These are challenging essays that ask you to think beyond the conventional about self-driving cars.

THE MOTHER OF ALL AI PROJECTS

In June 2017, Apple CEO Tim Cook came out and finally admitted that Apple has been working on a self-driving car. As you'll see in my essays, Apple was enmeshed in secrecy about their self-driving car efforts. We have only been able to read the tea leaves and guess at what Apple has been up to. The notion of an iCar has been floating for quite a while, and self-driving engineers and researchers have been signing tight-lipped Non-Disclosure Agreements (NDA's) to work on projects at Apple that were as shrouded in mystery as any military invasion plans might be.

Tim Cook said something that many others in the Artificial Intelligence (AI) field have been saying, namely, the creation of a self-driving car has got to be the mother of all AI projects. In other words, it is in fact a tremendous moonshot for AI. If a self-driving car can be crafted and the AI works as we hope, it means that we have made incredible strides with AI and that therefore it opens many other worlds of potential breakthrough accomplishments that AI can solve.

Is this hyperbole? Am I just trying to make AI seem like a miracle worker and so provide self-aggrandizing statements for those of us writing the AI software for self-driving cars? No, it is not hyperbole. Developing a true self-driving car is really, really, really hard to do. Let me take a moment to explain why. As a side note, I realize that the Apple CEO is known for at times uttering hyperbole, and he had previously said for example that the year 2012 was "the mother of all years," and he had said that the release of iOS 10 was "the mother of all releases" – all of which does suggest he likes to use the handy "mother of" expression. But, I assure you, in terms of true self-driving cars, he has hit the nail on the head. For sure.

When you think about a moonshot and how we got to the moon, there are some identifiable characteristics and those same aspects can be applied to creating a true self-driving car. You'll notice that I keep putting the word "true" in front of the self-driving car expression. I do so because as per my essay about the various levels of self-driving cars, there are some self-driving cars that are only somewhat of a self-driving car. The somewhat versions are ones that require a human driver to be ready to intervene. In my view, that's not a true self-driving car. A true self-driving car is one that requires no human driver intervention at all. It is a car that can entirely undertake via automation the driving task without any human driver needed. This is the essence of what is known as a Level 5 self-driving car. We are currently at the Level 2 and Level 3 mark, and not yet at Level 5.

Getting to the moon involved aspects such as having big stretch goals, incremental progress, experimentation, innovation, and so on. Let's review how this applied to the moonshot of the bygone era, and how it applies to the self-driving car moonshot of today.

Big Stretch Goal

Trying to take a human and deliver the human to the moon, and bring them back, safely, was an extremely large stretch goal at the time. No one knew whether it could be done. The technology wasn't available yet. The cost was huge. The determination would need to be fierce. Etc. To reach a Level 5 self-driving car is going to be the same. It is a big stretch goal. We can readily get to the Level 3, and we are able to see the Level 4 just up ahead, but a Level 5 is still an unknown as to if it is doable. It should eventually be doable and in the same way that we thought we'd eventually get to the moon, but when it will occur is a different story.

Incremental Progress

Getting to the moon did not happen overnight in one fell swoop. It took years and years of incremental progress to get there. Likewise, for self-driving cars. Google has famously been striving to get to the Level 5, and pretty much been willing to forgo dealing with the intervening levels, but most of the other self-driving car makers are doing the incremental route. Let's get a good Level 2 and a somewhat Level 3 going. Then, let's improve the Level 3 and get a somewhat Level 4 going. Then, let's improve the Level 4 and finally arrive at a Level 5. This seems to be the prevalent way that we are going to achieve the true self-driving car.

Experimentation

You likely know that there were various experiments involved in perfecting the approach and technology to get to the moon. As per making incremental progress, we first tried to see if we could get a rocket to go into space and safety return, then put a monkey in there, then with a human, then we went all the way to the moon but didn't land, and finally we arrived at the mission that actually landed on the moon.

Self-driving cars are the same way. We are doing simulations of self-driving cars. We do testing of self-driving cars on private land under controlled situations.

We do testing of self-driving cars on public roadways, often having to meet regulatory requirements including for example having an engineer or equivalent in the car to take over the controls if needed. And so on. Experiments big and small are needed to figure out what works and what doesn't.

Innovation

There are already some advances in AI that are allowing us to progress toward self-driving cars. We are going to need even more advances. Innovation in all aspects of technology are going to be required to achieve a true self-driving car. By no means do we already have everything in-hand that we need to get there. Expect new inventions and new approaches, new algorithms, etc.

Setbacks

Most of the pundits are avoiding talking about potential setbacks in the progress toward self-driving cars. Getting to the moon involved many setbacks, some of which you never have heard of and were buried at the time so as to not dampen enthusiasm and funding for getting to the moon. A recurring theme in many of my included essays is that there are going to be setbacks as we try to arrive at a true self-driving car. Take a deep breath and be ready. I just hope the setbacks don't completely stop progress. I am sure that it will cause progress to alter in a manner that we've not yet seen in the self-driving car field. I liken the self-driving car of today to the excitement everyone had for Uber when it first got going. Today, we have a different view of Uber and with each passing day there are more regulations to the ride sharing business and more concerns raised. The darling child only stays a darling until finally that child acts up. It will happen the same with self-driving cars.

SELF-DRIVING CARS CHALLENGES

But what exactly makes things so hard to have a true self-driving car, you might be asking. You have seen cruise control for years and years. You've lately seen cars that can do parallel parking. You've seen YouTube videos of Tesla drivers that put their hands out the window as their car zooms along the highway, and seen to therefore be in a self-driving car. Aren't we just needing to put a few more sensors onto a car and then we'll have in-hand a true self-driving car? Nope.

Consider for a moment the nature of the driving task. We don't just let anyone at any age drive a car. Worldwide, most countries won't license a driver until the age of 18, though many do allow a learner's permit at the age of 15 or 16. Some suggest that a younger age would be physically too small to reach the controls of the car. Though this might be the case, we could easily adjust the controls to allow for younger aged and thus smaller stature. It's not their physical size that matters. It's their cognitive development that matters.

To drive a car, you need to be able to reason about the car, what the car can and cannot do. You need to know how to operate the car. You need to know about how other cars on the road drive. You need to know what is allowed in driving such as speed limits and driving within marked lanes. You need to be able to react to situations and be able to avoid getting into accidents. You need to ascertain when to hit your brakes, when to steer clear of a pedestrian, and how to keep from ramming that motorcyclist that just cut you off.

Many of us had taken courses on driving. We studied about driving and took driver training. We had to take a test and pass it to be able to drive. The point being that though most adults take the driving task for granted, and we often "mindlessly" drive our cars, there is a significant amount of cognitive effort that goes into driving a car. After a while, it becomes second nature. You don't especially think about how you drive, you just do it. But, if you watch a novice driver, say a teenager learning to drive, you suddenly realize that there is a lot more complexity to it than we seem to realize.

Furthermore, driving is a very serious task. I recall when my daughter and son first learned to drive. They are both very conscientious people. They wanted to make sure that whatever they did, they did well, and that they did not harm anyone. Every day, when you get into a car, it is probably around 4,000 pounds of hefty metal and plastics (about two tons), and it is a lethal weapon. Think about it. You drive down the street in an object that weighs two tons and with the engine it can accelerate and ram into anything you want to hit. The damage a car can inflict is very scary. Both my children were surprised that they were being given the right to maneuver this monster of a beast that could cause tremendous harm entirely by merely letting go of the steering wheel for a moment or taking your eyes off the road.

In fact, in the United States alone there are about 40,000 deaths per year by auto accidents, which is more than 100 per day. Given that there are about 263 million cars in the United States, I am actually more amazed that the number of fatalities is not a lot higher.

During my morning commute, I look at all the thousands of cars on the freeway around me, and I think that if all of them decided to go zombie and drive in a crazy maniac way, there would be many people dead. Somehow, incredibly, each day, most people drive relatively safely. To me, that's a miracle right there. Getting millions and millions of people to be safe and sane when behind the wheel of a two-ton mobile object, it's a feat that we as a society should admire with pride.

So, hopefully you are in agreement that the driving task requires a great deal of cognition. You don't' need to be especially smart to drive a car, and we've done quite a bit to make car driving viable for even the average dolt. There isn't an IQ test that you need to take to drive a car. If you can read and write, and pass a test, you pretty much can legally drive a car. There are of course some that drive a car and are not legally permitted to do so, plus there are private areas such as farms where drivers are young, but for public roadways in the United States, you can be generally of average intelligence (or less) and be able to legally drive.

This though makes it seem like the cognitive effort must not be much. If the cognitive effort was truly hard, wouldn't we only have Einstein's that could drive a car? We have made sure to keep the driving task as simple as we can, by making the controls easy and relatively standardized, and by having roads that are relatively standardized, and so on. It is as though Disneyland has put their Autopia into the real-world, by us all as a society agreeing that roads will be a certain way, and we'll all abide by the various rules of driving.

A modest cognitive task by a human is still something that stymies AI. You certainly know that AI has been able to beat chess players and be good at other kinds of games. This type of narrow cognition is not what car driving is about. Car driving is much wider. It requires knowledge about the world, which a chess playing AI system does not need to know. The cognitive aspects of driving are on the one hand seemingly simple, but at the same time require layer upon layer of knowledge about cars, people, roads, rules, and a myriad of other "common sense" aspects. We don't have any AI systems today that have that same kind of breadth and depth of awareness and knowledge.

As revealed in my essays, the self-driving car of today is using trickery to do particular tasks. It is all very narrow in operation. Plus, it currently assumes that a human driver is ready to intervene. It is like a child that we have taught to stack blocks, but we are needed to be right there in case the child stacks them too high and they begin to fall over.

AI of today is brittle, it is narrow, and it does not approach the cognitive abilities of humans. This is why the true self-driving car is somewhere out in the future.

Another aspect to the driving task is that it is not solely a mind exercise. You do need to use your senses to drive. You use your eyes as vision sensors to see the road ahead. You vision capability is like a streaming video, which your brain needs to continually analyze as you drive. Where is the road? Is there a pedestrian in the way? Is there another car ahead of you? Your senses are relying a flood of info to your brain. Self-driving cars are trying to do the same, by using cameras, radar, ultrasound, and lasers. This is an attempt at mimicking how humans have senses and sensory apparatus.

Thus, the driving task is mental and physical. You use your senses, you use your arms and legs to manipulate the controls of the car, and you use your brain to assess the sensory info and direct your limbs to act upon the controls of the car. This all happens instantly. If you've ever perhaps gotten something in your eye and only had one eye available to drive with, you suddenly realize how dependent upon vision you are. If you have a broken foot with a cast, you suddenly realize how hard it is to control the brake pedal and the accelerator. If you've taken medication and your brain is maybe sluggish, you suddenly realize how much mental strain is required to drive a car.

An AI system that plays chess only needs to be focused on playing chess. The physical aspects aren't important because usually a human moves the chess pieces or the chessboard is shown on an electronic display. Using AI for a more life-and-death task such as analyzing MRI images of patients, this again does not require physical capabilities and instead is done by examining images of bits.

Driving a car is a true life-and-death task. It is a use of AI that can easily and at any moment produce death. For those colleagues of mine that are developing this AI, as am I, we need to keep in mind the somber aspects of this. We are producing software that will have in its virtual hands the lives of the occupants of the car, and the lives of those in other nearby cars, and the lives of nearby pedestrians, etc. Chess is not usually a life-or-death matter.

Driving is all around us. Cars are everywhere. Most of today's AI applications involve only a small number of people. Or, they are behind the scenes and we as humans have other recourse if the AI messes up. AI that is driving a car at 80 miles per hour on a highway had better not mess up. The consequences are grave.

Multiply this by the number of cars, if we could put magically self-driving into every car in the USA, we'd have AI running in the 263 million cars. That's a lot of AI spread around. This is AI on a massive scale that we are not doing today and that offers both promise and potential peril.

There are some that want AI for self-driving cars because they envision a world without any car accidents. They envision a world in which there is no car congestion and all cars cooperate with each other. These are wonderful utopian visions.

They are also very misleading. The adoption of self-driving cars is going to be incremental and not overnight. We cannot economically just junk all existing cars. Nor are we going to be able to affordably retrofit existing cars. It is more likely that self-driving cars will be built into new cars and that over many years of gradual replacement of existing cars that we'll see the mix of self-driving cars become substantial in the real-world.

In these essays, I have tried to offer technological insights without being overly technical in my description, and also blended the business, societal, and economic aspects too. Technologists need to consider the non-technological impacts of what they do. Non-technologists should be aware of what is being developed.

We all need to work together to collectively be prepared for the enormous disruption and transformative aspects of true self-driving cars.

WHAT THIS BOOK PROVIDES

What does this book provide to you? It introduces many of the key elements about self-driving cars and does so with an AI based perspective. I weave together technical and non-technical aspects, readily going from being concerned about the cognitive capabilities of the driving task and how the technology is embodying this into self-driving cars, and in the next breath I discuss the societal and economic aspects.

They are all intertwined because that's the way reality is. You cannot separate out the technology per se, and instead must consider it within the milieu of what is being invented and innovated, and do so with a mindset towards the contemporary mores and culture that shape what we are doing and what we hope to do.

WHY THIS BOOK

I wrote this book to try and bring to the public view many aspects about self-driving cars that nobody seems to be discussing.

For business leaders that are either involved in making self-driving cars or that are going to leverage self-driving cars, I hope that this book will enlighten you as to the risks involved and ways in which you should be strategizing about how to deal with those risks.

For entrepreneurs, startups and other businesses that want to enter into the self-driving car market that is emerging, I hope this book sparks your interest in doing so, and provides some sense of what might be prudent to pursue.

For researchers that study self-driving cars, I hope this book spurs your interest in the risks and safety issues of self-driving cars, and also nudges you toward conducting research on those aspects.

For students in computer science or related disciplines, I hope this book will provide you with interesting and new ideas and material, for which you might conduct research or provide some career direction insights for you.

For AI companies and high-tech companies pursuing self-driving cars, this book will hopefully broaden your view beyond just the mere coding and development needed to make self-driving cars.

For all readers, I hope that you will find the material in this book to be stimulating. Some of it will be repetitive of things you already know. But I am pretty sure that you'll also find various eureka moments whereby you'll discover a new technique or approach that you had not earlier thought of. I am also betting that there will be material that forces you to rethink some of your current practices.

I am not saying you will suddenly have an epiphany and change what you are doing. I do think though that you will reconsider or perhaps revisit what you are doing.

For anyone choosing to use this book for teaching purposes, please take a look at my suggestions for doing so, as described in the Appendix. I have found the material handy in courses that I have taught, and likewise other faculty have told me that they have found the material handy, in some cases as extended readings and in other instances as a core part of their course (depending on the nature of the class).

In my writing for this book, I have tried carefully to blend both the practitioner and the academic styles of writing.

It is not as abstract as is typical academic journal writing, but at the same time offers depth by going into the nuances and trade-offs of various practices.

The word "deep" is in vogue today, meaning getting deeply into a subject or topic, and so is the word "unpack" which means to tease out the underlying aspects of a subject or topic. I have sought to offer material that addresses an issue or topic by going relatively deeply into it and make sure that it is well unpacked.

In any book about AI, it is difficult to use our everyday words without having some of them be misinterpreted. Specifically, it is easy to anthropomorphize AI. When I say that an AI system "knows" something, I do not want you to construe that the AI system has sentience and "knows" in the same way that humans do. They aren't that way, as yet. I have tried to use quotes around such words from time-to-time to emphasize that the words I am using should not be misinterpreted to ascribe true human intelligence to the AI systems that we know of today. If I used quotes around all such words, the book would be very difficult to read, and so I am doing so judiciously. Please keep that in mind as you read the material, thanks.

Some of the material is time-based in terms of covering underway activities, and though some of it might decay, nonetheless I believe you'll find the material useful and informative.

COMPANION BOOKS BY DR. ELIOT

1. **"Introduction to Driverless Self-Driving Cars"** by Dr. Lance Eliot
2. **"Innovation and Thought Leadership on Self-Driving Driverless Cars"**
3. **"Advances in AI and Autonomous Vehicles: Cybernetic Self-Driving Cars"**
4. **"Self-Driving Cars: The Mother of All AI Projects"** by Dr. Lance Eliot
5. **"New Advances in AI Autonomous Driverless Self-Driving Cars"**
6. **"AV Driverless Self-Driving Cars & AI"** by Dr. Lance Eliot and Michael B. Eliot
7. **"Transformative Artificial Intelligence Driverless Self-Driving Cars"**
8. **"Disruptive Artificial Intelligence and Driverless Self-Driving Cars"**
9. **"State-of-the-Art AI Driverless Self-Driving Cars"** by Dr. Lance Eliot
10. **"Top Trends in AI Self-Driving Cars"** by Dr. Lance Eliot
11. **"AI Innovations and Self-Driving Cars"** by Dr. Lance Eliot
12. **"Crucial Advances for AI Driverless Cars"** by Dr. Lance Eliot
13. **"Sociotechnical Insights and AI Driverless Cars"** by Dr. Lance Eliot.
14. **"Pioneering Advances for AI Driverless Cars"** by Dr. Lance Eliot
15. **"Leading Edge Trends for AI Driverless Cars"** by Dr. Lance Eliot
16. **"The Cutting Edge of AI Autonomous Cars"** by Dr. Lance Eliot
17. **"The Next Wave of AI Self-Driving Cars"** by Dr. Lance Eliot
18. **"Revolutionary Innovations of AI Driverless Cars"** by Dr. Lance Eliot
19. **"AI Self-Driving Cars Breakthroughs"** by Dr. Lance Eliot
20. **"Trailblazing Trends for AI Self-Driving Cars"** by Dr. Lance Eliot
21. **"Ingenious Strides for AI Driverless Cars"** by Dr. Lance Eliot
22. **"AI Self-Driving Cars Inventiveness"** by Dr. Lance Eliot
23. **"Visionary Secrets of AI Driverless Cars"** by Dr. Lance Eliot
24. **"Spearheading AI Self-Driving Cars"** by Dr. Lance Eliot
25. **"Spurring AI Self-Driving Cars"** by Dr. Lance Eliot
26. **"Avant-Garde AI Driverless Cars"** by Dr. Lance Eliot
27. **"AI Self-Driving Cars Evolvement"** by Dr. Lance Eliot
28. **"AI Driverless Cars Chrysalis"** by Dr. Lance Eliot
29. **"Boosting AI Autonomous Cars"** by Dr. Lance Eliot
30. **"AI Self-Driving Cars Trendsetting"** by Dr. Lance Eliot
31. **"AI Autonomous Cars Forefront"** by Dr. Lance Eliot
32. **"AI Autonomous Cars Emergence"** by Dr. Lance Eliot
33. **"AI Autonomous Cars Progress"** by Dr. Lance Eliot
34. **"AI Self-Driving Cars Prognosis"** by Dr. Lance Eliot
35. **"AI Self-Driving Cars Momentum"** by Dr. Lance Eliot
36. **"AI Self-Driving Cars Headway"** by Dr. Lance Eliot
37. **"AI Self-Driving Cars Vicissitude"** by Dr. Lance Eliot
38. **"AI Self-Driving Cars Autonomy"** by Dr. Lance Eliot
39. **"AI Driverless Cars Transmutation"** by Dr. Lance Eliot
40. **"AI Driverless Cars Potentiality"** by Dr. Lance Eliot
41. **"AI Driverless Cars Realities"** by Dr. Lance Eliot
42. **"AI Self-Driving Cars Materiality"** by Dr. Lance Eliot
43. **"AI Self-Driving Cars Accordance"** by Dr. Lance Eliot
44. **"AI Self-Driving Cars Equanimity"** by Dr. Lance Eliot
45. **"AI Self-Driving Cars Divulgement"** by Dr. Lance Eliot
46. **"AI Self-Driving Cars Consonance"** by Dr. Lance Eliot
47. **"Revelatory AI Self-Driving Cars"** by Dr. Lance Eliot
48. **"Edifying AI Self-Driving Cars"** by Dr. Lance Eliot
49. **"Apprising AI Driverless Cars"** by Dr. Lance Eliot

These books are available on Amazon and at other major global booksellers.

CHAPTER 1

ELIOT FRAMEWORK FOR AI SELF-DRIVING CARS

This chapter is a core foundational aspect for understanding AI self-driving cars and I have used this same chapter in several of my other books to introduce the reader to essential elements of this field. Once you've read this chapter, you'll be prepared to read the rest of the material since the foundational essence of the components of autonomous AI driverless self-driving cars will have been established for you.

When I give presentations about self-driving cars and teach classes on the topic, I have found it helpful to provide a framework around which the various key elements of self-driving cars can be understood and organized (see diagram at the end of this chapter). The framework needs to be simple enough to convey the overarching elements, but at the same time not so simple that it belies the true complexity of self-driving cars. As such, I am going to describe the framework here and try to offer in a thousand words (or more!) what the framework diagram itself intends to portray.

The core elements on the diagram are numbered for ease of reference. The numbering does not suggest any kind of prioritization of the elements. Each element is crucial. Each element has a purpose, and otherwise would not be included in the framework. For some self-driving cars, a particular element might be more important or somehow distinguished in comparison to other self-driving cars.

You could even use the framework to rate a particular self-driving car, doing so by gauging how well it performs in each of the elements of the framework. I will describe each of the elements, one at a time. After doing so, I'll discuss aspects that illustrate how the elements interact and perform during the overall effort of a self-driving car.

At the AI Self-Driving Car Institute, we use the framework to keep track of what we are working on, and how we are developing software that fills in what is needed to achieve Level 5 self-driving cars.

D-01: Sensor Capture

Let's start with the one element that often gets the most attention in the press about self-driving cars, namely, the sensory devices for a self-driving car.

On the framework, the box labeled as D-01 indicates "Sensor Capture" and refers to the processes of the self-driving car that involve collecting data from the myriad of sensors that are used for a self-driving car. The types of devices typically involved are listed, such as the use of mono cameras, stereo cameras, LIDAR devices, radar systems, ultrasonic devices, GPS, IMU, and so on.

These devices are tasked with obtaining data about the status of the self-driving car and the world around it. Some of the devices are continually providing updates, while others of the devices await an indication by the self-driving car that the device is supposed to collect data. The data might be first transformed in some fashion by the device itself, or it might instead be fed directly into the sensor capture as raw data. At that point, it might be up to the sensor capture processes to do transformations on the data. This all varies depending upon the nature of the devices being used and how the devices were designed and developed.

D-02: Sensor Fusion

Imagine that your eyeballs receive visual images, your nose receives odors, your ears receive sounds, and in essence each of your distinct sensory devices is getting some form of input. The input befits the nature of the device. Likewise, for a self-driving car, the cameras provide visual images, the radar returns radar reflections, and so on. Each device provides the data as befits what the device does.

At some point, using the analogy to humans, you need to merge together what your eyes see, what your nose smells, what your ears hear, and piece it all together into a larger sense of what the world is all about and what is happening around you. Sensor fusion is the action of taking the singular aspects from each of the devices and putting them together into a larger puzzle.

Sensor fusion is a tough task. There are some devices that might not be working at the time of the sensor capture. Or, there might some devices that are unable to report well what they have detected. Again, using a human analogy, suppose you are in a dark room and so your eyes cannot see much. At that point, you might need to rely more so on your ears and what you hear. The same is true for a self-driving car. If the cameras are obscured due to snow and sleet, it might be that the radar can provide a greater indication of what the external conditions consist of.

In the case of a self-driving car, there can be a plethora of such sensory devices. Each is reporting what it can. Each might have its difficulties. Each might have its limitations, such as how far ahead it can detect an object. All of these limitations need to be considered during the sensor fusion task.

D-03: Virtual World Model

For humans, we presumably keep in our minds a model of the world around us when we are driving a car. In your mind, you know that the car is going at say 60 miles per hour and that you are on a freeway.

You have a model in your mind that your car is surrounded by other cars, and that there are lanes to the freeway. Your model is not only based on what you can see, hear, etc., but also what you know about the nature of the world. You know that at any moment that car ahead of you can smash on its brakes, or the car behind you can ram into your car, or that the truck in the next lane might swerve into your lane.

The AI of the self-driving car needs to have a virtual world model, which it then keeps updated with whatever it is receiving from the sensor fusion, which received its input from the sensor capture.

D-04: System Action Plan

By having a virtual world model, the AI of the self-driving car is able to keep track of where the car is and what is happening around the car. In addition, the AI needs to determine what to do next. Should the self-driving car hit its brakes? Should the self-driving car stay in its lane or swerve into the lane to the left? Should the self-driving car accelerate or slow down?

A system action plan needs to be prepared by the AI of the self-driving car. The action plan specifies what actions should be taken. The actions need to pertain to the status of the virtual world model. Plus, the actions need to be realizable.

This realizability means that the AI cannot just assert that the self-driving car should suddenly sprout wings and fly. Instead, the AI must be bound by whatever the self-driving car can actually do, such as coming to a halt in a distance of X feet at a speed of Y miles per hour, rather than perhaps asserting that the self-driving car come to a halt in 0 feet as though it could instantaneously come to a stop while it is in motion.

D-05: Controls Activation

The system action plan is implemented by activating the controls of the car to act according to what the plan stipulates.

This might mean that the accelerator control is commanded to increase the speed of the car. Or, the steering control is commanded to turn the steering wheel 30 degrees to the left or right.

One question arises as to whether or not the controls respond as they are commanded to do. In other words, suppose the AI has commanded the accelerator to increase, but for some reason it does not do so. Or, maybe it tries to do so, but the speed of the car does not increase.

The controls activation feeds back into the virtual world model, and simultaneously the virtual world model is getting updated from the sensors, the sensor capture, and the sensor fusion. This allows the AI to ascertain what has taken place as a result of the controls being commanded to take some kind of action.

By the way, please keep in mind that though the diagram seems to have a linear progression to it, the reality is that these are all aspects of the self-driving car that are happening in parallel and simultaneously. The sensors are capturing data, meanwhile the sensor fusion is taking place, meanwhile the virtual model is being updated, meanwhile the system action plan is being formulated and reformulated, meanwhile the controls are being activated.

This is the same as a human being that is driving a car. They are eyeballing the road, meanwhile they are fusing in their mind the sights, sounds, etc., meanwhile their mind is updating their model of the world around them, meanwhile they are formulating an action plan of what to do, and meanwhile they are pushing their foot onto the pedals and steering the car. In the normal course of driving a car, you are doing all of these at once. I mention this so that when you look at the diagram, you will think of the boxes as processes that are all happening at the same time, and not as though only one happens and then the next.

They are shown diagrammatically in a simplistic manner to help comprehend what is taking place. You though should also realize that they are working in parallel and simultaneous with each other. This is a tough aspect in that the inter-element communications involve latency and other aspects that must be taken into account. There can be delays in one element updating and then sharing its latest status with other elements.

D-06: Automobile & CAN

Contemporary cars use various automotive electronics and a Controller Area Network (CAN) to serve as the components that underlie the driving aspects of a car.

There are Electronic Control Units (ECU's) which control subsystems of the car, such as the engine, the brakes, the doors, the windows, and so on.

The elements D-01, D-02, D-03, D-04, D-05 are layered on top of the D-06, and must be aware of the nature of what the D-06 is able to do and not do.

D-07: In-Car Commands

Humans are going to be occupants in self-driving cars. In a Level 5 self-driving car, there must be some form of communication that takes place between the humans and the self-driving car. For example, I go into a self-driving car and tell it that I want to be driven over to Disneyland, and along the way I want to stop at In-and-Out Burger. The self-driving car now parses what I've said and tries to then establish a means to carry out my wishes.

In-car commands can happen at any time during a driving journey. Though my example was about an in-car command when I first got into my self-driving car, it could be that while the self-driving car is carrying out the journey that I change my mind. Perhaps after getting stuck in traffic, I tell the self-driving car to forget about getting the burgers and just head straight over to the theme park. The self-driving car needs to be alert to in-car commands throughout the journey.

D-08: V2X Communications

We will ultimately have self-driving cars communicating with each other, doing so via V2V (Vehicle-to-Vehicle) communications. We will also have self-driving cars that communicate with the roadways and other aspects of the transportation infrastructure, doing so via V2I (Vehicle-to-Infrastructure).

The variety of ways in which a self-driving car will be communicating with other cars and infrastructure is being called V2X, whereby the letter X means whatever else we identify as something that a car should or would want to communicate with.

The V2X communications will be taking place simultaneous with everything else on the diagram, and those other elements will need to incorporate whatever it gleans from those V2X communications.

D-09: Deep Learning

The use of Deep Learning permeates all other aspects of the self-driving car. The AI of the self-driving car will be using deep learning to do a better job at the systems action plan, and at the control's activation, and at the sensor fusion, and so on.

Currently, the use of artificial neural networks is the most prevalent form of deep learning. Based on large swaths of data, the neural networks attempt to "learn" from the data and therefore direct the efforts of the self-driving car accordingly.

D-10: Tactical AI

Tactical AI is the element of dealing with the moment-to-moment driving of the self-driving car. Is the self-driving car staying in its lane of the freeway? Is the car responding appropriately to the controls commands? Are the sensory devices working?

For human drivers, the tactical equivalent can be seen when you watch a novice driver such as a teenager that is first driving. They are focused on the mechanics of the driving task, keeping their eye on the road while also trying to properly control the car.

D-11: Strategic AI

The Strategic AI aspects of a self-driving car are dealing with the larger picture of what the self-driving car is trying to do. If I had asked that the self-driving car take me to Disneyland, there is an overall journey map that needs to be kept and maintained.

There is an interaction between the Strategic AI and the Tactical AI. The Strategic AI is wanting to keep on the mission of the driving, while the Tactical AI is focused on the particulars underway in the driving effort.

If the Tactical AI seems to wander away from the overarching mission, the Strategic AI wants to see why and get things back on track. If the Tactical AI realizes that there is something amiss on the self-driving car, it needs to alert the Strategic AI accordingly and have an adjustment to the overarching mission that is underway.

D-12: Self-Aware AI

Very few of the self-driving cars being developed are including a Self-Aware AI element, which we at the Cybernetic Self-Driving Car Institute believe is crucial to Level 5 self-driving cars.

The Self-Aware AI element is intended to watch over itself, in the sense that the AI is making sure that the AI is working as intended. Suppose you had a human driving a car, and they were starting to drive erratically. Hopefully, their own self-awareness would make them realize they themselves are driving poorly, such as perhaps starting to fall asleep after having been driving for hours on end. If you had a passenger in the car, they might be able to alert the driver if the driver is starting to do something amiss.

This is exactly what the Self-Aware AI element tries to do, it becomes the overseer of the AI, and tries to detect when the AI has become faulty or confused, and then find ways to overcome the issue.

D-13: Economic

The economic aspects of a self-driving car are not per se a technology aspect of a self-driving car, but the economics do indeed impact the nature of a self-driving car. For example, the cost of outfitting a self-driving car with every kind of possible sensory device is prohibitive, and so choices need to be made about which devices are used. And, for those sensory devices chosen, whether they would have a full set of features or a more limited set of features.

We are going to have self-driving cars that are at the low-end of a consumer cost point, and others at the high-end of a consumer cost point. You cannot expect that the self-driving car at the low-end is going to be as robust as the one at the high-end.

I realize that many of the self-driving car pundits are acting as though all self-driving cars will be the same, but they won't be. Just like anything else, we are going to have self-driving cars that have a range of capabilities. Some will be better than others. Some will be safer than others. This is the way of the real-world, and so we need to be thinking about the economics aspects when considering the nature of self-driving cars.

D-14: Societal

This component encompasses the societal aspects of AI which also impacts the technology of self-driving cars. For example, the famous Trolley Problem involves what choices should a self-driving car make when faced with life-and-death matters. If the self-driving car is about to either hit a child standing in the roadway, or instead ram into a tree at the side of the road and possibly kill the humans in the self-driving car, which choice should be made?

We need to keep in mind the societal aspects will underlie the AI of the self-driving car. Whether we are aware of it explicitly or not, the AI will have embedded into it various societal assumptions.

D-15: Innovation

I included the notion of innovation into the framework because we can anticipate that whatever a self-driving car consists of, it will continue to be innovated over time. The self-driving cars coming out in the next several years will undoubtedly be different and less innovative than the versions that come out in ten years hence, etc.

Framework Overall

For those of you that want to learn about self-driving cars, you can potentially pick a particular element and become specialized in that aspect. Some engineers are focusing on the sensory devices. Some engineers focus on the controls activation. And so on. There are specialties in each of the elements.

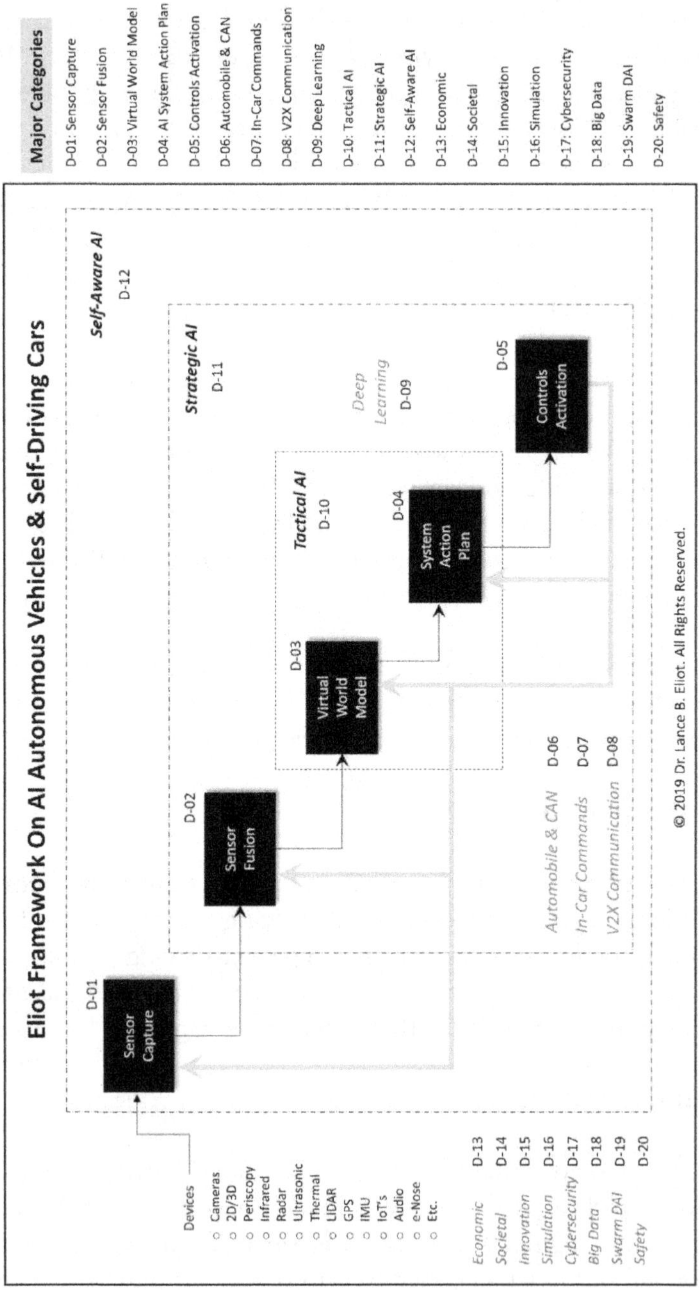

Eliot Framework On AI Autonomous Vehicles & Self-Driving Cars
Self-Aware AI
D-12
Strategic AI
D-11
Tactical AI
D-10
Deep Learning
D-09
Sensor Capture
D-01
Sensor Fusion
D-02
Virtual World Model
D-03
System Action Plan
D-04
Controls Activation
D-05
Automobile & CAN D-06
In-Car Commands D-07
V2X Communication D-08
Devices
Cameras
2D/3D
Periscopy
Infrared
Radar
Ultrasonic
Thermal
LIDAR
GPS
IMU
IoT's
Audio
e-Nose
Etc.
Economic D-13
Societal D-14
Innovation D-15
Simulation D-16
Cybersecurity D-17
Big Data D-18
Swarm DAI D-19
Safety D-20
© 2019 Dr. Lance B. Eliot. All Rights Reserved.
Major Categories
D-01: Sensor Capture
D-02: Sensor Fusion
D-03: Virtual World Model
D-04: AI System Action Plan
D-05: Controls Activation
D-06: Automobile & CAN
D-07: In-Car Commands
D-08: V2X Communication
D-09: Deep Learning
D-10: Tactical AI
D-11: Strategic AI
D-12: Self-Aware AI
D-13: Economic
D-14: Societal
D-15: Innovation
D-16: Simulation
D-17: Cybersecurity
D-18: Big Data
D-19: Swarm DAI
D-20: Safety

CHAPTER 2
MOVE OVER AND SELF-DRIVING CARS

You are driving along on a long stretch of highway and minding your own business. So far, your driving journey has been relatively uneventful.

Upon reaching a curve in the highway, you suddenly spy a tow truck that is trying to hook-up a stranded car at the edge of the roadway. Both the tow truck and the incapacitated car are just barely out of the lane that you are in. Turns out that this portion of the highway has a very thin emergency lane and thus there are going to be just inches between your car and those two vehicles attempting to get connected and ultimately get off the highway.

What do you do?

What should you do?

The usual rule-of-thumb would be to try and get over into the next lane. This would enable you to pass those two vehicles and be plenty of distance from them as you do so. Not only won't you skirt the sides of the tow truck and the standing car, but you'll also be safer and so will the tow truck driver and any of the passengers in the stranded car if they perchance decide to walk around nearby their vehicles.

Though it seems unimaginable, there are sometimes people that get out of their stranded cars and stand adjacent to their vehicle, being within a whisker's distance of cars zipping along at 65 miles per hour (or faster). Somehow these people do not realize the gravity of their situation. All it takes is for a car on the highway to veer a few inches or feet into the emergency lane and someone is going to be pushing up daisies, horrifically so.

For reasons that aren't very clear cut, those motorists that stand or walk around on an active highway or freeway are playing a daring door-die kind of game. One supposes that it is easy to assume that no car is going to purposely divert from the normal lane and come into the emergency lane, though this does indeed happen with more regularity than is expected. Also, there are those drunk drivers that see a car in the emergency lane and seem to be drawn to it like a moth to light, as though the stranded car suggests that there is another viable lane available for use.

Another factor consists of daytime versus nighttime driving. At night, the vision for drivers tends to be obscured or otherwise diminished. It is possible to mistakenly believe that an emergency lane is perhaps an exit lane or has some other purpose such that it can be used for cars already in motion and that wish to use it. There are those outright scofflaws that use the emergency lane as a means of scooting around other cars, which is a definite no-no and once again a high-risk form of devious driving that is decidedly illegal.

Returning to the notion of moving over to avoid those that are sitting in an emergency lane, this is not necessarily as simple a maneuver as it might seem.

You might be caught off-guard about the brewing situation up ahead and not have enough time to switch lanes. At times, you need to weigh the challenge of making a risky lane change against the sour odds of staying in the lane and breezing right next to the vehicles on the side of the highway. There is also the possibility of other cars in the lane that you wish to switch into, and thus you might disturb those cars by making a seemingly rash switcheroo. It does little good to avoid the emergency lane calamity by instead starting a lane change calamity that could just as likely start a cavalcade of car crashes.

You've undoubtedly seen car drivers that are frantically trying to switch lanes and it is obvious they are doing so to get over and away from vehicles at the side of the road. If you are in the lane they want to barge into, presumably, you would politely let them in. Of course, if they are now going much slower than the prevailing traffic, you have to decide whether to hit the brakes to let them in or try to zip past them and assume they will enter into your lane once you've gone past. This can be a delicate dance and one that gets all parties frustrated.

The driver wanting to get into your lane is bound to be giving you the evil eye for not slowing down and giving them a chance to get in. You are going to be giving that driver your evil eye since they are unduly disrupting the flow of traffic. If the driver in the running lane doesn't see why the other driver wants to feverishly change lanes, this ups the ante in terms of exasperation and irksomeness. It might appear as though there is no reason for that driver to make such a rash switch and therefore the driver zipping along is more determined to not let the interloper into the lane.

This brings up another facet about what to do when in the lane that is adjacent to the emergency lane, namely slow down.

The assumption is that by slowing down, you'll have less chance of striking the vehicles or any wandering people, and be able to come to a stop quickly if absolutely necessary. The act of slowing down also means that if push does come to shove, heaven forbid, the resulting collision will be a lot less impactful at a lower speed. Slow speed also means more mental processing time is available and adds leeway somewhat to the decision making process about what driving action is best to be undertaken.

Many states have a "move over, slow down" law that is a mandatory requirement for driving on their highways and byways.

California recently amended its version of the "move over, slow down" provision, which encompasses all manner of vehicles that might be standing alongside the roadway, including tow trucks, fire trucks, ambulances, police cars, and so on. The existing law as per the DMV says that "a person driving a vehicle on a freeway approaching, among other things, a stationary authorized emergency vehicle that is displaying emergency lights to approach with due caution and, before passing in a lane immediately adjacent to one of those specified vehicles, absent other direction by a peace officer, either proceed to make a lane change into an available lane not immediately adjacent to one of those specified vehicles, or slow to a reasonable and prudent speed that is safe for existing weather, road, and vehicular or pedestrian traffic conditions, as specified." Part of the expanded scope includes that not only are the state highways part of the rule, so too are local ones.

Hopefully, drivers in California and other states are mindful about trying to avoid anyone or anything that is standing alongside the roadway. Prudence dictates that it is wise to get over and avoid the standing particulars if you can safely navigate away and that it is advisable to slow down as you pass such situations. We would not seem to need a law to instruct us as such, but then again, not everyone drives cautiously and mindfully, thus the law adds teeth and a reminder of the civil thing to be done.

Shifting gears, let's ponder what the future of driving might be like. There is going to gradually be the appearance of self-driving cars on our highways and byways.

This brings up an interesting question: *Should AI-based true self-driving cars also observe the "move over, slow down" provisions?*

Let's unpack the matter and see.

Self-Driving Cars And Move Over

For Level 4 and Level 5 true self-driving vehicles, there won't be a human driver involved in the driving task.

All occupants will be passengers.

The AI is doing the driving.

It is widely anticipated that self-driving cars will strictly abide by the laws of the road. In that case, we would certainly expect that the AI driving system would obediently do a "move over, slow down" whenever it detected a suitable circumstance.

That's part of the rub about this matter.

The question arises as to whether the AI driving system will be able to detect a situation that entails invoking the "move over, slow down" protocol.

Notice that the California law states that if there is a "stationary authorized emergency vehicle that is displaying emergency lights" the provision so applies. This makes things pretty clear cut that there needs to be a stationary vehicle, and for which it needs to be an authorized emergency vehicle. Furthermore, this said vehicle, if detectable as such, would also need to display emergency lights.

You might think that this is a rather obvious and abundantly detectable facet.

For humans, perhaps that is the case, though even humans admittedly can mess-up on doing so. In any case, most AI driving systems make use of a special sensory suite consisting of video cameras, radar, LIDAR, ultrasonic units, thermal imaging, and the like. These devices are mounted on the self-driving car and are used to collect data about the driving environment. They are essentially the eyes and ears, as it were, for the AI driving system.

Typically, AI driving systems are pre-trained on what different kinds of vehicles look like. This is usually done by presenting thousands upon thousands of pictures or videos to a Machine Learning or Deep Learning (ML/DL) algorithm which uses computational pattern matching to try and figure out what those objects consist of. You might provide an ML/DL with a large set of images that showcase say an ambulance, and the computational pattern matching attempts to ferret out the visual characteristics that seem to pertain to ambulances.

When a self-driving car is cruising along on a highway, it is capturing the video streams and applying the ML/DL to try and identify what else is around the self-driving car. Coming upon a scene that has an ambulance at the side of the road and standing still, the video is examined by the ML/DL and a probability associated with what the vehicle is will then be provided to the rest of the AI driving system. Once the rest of the AI driving system has a semblance of what is around the self-driving car, there is an internal virtual world database that is marked with what objects are nearby and what they signify.

It is readily conceivable that the emergency vehicle might not be recognized via the pattern matching and therefore not necessarily be classified as an emergency vehicle. There is also the chance that the object will be classified as an emergency vehicle though with an assigned probability, such that the pattern matching only perhaps got a partial impression and has stipulated that there is say a 60% chance that the vehicle is an ambulance.

This has to do with the kind of "facial recognition" per se associated with spotting an emergency vehicle. You might be thinking that it doesn't matter much since there is also the stated requirement of the emergency lights. It would seem trivial to be able to spot the use of emergency lights. As such, put aside whether the vehicle is an authorized emergency vehicle and focus solely on those emergency lights.

Well, once again, this can be somewhat tricky to figure out. Suppose the emergency lights are hard to see because they are obscured by a stranded vehicle that is behind the emergency truck or ambulance. Perhaps the emergency lights are on, but they are low to the ground, or maybe the sunlight is adding glare and it is not readily feasible to see the emergency lights. And so on.

The crux of this emphasis is that you cannot summarily assume that a self-driving car can readily detect an emergency vehicle and nor detect that emergency lights are being displayed. This is a harder problem than it might seem.

If the AI driving system does not detect the presence of the emergency vehicle and nor the emergency use of lights, what then?

One obvious answer is that if there is anything at the side of the road, regardless of flashing lights and even not an authorized emergency vehicle, by gosh the right thing to do is get over and slow down.

A counter-argument to that rule-of-thumb would be that the self-driving car might be continually switching lanes to avoid whatever might perchance be alongside the highway. Yes, this could be the safest idea when construed in a narrow viewpoint, but then again it could also mean that the self-driving car is making a lot of lane changes. Each lane change carries its own associated risks.

Okay, you say, then just have the self-driving car stay out of the lane that is adjacent to the side of the highway. In that case, there is presumably no need to generally be switching lanes, since the self-driving car is already in a "safer" lane to begin with. This has some merit, on the other hand, inevitably it would seem that a self-driving car has to get into the lane adjacent to the side of the highway if nothing else to prepare to exit or when coming onto the highway. And, notably, in either of those settings, there is always the chance that an emergency vehicle just so happens to be sitting on the side of the highway and needs to be dealt with.

As a measured stopgap, most of the automakers and self-driving tech makers are programming their self-driving cars to always attempt to get away from anything stranded on the side of the highway. The assumption is that this is the most prudent action.

That takes us into the other dicey part of this equation.

The act of moving over into another lane is fraught with potential problems. As mentioned earlier, human drivers are notorious for not letting other cars into their lane. The same kind of reluctance can assuredly be done to self-driving cars. This means that a self-driving car that wants to move over can be potentially stymied by the human drivers in the desired lane.

Another question comes up about the slowing down aspect. How slow should a self-driving car be programmed to go in these circumstances? In theory, a human driver might go just a tad slower than prevailing traffic or might drop down their speed to a crawl. It all depends.

There isn't a magic number that can be relied upon. As per the California DMV, the notion of slowing down is to "slow to a reasonable and prudent speed that is safe for existing weather, road, and vehicular or pedestrian traffic conditions."

Thus, we are expecting an AI driving system to essentially exercise a kind of human judgment about what speed is the proper one to use in such settings.

You can bet that this will inevitably be a contested issue in some future court cases, whereby a self-driving car slowed down, but arguably not enough, and somehow that led to a car crash or other injury. The other side of that coin is rife for attack too, namely that the self-driving car went too slow and therefore caused or generated a car collision or injury thereof.

If you are AI, you can lose either way.

Conclusion

Some pundits are quick to point out that we will be using V2V (vehicle-to-vehicle) electronic communications that allow self-driving cars to message each other. This implies that whenever a vehicle is stopped alongside the highway if a self-driving car spots this occurrence, it could rapidly use its V2V to message other nearby self-driving cars and give those AI driving systems a greater opportunity to move into a further lane.

Also, those vehicles stranded could be emitting a V2V message, letting any self-driving cars that are nearby be alerted to their presence, potentially doing so long before the self-driving car manages to reach that part of the highway.

An AI driving system might decide to go a different route entirely, or at least make sure to be in a further lane to avoid the stranded vehicle.

Yes, those are all handy possibilities. The issue is that it will be a while before V2V is widely adopted, and meanwhile, there will be lots of conventional cars that do not have V2V. Overall, the V2V usage has a more pronounced long-term advantage, while in the nearer term there is still going to be an expectation that a self-driving car can figure out what to do on its own and without any V2V forewarning being provided.

You can even argue that despite an eventual widespread use of V2V, you would still want a self-driving car to be able to undertake its own actions without V2V since it is always possible that the V2V might not be functioning or otherwise have some form of electronic communications difficulties.

A final twist.

Believe it or not, some argue whether it is "move over, slow down" or ought to be "slow down, move over" in terms of the appropriate phrasing. You can get yourself tied into a knot by trying to be finicky about that wording.

Perhaps we can all agree that moving over is a usually good idea, and slowing down is a usually good idea, for which you can mix or match those two driving rules, as long as they make sense and aim to avoid any disastrous roadway incidents.

We can assuredly get the AI to observe the rule in that manner, and so the question remains, what about those dogged human drivers that think they rule the road.

You might say that new tricks are hard to learn, but this is an old trick that ought to already be part and parcel of anyone behind the wheel.

CHAPTER 3

CROSSING CHICKEN AND SELF-DRIVING CARS

Why did the chicken cross the road?

To befuddle those newly emerging self-driving cars.

And, maybe, just maybe, in hopes of reaching the other side of the road.

Obviously, this is a bit of a tongue-in-cheek twist on a legendary and familiar joke, but there are nonetheless some useful and quite serious insights to be gleaned from this otherwise seemingly lighthearted topic.

Speaking of chickens, you might have seen in the news recently that some rambunctious and altogether live chickens in New Jersey were running loose in a McDonald's parking lot. Some drivers that were in the drive-thru line were annoyed when the chickens opted to peck at the car tires. Guess those drivers were hoping for sedate chicken sandwiches more so than rowdy chickens wreaking havoc (the police responded to a 911 call and nabbed the perps before they could fly the coop, it was so reported).

Chickens can be quite serious business.

As we approach the advent of self-driving cars, some various nuances and qualms still need to be worked out, including the seemingly innocuous matter of chickens crossing the road, along with other facets of anything or anyone that perchance crosses the road while in front of an oncoming self-driving car.

Do not though get into an undue panic about chickens and other living creatures that might find themselves staring at the headlights of a self-driving car that looms upon them.

The hope is that self-driving cars will be as safe, and presumably safer at driving than are human drivers. Logically, we can clear out the count of car crashes that occur due to drunk driving, simply because AI driving systems are not going to drink and drive. There is also the aspect that much of today's car accidents are based on distracted driving by humans, which will thankfully be avoided since the AI driving systems will be devoted to the driving chore and not watching cat videos or trying to sneak glances at their text messages while at the wheel.

All told, there are about 40,000 fatalities each year in the U.S. alone due to car crashes, and approximately 2.3 million injuries. Those numbers will inevitably be reduced whence self-driving cars become available and prevalent. This adoption won't happen overnight, and you can expect that the 250 million conventional cars in use today will take many decades to gradually be replaced by self-driving cars.

Also, for those that keep insisting we will achieve a goal of zero car crash-related deaths once there are self-driving cars, this is a decidedly false expectation and there will (sadly) still be car-related fatalities. The physics of cars is still valid, even for self-driving cars, and thus a pedestrian that suddenly darts in front of a self-driving car is going to get smacked, assuming that there were no viable means to stop in time or avoid the collision.

This brings us back to those vaunted chickens.

The reason that I'm picking on chickens, well, actually providing some added fame to chickens, dives into how self-driving cars are being crafted to try and detect and avoid objects in the roadway. Human drivers know that there are lots of ways in which objects get into the path of their moving cars. You might be on a long stretch of highway and spy a tumbleweed that is rolling and dancing across the roadway. Or maybe a truck ahead of you has some pieces of discarded wood from a construction site that manages to flop off the back of the truck and onto the highway, scattering and bouncing around to create a dangerous obstacle course.

When confronting non-living objects, you don't have to try and decide whether hitting the object involves sparing a life of that obstruction. You are certainly worried about your life, as a driver and trying to keep from hitting the object such that you lose control of your car or otherwise swerve and start a violent and death producing cascade of cars crashing into each other. The lives of those in your car and any nearby people will abundantly come to mind, but the non-living object is not in the living category and therefore can be struck if so needed.

I dare say, even if the object is the revered painting of the Mona Lisa, presumably striking that inanimate thing is at a lower priority than saving the lives of humans (for those that cherish famous paintings, please do not get upset at this example, and be relieved that the chances of having a famous artwork at severe risk in the middle of the road seem as remote as living on Pluto, one so assumes).

The matter of confronting a living object that perchance has come forth in front of your moving car is an altogether tougher proposition.

What do you do when that dreaded moment arrives?

If the living creature is a beloved type, such as a dog or cat, presumably you will take more desperate measures to avoid it. Suppose the living beast was a rat, I'd guess that most drivers would not give much thought to striking the interloper, assuming that doing so was the safest way to proceed and there were no other means to either stop in time or swerve to avoid striking the rodent (admittedly, there are some that might intentionally seek to strike it, depending upon prior biases and already formed opinions).

The use case of having a human that is in the roadway requires added attention, which is not to suggest that animals of all kinds ought to not be given proper due consideration. Generally, it seems relatively legally prudent to assert that avoiding a human while driving a car has got to be at the top of the driving tasks assigned via our laws and customs. You need to take whatever plausible avoidance tactics can be taken and try mightily to avoid such a collision.

Let's though get back to those chickens since they are waiting around for this discussion to turn in their direction.

Here is an interesting question: *Will chickens be able to successfully cross the road in an era of self-driving cars?*

Seems like a bit of an off-the-wall question (a reader kindly brought this weighty topic to my attention), and perhaps by delving closely into the answer we can find some notable points about the emergence and use of self-driving cars.

Time to unpack the matter and see.

Self-Driving Cars And Chickens Crossing

For Level 4 and Level 5 true self-driving vehicles, there won't be a human driver involved in the driving task.

All occupants will be passengers.

The AI is doing the driving.

Imagine the following scenario.

A self-driving car is making its way along a rural road. There are farms nearby. A chicken has wandered around, circumventing whatever perimeter might have existed to keep it fenced in. The chicken opts to meander out onto the roadway.

Why?

Maybe it spotted something enticing on the other side of the road and decided it made sense to skedaddle over to it. Perhaps the chicken liked the roadway surface and figured it would be fun to do a bit of a chicken dance on it. There are a plethora of reasons for that chicken to end-up in the roadway. We don't know for sure what is taking place inside the mind of the chicken, so we'll need to settle on the plain fact that there is a chicken in the road, for whatever reason or basis it has chosen to be there.

Consider two varying scenarios.

In one scenario, the chicken has been standing on that road for a while, and thus from a sizable distance, you could potentially spot the chicken long before you reach its position. We'll refer to this as the dillydally chicken.

A contrasting scenario is the instance of a chicken that was well-hidden off the side of the road, perhaps by some clump of bushes or whatever else might be there, and it suddenly and dramatically struts out into the roadway with essentially no due notice and just as a car happens to be zipping along. We'll refer to this as the spontaneous chicken (some might say it is the dead-duck chicken, though that seems like a foul pun).

What would a self-driving car do in these two scenarios?

We need to first realize that the chicken needs to be detected.

The AI driving system makes use of a suite of specialized sensors, typically consisting of a mix of video cameras, radar, LIDAR, ultrasonic units, thermal image devices, and so on. These are continually scanning the driving environment and the collected data is analyzed by the AI driving system. For example, video images are examined to visually identify recognizable shapes and objects. Most AI driving systems make use of Machine Learning and Deep Learning (ML/DL), a kind of computational pattern matching that tries to ascertain whether objects being sensed are akin to training sets that have included those shapes and patterns.

If the ML/DL training set did not encompass chickens, this implies that the AI driving system will not recognize what the object in the roadway is, though it nonetheless might still ascertain that there is an object there. Some argue that it doesn't matter if an AI driving system can connect the presence of an object to the nature of the object. Simply detecting an object is sufficient, they argue, and there is no particular need to go beyond the barebones fact that an object is there in the road.

I think we can undercut that abysmal logic.

Suppose the object is a tumbleweed. Most of the time, you are willing to simply strike a tumbleweed, rather than making any oddball swerving actions that could endanger you and anyone else nearby. On the other hand, if the object is a dog or cat, as mentioned earlier you are likely going to want to take evasive action if at all feasible. We also have the special case of humans in the roadway.

The point is that if the AI driving system only is established to find objects, doing so without any semblance of trying to associate those objects with what they are, you are summarily treating all objects as pretty much a blob. Per the comments already made, not all blobs are the same. A blob that is a dog or cat is different than a blob that is a tumbleweed.

In short, we ought to expect and perhaps demand that any viable and bona fide AI driving system should be doing what it can to not simply detect objects, but also try to figure out what those objects represent.

There is another reason to identify an object definitively. Suppose the object is a piece of wood and is residing on the roadway, planted right there in the middle of your lane. It is reasonable to generally expect that a piece of wood is not going to move on its own. You can predict it is going to be stationary, all else being equal.

Consider a chicken that is standing in the roadway. Is it like a piece of wood and therefore we can anticipate it won't move? Unless the chicken is pushing up daisies (and nailed to a perch, for those of you that are fans of Monty Python), we can abundantly anticipate that the chicken is going to go into motion.

In fact, the problem with a chicken is its unpredictability. A dog or a cat is probably going to be astute enough to try and get out of the roadway, and much of the time attempt to dart directly to the sides of the roadway. Unless you come upon a specially trained chicken, it does not seem as assured that the chicken will try to avoid the oncoming car, and even if it does do so, it will maybe circle around and not necessarily try to get out of the way by going directly to the sides of the road.

I apologize if that seems unfair to chickens as an overall characterization and please do know that some chickens would do just as well as a dog or a cat in such a circumstance. Hooray for chickens.

Anyway, we can dispense with the argument that there is no need for an AI driving system to do both detection and identification. The identification is also crucial and not be discounted. By identifying the object, there is a greater chance that the rest of the AI driving system will do a better job of figuring out what driving actions to take.

Returning to the dicey scenario, the doomed chicken, or earlier referred to as the spontaneous chicken, which hopefully has nine lives, this circumstance presents a quite difficult problem for the AI driving system. Assuming that the chicken gets detected, and assuming it is identified as a chicken, the amount of time available for then taking any evasive action is shortened and doesn't allow for many choices.

You need to use some form of calculus in that let's assume there is a passenger inside the self-driving car and that any radical driving action by the AI is going to shake up the passenger. Furthermore, suppose that a last-minute braking effort is not going to save the chicken because the stopping distance available is insufficient.

Should the AI driving system try to stop or not?

Should it just proceed and likely ram into the chicken?

If you insist that the self-driving car should come to an immediate halt, even though we've agreed that this won't save the chicken, you are then willing to potentially harm the passenger, either via a whiplash effect or other possible injury.

But that poor and innocent chicken, you exhort!

Well, not wanting to seem callous, you ought to know that there are an estimated eight billion chickens consumed in the United States alone each year. In that context, what risk are you willing to assign to harming a human passenger versus causing that chicken to go to chicken heaven?

The first scenario of the dillydally chicken is presumably a lot easier to solve. The AI driving system hopefully detects the chicken at a lengthy distance, identifies the chicken as a chicken, and opts to gradually slow down the self-driving car. Upon reaching the chicken, the self-driving car tries to see if there is a means to maneuver slowly around the chicken, doing so without ruffling any of its feathers. This can be hopefully done without also ruffling the human passenger.

Now that we've gotten those aspects onto our plate, let's add some twists and turns.

The human passenger happens to see the chicken in the road. The AI driving system does not seem to be slowing down. Assume this is the dillydally chicken instance.

What should or can the human passenger do?

You might assume that the passenger can merely yell out to the AI driving system to slow down, darn it before that chicken gets whacked. This raises a slew of other considerations.

First, is there a means for the passenger to warn the AI driving system about this predicament? Some automakers and self-driving tech firms are focusing solely on having passengers indicate a destination of where they want to be driven, and there is not much other interaction involved. The added interaction is something on the so-called edge or corner cases list, meaning that it will someday get attention but not now.

Second, even if there is AI interaction provided, should the AI driving system do what the passenger says? You might insist that the human is always right and always to be obeyed. Sorry, there are lots of possibilities of a human passenger being absolutely wrong, such as suppose they are drunk or suppose they are mistaken about what they see, etc. Blindly abiding by the wishes of a human passenger is not a sensible way to program the AI.

Third, most self-driving cars will undoubtedly be outfitted with an OnStar-like remote human agent access capability. The idea is that a passenger can invoke this capacity and discuss whatever is happening, and the remote agent might be able to somehow instruct the self-driving car accordingly. The problem with this approach is that you never know for sure that a communication line is going to be working, such as this case of being in a rural area and there might be little or spotty connections.

There is also the timing aspect that once again rears its ugly head.

Even the dillydally chicken would need to be spotted a heck of a long distance away, as they say at least at a country mile, so to speak, in order to allow time for the passenger to invoke the remote communication, get connected, explain the situation to the remote agent, and have the remote agent take some kind of action.

Regrettably, if the AI driving system didn't detect the chicken, and you are betting that the passenger will be able to persuade a remote human agent to do something, the odds are that this wandering chicken is going to be on someone's food platter later that day.

The life of a chicken is not an easy one.

Conclusion

There are quite a lot of additional permutations and combinations that can be divined about this chicken trying to cross the road.

For example, suppose the AI driving system misclassified the chicken, perhaps assigning it the label of a dog. If the AI driving system has been built to try and take riskier saving actions for a dog rather than a chicken, this suggests that the self-driving car will possibly go through some extreme maneuvers. The passenger gets heavily jostled.

When the passenger realizes that the AI driving system took this crazed evasive action for a chicken, there is likely going to be heck to be paid. Perhaps a lawsuit is filed against the automaker or self-driving tech firm. During the discovery process, it comes out that the AI misclassified the chicken as a dog. Oops. This could be an oopsie that wins the day for the passenger and gets the self-driving car maker into the doghouse.

I'll leave things to your imagination to come up with the myriad of scenarios and how they can aid in revealing the nuances and societal aspects underlying the advent of self-driving cars.

One last point.

Why did the horse decide to cross the road?

Because the chicken needed a day off.

A round of applause for all of the chickens on our planet and their ongoing sacrifices for humanity, including when crossing the road, albeit coming under the (sometimes) watchful eye of human drivers and AI driving systems.

CHAPTER 4
CODE BREACHES AND SELF-DRIVING CARS

It is said that software eats the world.

If that is indeed the case, presumably the source code underlying the software must be the atomic core that drives this global consuming beast.

They used to say that no bucks meant no Buck Rodgers, while today's witticism might be that no source code means no supercilious software planetary takeover (or something like that). The effort to craft software requires hours upon hours of laborious and at times mind-numbing concentration to stipulate all the painstaking steps and activities that a system is supposed to undertake. Software developers use a variety of programming languages and can be at times perniciously cryptic and succinct in their coding, while in other cases the source code is quite elaborately expressed and somewhat self-evident in what it indicates.

There are two major opposition camps or heated viewpoints about how to best treat source code.

One belief is that source code ought to be kept close to the vest.

Keep the source code proprietary, hidden from view, and treat it like a deep dark secret that can only be seen by those that have an absolute need to take a glimpse. The thinking on this is that the source code is a form of revered Intellectual Property (IP) and should be housed under abundant lock-and-key safeguards. This is not simply due to retaining legal protections (which, certainly seems warranted as a result of significant costs involved in the labor to craft the programming code), but also because the source code might reveal the inner workings of the secret sauce or other vital machinations that should not be widely known (so it is believed).

The moment someone whispers or somehow leaks even the tiniest snippet of your source code, you need to immediately and with a great show of force put a stop to the leakage.

The other side of that secretive mantra is the polar opposite, namely, let all source code be free to roam.

Often referred to as open-source, the assertion is that you'll never really be able to keep source code tightly under wraps, thus you might as well throw in the towel and make it readily available. Anyone that wants to see the source code is welcome to do so. In a sense, by proclaiming your source code to be free from the bonds of locked room confinement, the otherwise overbearing stress of trying to prevent others from seeing the code is completely deflated and not one iota of concern remains in that regard.

Like most things in life, some depict these two diametrically opposed stances as regrettable and altogether unnecessary extremes on a spectrum that might instead allow for a type of middle ground. These centrist proponents would likely suggest that some of your source code is fine to be padlocked and kept unseen, meanwhile other parts of the source should be openly displayed to the world at large. This seems like a potentially reasonable perspective, these mediators assert.

Not so, say the extremists, since this is the *worst* of both worlds' contrivance rather than a best of both kinds of compromise.

By opening the door to any of your source code, it is said to be an invitation for further intrusion. The teasers revealed will simply whet appetites for more to be divulged. Furthermore, it could showcase aspects that make breaking into the rest of the source code a lot easier or at least allows for doing some mental reverse engineering to figure out what the remaining code consists of. Ergo, per the avid clampdown camp, whatever you do, assuredly do not allow your source code to see the light of day.

The opposing viewpoint by the open-source advocates is that you are never going to be able to prevent your source code from being inevitably seen. It will dribble out, one way or another. You will falsely lull yourself into thinking that you've got this caged animal and that there are no apparent means of escape. Instead, there is a likelihood that the creature is already out and about, you just do not know it, and you failed to take sufficient precautions because you foolishly assumed and continue blindly to assume that the enclosure is locked shut as tight as a drum.

Round and round this Merry-go-round we go on this contested topic.

Speaking of source code, consider a recent spate of newsworthy reports about high profile source code incursions.

In the headlines recently, Microsoft acknowledged that some of its source code was viewed in an unauthorized manner (per their press release on the matter): "We detected unusual activity with a small number of internal accounts and upon review, we discovered one account had been used to view source code in a number of source code repositories. The account did not have permissions to modify any code or engineering systems and our investigation further confirmed no changes were made. These accounts were investigated and remediated."

You might also recall that recently there have been reports of leaked source code from Nissan, reportedly due to a misconfigured Git server (a Git server is an online facility to store source code and other related configuration facets for programming).

And, last year, there was a news report that Mercedes had encountered a source code reveal. Apparently, a Git site being used by Daimler AG was used by an unauthorized party to take a look at source code for the Onboard Logic Units (OLU) software used in some models of Mercedes-Benz vans.

There have been mixed reactions to these source code eyeball infiltrations.

To some, this emerging wave of known source code exposures is an obvious sign that trying to keep source code tucked away is bereft with issues and ultimately untenable as an approach to handling your source code (keeping in mind that the reported cases are probably just a tiny portion of the actual number of such instances). Others though point out that this merely indicates that there are people out there that will undercut the hard work of others and be willing to perform seemingly evil acts. There will always be evildoers and there will always be a need to have steel vaults and electrified fences to keep out intruders.

One aspect that is notable about source code breaches is how readily these incursions tend to be downplayed. The firms so struck are bound to paint a picture that these events are not especially earth-shattering, and thus in a Yoda-like way attempt to get you to look elsewhere and not become focused on the ramifications of such break-ins.

For the general public, they are oftentimes not quite sure what to make of these matters.

Just because someone was able to see your source code, it doesn't appear to be anything to write home about and, though certainly disturbing and ought not to have taken place, appears to be a classic instance of no harm, no foul. Well, yes, it was assuredly foul to have dipped into the treasures of another, but merely looking seems harmless and ineffectual. Perhaps it is akin to breaking into a prized art museum and with rapt attention eyeing the works of art on the walls. As long as you don't mar the artwork or spray graffiti, this seems like a peculiar though meaningless act.

Actually, there is harm being had.

I'll get to those harms in a moment, and also poke holes in the aforementioned analogy to an art museum. Let's be aboveboard and acknowledge that there are demonstrative problems associated with the unlawful revealing of proprietary source code.

Furthermore, we can up the ante.

Consider code that is quite serious stuff, namely the source code developed for self-driving cars.

Cars are life-or-death machines that roll around on our highways and byways. I say they are life-or-death due to the aspect that anyone driving a car, whether human or AI, have at their command the capability to determine where the car goes and what it does. Passengers inside a car are at risk, and so are nearby occupied cars, bike riders, and likewise, meandering pedestrians are at risk too.

You probably do not think of driving as a life-or-death matter, but it indeed is, and each time you are at the wheel, you are deciding the fate of others all around you. So are all the other drivers.

Time to unpack all this as it especially relates to self-driving cars.

Self-Driving Cars And Source Code Handling

For Level 4 and Level 5 true self-driving vehicles, there won't be a human driver involved in the driving task.

All occupants will be passengers.

The AI is doing the driving.

How does the AI "know" how to drive a car?

For those that assume that an AI system that can drive requires human-like sentience, sorry to burst that bubble, the AI is just software (at least for now, though there is a lot of speculation about what AI of the future might be).

Underlying the AI-based driving systems there is source code that consists of conventional programming, millions upon millions of lines of code. Also, there are the use of Machine Learning and Deep Learning algorithms, which again are based on source code, along with the tons of data that is used to aid in training the computational pattern matching that is needed for driving a car.

Similar to the discussion earlier about the two divergent camps approach to source code, the self-driving car industry is likewise divided.

Some are advocating a decidedly open-source avenue for self-driving cars. Companies are developing open-source code for AI driving systems, and research entities including university AI labs doing so. Nonetheless, by-and-large the commercial automakers and self-driving tech firms are currently pursuing the proprietary route more so than the open-source path (that being said, some are doing a mix-and-match of their own private stuff with the added use of open source).

Is the proprietary or private source code akin to artwork in a locked museum and for which any unauthorized incursion is relatively benign if it does not seemingly mar or alter the code in place?

Simply stated, the answer is no.

Here's why.

Those that get their eyes on the source code are just as likely able to copy it. In that case, they now have the source code in their own hands, separate and apart from wherever the source code was originally housed. With that copy, they can leisurely study it, and then make changes to their heart's content and try to redeploy the software (more on this in a moment).

In an art museum, you are presumably looking at the originals of the artwork. There is a desire to keep that original artwork pristine and pure, unaltered or damaged in any respect. Generally, you can discern the difference between the true original and any faked or fabricated version.

With source code, there is essentially no ready way to ascertain whether the copy is a copy, and essentially it is a complete and indistinguishable copy of the original (all else being equal).

Furthermore, the source code is malleable in a manner that an artwork does not quite equally imbue.

All in all, though news reports seem to suggest that someone only glanced at the source code, the reality is that they could very well have copied it, and also then opt to change it, as they might so desire.

Indeed, the intruder might not have changed the so-called original instance, since the source code might be maintained in a read-only status at its point of origin, though this also imbues a potential "hidden" unrealized danger for those that are relying upon the original source code (in essence, if the intruder could have altered the original source code at its point of normal storage, it bodes for quite grave concerns about what changes were made, and especially if the developers of the source code are unaware of what was altered and are not deliberately seeking to find any such changes).

Okay, so let's assume that the source code is still intact at its original point of storage (which might not necessarily be so) and that the intruder has "only" grabbed a copy of the source code.

Even if the intruder doesn't seek to change the code, they can at least inspect the code, doing so for nefarious purposes. They can look to find weaknesses in the source code.

This might allow the intruder to devise a means to crack into the system that is running the software based on that source code. Or it might enable the intruder to find a means to augment the software and get the system to accept a type of Trojan Horse. Even in the simplest form of manipulation, there might be a discovered means of getting the running software to react in a way that you wish to have it do so, seemingly by a kind of magical mannerism when it is actually due to knowing what the presumed unrevealed internal mechanisms are doing.

For self-driving cars, the range of exposures is hopefully kept to less crucial elements, perhaps controlling the air conditioning or whether the entertainment system is working properly. The more dire possibilities include being able to access the driving controls or otherwise confound or redirect the AI driving systems.

Realize that there is source code underlying the software that runs all of the specialized sensors on a self-driving car, including the video cameras, radar, LIDAR, ultrasonic units, thermal imaging, etc. Knowing the intricacies of that source might provide insights about how to confuse a sensor or get it to misreport what has been sensed.

There is the source code that underpins the AI driving system as it brings together the sensory data and attempts to merge and align what the sensors are indicating. This is referred to as Multi-Sensor Data Fusion (MSDF), and usually is source code that is held in tight control and only seen by the programmers responsible for that capability.

The same can be said for the source code that entails the virtual world capability of the AI driving system, which is used to keep track of real-world sensed objects and try to figure out the surrounding driving environment. There is source code for the AI driving system portion that plans driving actions to perform. There is source code for the interface of the AI driving system to the driving controls, controlling the accelerator, the brakes, the steering, and the like.

All told, it is a veritable boatload of software and a massive shipload of source code.

Another devious aspect involves rewriting or changing the code and then trying to either put the altered version back into the source code repository, as though it was there all along or attempt to see if you can replace the running software with your altered version based on the source code changes that you've made.

There are cybersecurity concerns that some evildoers might arrange to be a seemingly everyday passenger for a self-driving car, and yet upon getting inside, would surreptitiously attempt to infiltrate the AI driving system by loading their alternative code into the on-board hardware. Presumably, this would be prevented by hardware and software security precautions, though if the source code has been thoroughly inspected by a bad actor, perhaps they will have found a gap or loophole that can be exploited.

The same qualms can be applied to the use of OTA (Over-The-Air) electronic updating.

We generally think of OTA as a great means of being able to remotely update the software of a self-driving car, thus quickly and easily keeping the AI driving systems updated (doing so without having to drive over to a dealership to do the updating). Unfortunately, the OTA also provides a prime portal for the infecting of computer viruses and other malware directly into the on-board AI driving system. Various cybersecurity protections are being built into the OTA, but if the bad actors can see what those protections are, this raises the chances of figuring out tricks or bypasses to let in their verboten code.

In short, being able to get access to proprietary source code provides numerous potential cybersecurity issues that can subsequently playout by a determined hostile hacker or evildoer.

Conclusion

The rule-of-thumb for those that are ardent believers of the proprietary source code approach is that they must always and continually be working under the assumption that their source code will get out. Those that take that mantra to heart are fervently bent on trying to ferret out all possibilities of how the revealing of their source code could lead to troubles and thus aim stridently to plug those pitfalls before the code is possibly ever leaked.

Essentially, the default mode of the software developers is that the source code has been or will be breached. In that manner of a cornerstone assumption, they should be devising the source code so that even if it is seen, the revealing facets will not undercut the security of the resulting system.

Can that mindset be fully realized?

The open-source proponents say that it is foolhardy to make such an assumption. Better to let all eyes see the source code, which also means that the "wisdom of the crowd" will find loopholes and gotchas, rather than relying upon the handfuls of programmers assigned to coding the privately held source.

If the software involved is relatively unimportant, perhaps a security breach of the source code is not particularly important. When the source code is used for software that has life-or-death consequences, any breach is worthy of substantive attention, and those developing AI driving systems are hopefully and diligently taking to heart the significance therein.

May the source be with you.

But only if that's a good thing and not used for wrongdoing.

CHAPTER 5
CAR PAINT COLORS AND SELF-DRIVING CARS

What color is your car?

I'm sure that you've made a perfect choice for your car.

Go with me on a thought experiment about car colors, if you are willing to entertain some outsized thinking on this topic.

There are about 285 million cars in the United States, which is a whole lot of cars, and imagine if they were all painted the same color.

Besides being a somewhat drab approach to life for us all, you would undoubtedly find it very hard to readily discover your own car while walking through a crowded parking lot. Envision row after row of cars that are the same identical color.

Even if the color was bright and eye-catching, let's say a sparkling red, keep in mind that we are assuming for the moment that every car is that same color (i.e., all are red). In that sense, the seemingly look-at-me red color does nothing to make any particular car stand out in comparison to any other.

Some people eschew purchasing a car that is red since they believe that cops can more readily spot a speeding red car versus one of a more muted color.

In this imaginary scenario of all cars being painted red, apparently the red car as a speeding magnet is no longer going to hold true per se since all cars will be red and none sticks out more than any other. Score a point for those that want to get a red sports car and push the pedal to the metal, a dicey notion today but would be a blend-in proposition for our all-the-same color cars scenario.

Anyway, we know that cars are not all painted the same color and there seems to be a relatively wide array of colors being used.

Researchers claim that the color of your car is a reflection of your personality.

In other words, you ostensibly choose a color for your car that tends to match your personality traits. You might not even be aware that you are doing this. When buying a car, you might gravitate toward a car with a particular color, and it is seemingly a natural fit for you. Thus, you are not first saying to yourself that you have personality X and ergo you ought to get a car with painted color Y. Instead, the car color is just a natural outgrowth of your selection process for picking a car.

That's not to suggest that some people aren't aware of their car color preferences and how it befits their personal style. Many people have a hunch or extrasensory feeling that a specific color is somehow right for them. They therefore will only buy a car that matches their color preference. Indeed, some people are so adamant about this aspect that when they rent a car, they insist on the color of the rental vehicle, despite the obvious fact that they aren't buying it and are only using it for a little while.

You might say it is a stubbornness aspect, or perhaps they believe in car color karma.

Can you guess what car colors are the most popular to the least popular?

Also, how does your car color preference fit into the rankings?

Let's take a look at the rankings.

Please note that the rankings are based on published research of new car sales in the approximate last five years and as only for cars sold in the United States. The percentage of cars is shown in a rounded fashion and the ranking goes from one to twelve. Other colors beyond the ones indicated below are beyond the twelfth ranking and not listed here (though, yes, those other colors are still important and maybe you can be proud that your chosen car color is relatively unique in comparison to everyone else if it perchance falls below the end of this abbreviated listing).

Here then are the rankings:

1) White Painted Cars (24%)
2) Black Painted Cars (23%)
3) Gray Painted Cars (16%)
4) Silver Painted Cars (15%)
5) Red Painted Cars (10%)
6) Blue Painted Cars (9%)
7) Brown Painted Cars (1%)
8) Green Painted Cars (0.7%)
9) Beige Painted Cars (0.4%)
10) Orange Painted Cars (0.4%)
11) Gold Painted Cars (0.3%)
12) Yellow Painted Cars (0.2%)

Mull over those percentages.

A whopping 63% or roughly two-thirds of cars are painted either white, black, or gray. That might seem surprising, though if you wander around a mall parking lot, it becomes rather evident quickly that this does seem to describe the preponderance of car colors.

The red that we were earlier pretending was the color of all cars is only about one-tenth of them today. For those that love red colored cars, imagine their joy if all cars were painted red. Well, maybe this would irk those red favoring car owners since all of a sudden everyone was using their chosen color. It might undercut their sense of being a maverick and gloomily would find themselves now simply in the same red color camp like everyone else.

This brings us round to the assertion that there are personality types associated with car colors.

Some believe that the car color relationship to personalities is a bit of a reach and marginally valid, likening the topic to astrological fortune-telling. Others take umbrage at such a posture. They point out that you can readily find in-depth research on the topic that has attempted to statistically connect a tie between the car color preference and personality tendencies of the car owner or car driver.

Anyway, believe as you wish, and here is the usual characterization (using the same ranking as earlier shown):

1) White Painted Cars – someone that strives for perfection, relishes purity, modernness
2) Black Painted Cars – timeless choice, prefers air of mystery, luxury-seeking
3) Gray Painted Cars – someone that prefers to blend in, traditionalist
4) Silver Painted Cars – innovator, hard worker, practical
5) Red Painted Cars – has a zest for life, outgoing, impulsive
6) Blue Painted Cars – serene and compassionate, introspective
7) Brown Painted Cars – thrifty, down-to-earth
8) Green Painted Cars – peace-loving marches to their own tune
9) Beige Painted Cars – persistent, loyal, stay the distance
10) Orange Painted Cars - someone that is economic, wants to be different
11) Gold Painted Cars – bold, optimistic
12) Yellow Painted Cars – joyful, always happy

Please consider those as rather broad depictions and that exception certainly apply. As they say, your mileage may vary.

Now that we've covered the present day of car colors, maybe we ought to noodle on the future and how there might be changes afoot in all of this.

Why would things change?

The anticipated future is one of using self-driving cars.

This raises an interesting question: *Will the advent of AI-based true self-driving cars cause disruption or repainting as it were of the car colors that are prevalent on automobiles?*

Time to unpack the matter and see.

Self-Driving Cars And Source Code Handling

For Level 4 and Level 5 true self-driving vehicles, there won't be a human driver involved in the driving task.

All occupants will be passengers.

The AI is doing the driving.

Your first thought about the use of self-driving cars is that there doesn't seem to be any obvious reason that the color of cars would be any different in terms of the preferences of today versus the future.

Actually, there is a likely big difference, namely that there isn't a human driving the car.

This is significant because many people associate the act of driving a car as a kind of extension of their personality and their persona. But there won't be people behind the steering wheel. The AI presumably has no stake in the game of what the color of a car might be. Unless you believe in an AI that becomes sentient someday and perhaps starts incurring the same cravings as humans, there is no reason to believe that the AI driving system gives one iota about the painted color of the car.

In short, from the perspective of the driver, a true self-driving car can be any painted color and it just doesn't matter which color is chosen.

There is someone else though involved in the car color choosing gambit.

The owner of the car.

We usually associate the owner of a car as generally being the driver of the car too. In that way of things, the owner picks a color for the car that matches their preferences and that will be exhibited by them while also being at the steering wheel of the vehicle.

There is a humongous open question about the ownership of self-driving cars.

The AI that's driving the car is not the owner, at least not for the foreseeable future and not presumably until (or if) we ever can somehow craft or spur AI to become sentient.

Pundits believe that the owners of self-driving cars will be large corporations.

These firms will opt to buy self-driving cars and deploy those autonomous vehicles in large-scale fleets. It might be that a company that has nothing to do with transportation might decide that being in the ridesharing business by using self-driving cars is a profitable line, and thus the company purchases a slew of self-driving cars for that purpose. Or, it could be an automaker that makes self-driving cars decides to do the same (they make the vehicles, and they rideshare them as a paying service).

The most obvious guess is that existing ridesharing firms would do this.

All told, the point being that there will apparently no longer be individual ownership of cars, at least not for self-driving cars. All self-driving cars will be bought up by companies that do so in fleets and either use those vehicles for their own purposes or ridesharing (some assert).

What's the big deal about this related to car colors?

Right now, there are about 250 million individual car owners and drivers in the U.S. that individually are essentially choosing the colors of cars. Of course, the reality is that the automakers are painting the cars to match the color preferences of those that are buying their cars. If people want gray painted cars, so be it. If people want cars that are painted purple, this can be done. The whole machination is pretty much based on a semblance of supply and demand.

In any case, suppose that individuals aren't going to be owning self-driving cars and nor driving self-driving cars. This means that those fleet owners are going to be able to choose the car colors. Instead of millions upon millions of people individually choosing car colors, it will be a handful of corporate executives that will do so.

If that is the case, you need to consider what would you do in terms of choosing car colors.

Probably the easiest and cheapest thing to do would be to decide that all of your self-driving cars ought to be the same color. Pick one color and stick with it. This would help to provide a sense of the branding of your vehicles. The marketplace would come to realize that your ridesharing self-driving cars are all the color of Z, whether that might be red, blue, green, white, black, or whatever color you have chosen.

You probably would not want to pick a color that a competitor is using. This would not allow your self-driving cars to stand out. On the other hand, maybe this could be a useful strategy if you are the underdog and want people that are using ridesharing to be somewhat confused about the leading brand versus your self-driving cars.

This also brings up the notion of consumer preference.

Will people that ride in self-driving cars be aware of or choosy about what the car color is?

You might think it odd that passengers are going to care what car color the self-driving car is. All that would seem to matter to a passenger is that the self-driving car is safe, available, least costly, and thus the car color would be an altogether unimportant matter.

That might be the case at first, but once self-driving cars become widely available, there might emerge a societal cultural semblance around the car colors. Initially, no one cares about the car colors and only that the darned things work. Once all of the self-driving car brands can showcase that they work, it could be that the nitty-gritty of other less crucial elements looms larger than would otherwise be justified.

This might translate into a fleet of self-driving cars that a fleet owner has purposefully painted some unusual or considered outlandish colors. They hope that their ridesharing self-driving cars will be sought by the public that wants a ride in a "maverick" and not just an everyday self-driving car. You can easily imagine the marketing by a fleet operator that tries to convince the public that the car color is important and still makes a statement about your personality, even though you aren't driving the vehicle and are not the owner of it.

In short, we might end-up with nearly all of the roadway self-driving cars being just a few colors and almost none in the more "extravagant" car colors. Since today the car colors of white, black, and gray for quite popular, perhaps this two-thirds or so of today's cars will rise to maybe 90% of self-driving cars. The remaining ten percent would be across the other car colors and done to try and have smaller fleet operators be able to appear distinctive.

Given the preceding viewpoint, please be aware that not all pundits are sold on the idea that self-driving cars will be owned solely by large companies.

I am known as a contrarian on this topic. My position is that we will certainly have large entities owning fleets, there is no argument there, but that we will still have individual ownership too. In brief, people are going to want to join the gravy train of ridesharing self-driving cars and this will spur a cottage industry of individuals and pods of people that opt to buy a self-driving car and deploy it as both a personally used vehicle and as a ridesharing vehicle.

In that contrarian outlook, the possibility of car colors being important is something that will be indeed a notable issue. We are back to the notion of thousands upon thousands of individual owners making such a choice, even if they aren't driving those vehicles. They will want to select a car color that they believe is suitable for their personal tastes as a passenger and as an owner, and that will be alluring in a ridesharing network for deploying their self-driving car.

Conclusion

There is a bit of a knockout punch that can quickly undermine the entire discussion about the car colors topic.

Are you ready?

Some believe that by the time self-driving cars are prevalent, there will also be a new kind of electronic skin, as it were, whereby you can stretch this electronic mesh across the entire exterior of a car, and it will be the same as if you had a car engulfed in an LED screen.

The outside of a car will be used for advertising, allowing the showcasing of video ads. People sitting inside a self-driving car won't necessarily know what ads are being displayed on the exterior. Meanwhile, as those passengers look outside the windows of the self-driving car, they will see tons of ads that are being displayed on all of the nearby passing self-driving cars.

This raises concerns of an overabundance of visual blot and our world becoming garish.

If there is a buck to be made, you can anticipate this use of car exteriors for displaying ads is going to happen and likely to a great profusion. Some believe that new laws or regulatory action will be needed to clamp down on the visual "polluting" aspects of widespread video on the outside of cars.

The related matter is the car painted colors topic.

Via the electronic mesh that encompasses a self-driving car, the vehicle can be any color at any point in time.

A fleet owner might decide that on say a Monday their self-driving cars are all blue.

On Tuesday, the autonomous vehicles might be turned to orange at the switch of a button (all the self-driving cars being connected via OTA or Over-The-Air to the cloud system that is centrally able to communicate with the vehicles). Whatever seems to be the best and most attractive choice toward getting ridesharing riders will be the key criteria for choosing the daily or even moment-to-moment selection of colors.

Finally, there's the ultimate in customization that this brings forth too.

You request a ridesharing self-driving car to come to pick you up. The ridesharing network systems know that you prefer the color pink. Upon arrival at your house, the self-driving car is entirely pink in color. You are elated.

You might be able to alter the car colors. Suppose you decide that it doesn't seem like a day for pink and you prefer purple instead. Once you get into the self-driving car, you merely tell the AI via its Natural Language Processing (NLP) to change the color.

Or, the AI scans your face, decides what kind of personality you have, and opts to select a car color on your behalf.

Maybe that is a bridge too far and overly intrusive by the AI.

Sometimes, those AI driving systems get a bit overexcited about things.

CHAPTER 6
BAIT CARS
IN
SELF-DRIVING CARS

Bait cars are said to be the equivalent of a four-wheeled mousetrap.

In case you've never heard the expression "bait cars" before, the notion is that an ordinary car is used as bait to lure prospective car thieves into trying to steal the seemingly innocuous vehicle. The way that this usually works is that the police opt to park an everyday looking car in a locale that is known for having a lot of car thefts, and then nab any car thieves that get into the car and attempt to drive away with the baited automobile.

Sometimes the cops are parked nearby and eyeballing the bait car in a classic stakeout protocol, though if they are too close it could inadvertently deter the car thieves if they perchance spy the police vehicle and are either scared off or become suspicious that the "sitting duck" car is indeed a kind of mousetrap. To avoid the chance of tipping their hand to the potential lawbreakers, modern-day uses of bait cars involve rigging the vehicle with hidden cameras and various remote-control devices. This allows law enforcement to be relatively far away and yet still know when the bait has been taken. An alerting signal is typically emanated from the bait car once the car doors have been opened and someone has gotten inside.

Are you wondering what happens once the thieves have taken the bait?

Well, there are plenty of online videos posted on numerous social media platforms that showcase the car thieves as they steal a bait car. If it weren't for the seriousness of the crime being committed, these videos are ostensibly laughable when you watch the recorded results of the crooks going from initial elation that they are getting away with stealing a car and then their shock and awe upon realizing they are being busted for the crime.

Many of the videos begin with the prospective crooks opting to look around inside the vehicle and searching for any "goodies" that might be laying around. To make bait cars especially alluring, the police will sometimes place a laptop computer in the backseat or put a bunch of cash in the dashboard cubby or possibly place a cellphone on the driver's seat as though it might have fallen out of the owner's pocket when they were driving the car.

Besides providing an added allure, these honey trap contraptions seem to embolden the thieves as to their perceived good luck and avid fortune toward possibly stealing the car. The bandits could potentially just take the goodies and leave the car, but it seems as though they begin to believe this is their perfect opportunity to steal the car since they already have gotten some pirated treasure from the intrusion.

Some assert that this illustrates that greed works and can prod added untoward action by those that are bent on being crooks. Others liken it to putting a small worm on a baited hook and getting a fish to take a taste, which then perhaps the hook has an ever larger and more alluring appearance, and the fish opts to take a larger gulp upon initial success.

In any case, the car thieves that are determined to take the car will start the engine and proceed to drive away from the parking spot. As they do so, the thieves tend to discuss what to do next. Sometimes there is a heated debate over where to take the vehicle and what to do with it. In other cases, the car thieves appear to be quite practiced on these matters and already have figured out where to go and have prearranged with other accomplices regarding the disposition of the stolen vehicle.

While they are having these deliberative chats, unbeknownst to them the police have been alerted and are closing in on the moving vehicle.

You might be worried that this is going to spark a car chase and could harm other innocents if the car thieves try to escape via a wild and death-defying driving escapade. For modern bait cars, law enforcement places a remote switch in the engine of the vehicle and can at the press of a button cause the engine to stop running. The car will briefly coast forward and then come to a halt. At that juncture, the police cars that were triangulating on the position of the bait car will surround the vehicle, turn on sirens, and announce to the occupants that the gig is up.

Via the internal cameras that were hidden inside the bait car, a handy video recording of what the car thieves did is presumably ironclad evidence of the theft.

There are some culprits that when the car engine freezes up begin to realize that they are perhaps inside a bait car. They might try to make a run for it, but another remote-control feature is that the door locks can be controlled remotely by the police. This makes any effort to try and dart out of the vehicle rather difficult if not nearly impossible to do since the doors and windows are kept locked at the time of the capture.

Believe it or not, in some areas the use of bait cars is so prevalent that the crooks will comment during the theft that they hope the vehicle is not a bait car (word has spread that bait cars are being used). The scofflaws will argue during the driving of the vehicle about whether or not the car is a legitimately ordinary car or one that has been surreptitiously set up by the cops. Perhaps one of the most frequent comments upon seeing the police car flashing lights is that one of the thieves will turn to the other one and insist they "told them so" about forewarning they were taking a bait car.

This last point about the awareness of bait cars by potential car thieves makes the situation one of a cat and mouse affair. If the bait car looks like it is a setup, the car thieves will presumably be leery and will not try to steal it.

Consider then that the bait car has to be ordinary looking and cannot have cameras protruding or appear as though it has been prearranged as bait. Indeed, it ought to look like any other vehicle that might be normally parked in the locale and that would blend into the street scene. People do at times leave laptops laying in their backseat, and forgetfully leave their cellphone inside their vehicles, thus these are reasonably everyday aspects and not a facet that would somehow serve as a blazing clue that the vehicle is bait (in contrast, a car loaded with high-def TV screens, toasters, and the kitchen sink might be more suspect).

As an aside, some argue that bait cars are a form of entrapment and unfairly spur someone to break into the vehicles to get those showcased goodies or spark them to steal the car entirely. There are various legal and moral arguments and counterarguments involved. That's also why some locales use the approach and others do not, depending upon their belief about the legality and whether this is an appropriate form of law enforcement.

Shifting gears, we might ponder the future of cars and how the nature of a bait car activity might take place once there are self-driving cars prevalent on our roadways.

Today's interesting question is this: *Might AI-based true self-driving cars be used as bait cars, or does that not make sense in an era of driverless or fully autonomous vehicles?*

Let's unpack the matter and see.

Self-Driving Cars And Bait Cars

For Level 4 and Level 5 true self-driving vehicles, there won't be a human driver involved in the driving task.

All occupants will be passengers.

The AI is doing the driving.

Today's self-driving cars can be readily spotted due to the rack of specialized sensory devices mounted on top of the vehicle, usually consisting of video cameras, radar, LIDAR, ultrasonic units, thermal imaging devices, and so on.

By-and-large, most automakers, and self-driving tech firms are using ordinary cars that are retrofitted with the high-tech needed for self-driving purposes. I point this out because some assert that we will eventually see a shift from using everyday cars to instead having an altogether new kind of car that is built solely and intentionally for self-driving proficiency.

How does this relate to the notion of bait cars?

If a self-driving car stands out as something other than an ordinary car, this will seem to make the self-driving car a chancy choice as a bait car. Presumably, car thieves would right away be worried that something is afoot, and they are being set up.

The irony, of sorts, is that a self-driving car has the kind of electronics and likely remote-control capabilities that makes it ideally suited as a bait car, at least with respect to the law enforcement perspective. Rather than the usual path of taking a car and trying to outfit it with remote control features, the likelihood is that an "ordinary" self-driving car already has all those facilities included.

In that manner of speaking, a self-driving car is a ready-to-go bait car.

The thing is, it won't do much good as a bait car if the crooks realize it is a baited trick. We don't know how smart fish are, but if a fish realizes that a worm on the hook is somehow suspicious, ostensibly the fish will swim right on past and not take the bait.

So, the point being that right now, using a self-driving car as a bait car is not particularly in the cards because it sticks out like a sore thumb. Car thieves would be hesitant to take it and thus the alluring characteristic as bait is over-the-top and unsavory therein. Also, they presumably might be especially suspicious concerning the boatload of electronics being able to track them, even if the self-driving car they are eyeing is not necessarily a bait car per se.

On that point, there is indeed merit.

Self-driving cars are going to be rolling along and recording their whereabouts, capturing video of anything around the vehicle, and likewise storing the other sensory data. This means that anyone that approaches the vehicle is essentially going to be automatically recorded. That's not a desired trait for a car thief. I've emphasized that this also bodes for serious concerns about the privacy of us all since the self-driving car portends a "roving eye" that can note our daily movement and activities (for more on this qualm, see **the link here**).

In one manner of thinking, self-driving cars have a possibility of reducing crime due to the roving eye aspects, but this also potentially comes at the cost of keeping track of all of our whereabouts. Nobody can yet say how this will ultimately play out. Are we putting in place a Big Brother apparatus and we'll relish doing so since it helps to undercut crime, or will the offset reduction in crime not be worth the loss of everyone's privacy?

Returning to the focus on self-driving cars as a potential bait car, another reason that self-driving cars are not currently suitable candidates as a bait car is that there are so few of them. Car thieves usually want to steal a car that will not be immediately spotted as a stolen vehicle. Even if they could somehow steal a self-driving car, it would be easy to spot on our highways and byways.

Furthermore, self-driving cars are right now being pampered by the firms trying to get autonomous vehicles to work. Usually, at the end of a daily tryout on the streets and freeways, the self-driving car is brought to a special warehouse that exists as the maintenance and upkeep facility. Data is downloaded, new software patches are uploaded, and the vehicle is given a full inspection to make sure it is ready for the next day of experimental runs. In that semblance of things, self-driving cars are usually kept under rather strict lock-and-key and you aren't going to just find them parked on the street in an everyday neighborhood.

We can somewhat reasonably cross-out today's self-driving cars as bait cars.

But what about in the future?

Assuming that self-driving cars gradually become tenable, we can expect that there will be more of them deployed onto our roadways. Eventually, perhaps thousands upon many thousands will be deployed, and ultimately many millions.

There are about 250 million conventional cars in the United States alone, and it is anticipated that those will inevitably be usurped by the advent of self-driving cars. Whether we will need 250 million self-driving cars is an open question. Some contend that we can suffice with a much lower number of self-driving cars instead of today's conventional and consumer-owned cars. Others believe that we will become quite dependent upon self-driving cars and will expand our number of driven miles extraordinarily, unleashing a kind of untapped demand, thus we will need zillions of self-driving cars, potentially raising far beyond the 250 million conventional cars of today.

Regardless of your opinion on the number of self-driving cars, we can all likely agree there will be a lot of them. This is an important point in the context of bait cars.

Imagine those self-driving cars are prevalent and no longer being pampered as they are today. We have gotten used to seeing self-driving cars. They are everywhere. In fact, on a daily journey, you see predominantly self-driving cars and very few conventional cars.

Guess what?

This means that self-driving cars could be used as bait cars. They would now be considered the norm of what is seen on the roadways. Having a self-driving car parked on a neighborhood street might be a common sight. Nobody gives a second glance toward a self-driving car.

In that way of thinking, pretty much all cars are once again looking the same, namely that they all look like self-driving cars. If you were to steal one, it will blend in as merely yet another self-driving car roaming around. Nobody would point and stare at the self-driving car. It has become part of the pack or herd of daily self-driving cars and no longer raises an eyebrow when spotted.

Law enforcement might be beset with criminals stealing self-driving cars. As such, the bait car of choice becomes a self-driving car. Tossing some goodies into the backseat or placed onto the front seat might still be a viable added lure. Of course, the future will presumably no longer be using the kinds of laptops and cellphones of today. One can only imagine what those devices will look like.

The car thieves are also bolstered by the fact that they don't even have to drive the stolen vehicle. they can just get into the vehicle and have the AI drive off for them.

Keep in mind that true self-driving cars are being devised to disallow any human accessible driving controls. The idea, which has controversial considerations, would be that the AI driving system is always going to be driving the car and never a human passenger doing so (an added exception is the possibility of having a remotely placed human that can take over the driving controls, though this has tradeoffs too, see my column coverage on the matter).

Seems like a pretty sweet deal, allowing a car thief to steal a car, but not having to drive it, and merely go along for the ride to wherever they are intending to take the absconded vehicle.

All told, you can certainly then see why self-driving cars might be utilized in the future as bait cars. If self-driving cars are the norm, and if car thieves are stealing them, it makes obvious and straightforward sense to use self-driving cars as bait to catch the crooks.

Conclusion

There is a catch though, a big one.

Will it be possible to steal a self-driving car?

Some argue that it will be impossible to do so.

Here's why.

For a conventional car, you get into the vehicle, turn the key to start the engine, or jimmy the vehicle to get the engine to start. You then drive away. The vehicle usually has no provision for videotaping you or otherwise reporting anything about the vehicle being underway (bait cars are the exception).

Self-driving cars will be chockful of recording equipment. The vehicle is also likely connected with a network that electronically is communicating with the car. The assumption is that self-driving cars are going to be tracked continually, doing so by whoever owns the vehicle or via the automaker or self-driving tech firm that crafted the systems.

The means of even starting the vehicle is also likely to be different than the approach used today. Rather than using a key, you'll likely speak to the AI driving system, which might be using facial recognition to ascertain whether you are the appropriate passenger for the vehicle journey that the AI is going to undertake.

In short, the car thief would need to somehow convince the AI driving system to proceed, though presumably the car thief is not authorized to issue such commands or instructions. If somehow, they circumvented that aspect, the self-driving car is nonetheless likely to be conveying where it is going and doing so throughout a driving journey. And it will be recording who got into the vehicle and likely whatever they are doing while inside the self-driving car.

Thus, successfully stealing a self-driving car appears to be an unachievable crime.

You might be smarmy and say that you could potentially tow the self-driving car and steal it that way. Yes, maybe that is possible (though arguably so), but what do you do with the multi-ton paperweight once you get it to wherever you want to go? It still is presumably only going to work via the AI driving system.

Of course, where there is a will, there is a way.

Perhaps via cybersecurity aspects, it might be possible to fool or reprogram an AI driving system, convincing it to become, well, an accomplice in the crime. Will the everyday car thieve be familiar with those advanced techniques and technologies?

It is hard to say, though some believe that we are increasingly heading toward a crime sharing economy, whereby crooks will be savvy about high-tech embedded systems and readily buy and sell sneaky snippets of computer hacks to circumvent online systems security. One supposes that if that happens, the cat and mouse game will have to rachet up accordingly, and bait cars will be set up to seem like everyday self-driving cars but are actually rigged with booster-style capabilities that overcome the known hacks.

The final pinnacle will seem to be if AI becomes sentient, in which case, all bets are off and we really won't know which AI opts to be good and which AI might turn to a life of crime.

Let's hope that we won't see headlines about AI having stolen yet another self-driving car.

Those dastardly AI-based sentient crooks.

CHAPTER 7

JINXES AND SELF-DRIVING CARS

Do you believe it is possible for someone or something to be jinxed?

When you watch sports players get upset at a potential jinx that is wrecking their team due to getting a haircut during the midst of a world series or by the act of wearing mismatched socks, it sure seems like the possibility of getting jinxed is real.

Many do not realize that the idea of a jinx or being jinxed is a longstanding facet that can readily be found in Greek mythology. The belief of jinxes is often seen as a superstitious practice, one rooted in the possibility of curses and the like.

One viewpoint is that jinxes do indeed exist, while an alternative perspective is that if you believe in the essence of jinxing then you are bringing sour luck upon yourself. In other words, this latter way of looking at things is that there really isn't any kind of innate or intrinsic jinx existence per se, but that if you set your mind to believe in the concept of getting jinxed then you will allow yourself to fall into the jinx blaming mantra. You will convince yourself that bad luck is abundant therefore will end-up becoming immersed in it.

In any case, sometimes people are the focus of jinx manifestations, such as saying that a colleague or even a friend that you know is a jinxed person.

The poor soul being classified as a jinx carries quite a societal burden. No matter what they do and how hard they try, the tiniest guffaw or blemish is attributed to their alleged badge-wearing jinx. The stickiness of the jinx stigma is so great that the person could win the lottery, and whatever money won would be considered less than it could have been, merely because of the jinx cloud that they live under.

There is also the notion of objects or things that are jinxed, rather than a human being per se being jinxed.

In sports, there are particular numbers that if worn on your jersey will bring bad luck. Notice that the number is the jinxing element. A number is not a person, and yet it can ostensibly contaminate a person with jinx emanation. The same kind of jinxing powers are ascribed to all types of objects, perhaps a hat or cap that is worn on the head, a coffee mug can be considered a jinxing source, and so on.

What about a car?

Sure, some people are quick to claim that a specific brand or model of car is a jinxed line of automobiles. For example, the problems associated with the Edsel and later on with the Pinto are sometimes pointed out as cars that for whatever reason were perchance jinxed. This can be carried quite deeply in the sense that it wasn't just the manufactured vehicles that were jinxed, but you can go to the original designs and architectural renderings and supposedly contend that the jinx started there.

You've likely have known someone that believed they owned a jinxed car.

After driving the vehicle off the lot of the dealership, things immediately began to go wrong. The bumper of the car falls off, doing so without any provocation. The paint begins peeling and flaking, yet the car is brand new. Starting the engine is a wild gambit since sometimes it starts instantly and in other cases, it refuses to engage.

A person that doesn't believe in jinxes would assert that you bought a lemon.

We have lemon laws that aim to deal with buying a car that has faultiness. Forget about this irrational stuff and concentrate instead on the fact that your car is not working as it should. Probably a lousy job was done at the assembly plant or perhaps the dealership messed with the car. Set aside this ridiculous amorphous jinx notion and instead find the human hand that was the culprit in producing these fully explainable humans derived problems.

If you don't already believe in the seemingly mysterious existence of jinxes, you are bound to discount any such claims and try to steer attention to the scientific and mechanistic explanations for why things go wrong. Meanwhile, if you do believe in jinxes, at least somewhat, you probably walk a tightrope between wanting to disregard a jinx and nonetheless not let a jinxing activity or effort intrude upon your life. Those that are fully vested in the power of jinxes are apt to avoid them whenever possible and also interpret actions that go wrong as indubitably caused or inflamed as a result of a jinx.

Speaking of cars, consider the future of cars and the advent of self-driving cars.

Here's an interesting question to ponder: *Will AI-based true self-driving cars be susceptible to being jinxed?*

Let's unpack the matter and see.

Self-Driving Cars And Jinxes

For Level 4 and Level 5 true self-driving vehicles, there won't be a human driver involved in the driving task.

All occupants will be passengers.

The AI is doing the driving.

For some people, a self-driving car has two paths towards being jinxed. There is the usual path of the self-driving car being, well, a car.

As earlier mentioned, sometimes cars can be construed as being jinxed, though whether this is merely a label that is used to denote a car that happens to have troubles versus one that possesses some intangible aura of bad luck, you'll need to be the judge.

The second path for presumed availability of being jinxed is the AI side of things. Yes, you might be willing to assert that an AI driving system could be jinxed. This seems farfetched, but if you are open to believing that objects can be jinxed, the AI is a type of object and therefore falls within the jinx permissible categorization.

I'm betting that some of you know of computer programs that you swear are absolutely jinxed. Maybe you've written one yourself. The jinxed program will do oddball things and seems to defy efforts to debug it and figure out why. In your heart, you know that the program will only do what it has been programmed to do, and thus there must be a crisp and clear-cut underlying basis for any anomalies, yet those assumed axiomatic principles appear to be uprooted by enigmatic bugs and systems issues.

A smarmy software developer might wave off the unexplained glitches and say that the program has a mind of its own. Of course, there isn't any computer program that has crossed the line from simple code into a semblance of sentience. No matter what the headlines keep touting about the latest AI capabilities, be assured that none of it is anywhere close to being sentient.

That being said, at some future point in time, we might achieve AI that is sentient.

At that juncture, if it arrives, one supposes that you could assign the jinxing possibilities to the "soul" of the machine (cleverly got a Tracy Kidder reference subtly in there), though this is quite a leap of logic as to what sentience means and how it will be manifested in AI.

So, getting back to the focus on self-driving cars, there is the car as a cornerstone for being a jinx and there is also the AI driving system that can be the jinxed component.

Self-driving cars appear to provide a twofer for those that faithfully subscribe to the powers of jinxes.

Could a jinx ever befall a self-driving car?

Here's something that will potentially knock your socks off.

When Uber had the calamity of their self-driving car deadly incident in Arizona, some suggested that it was a sign or indication that the Uber self-driving car efforts were jinxed.

Later on, and for those that believed in the jinx aspects, they were relieved to see Uber decide to essentially selloff their self-driving car activities and apparently get out of the jinx abyss. Despite trying to tell those people that the Uber move was based on business logic and models of profitability, the jinx believers retorted that this was merely window dressing justification for something that was otherwise mired in the jinx milieu.

The odds are that we are going to see the jinx moniker getting associated with self-driving cars, one way or another.

Consider this scenario.

Someone gets into a self-driving car, doing so for an easy and straightforward ride to the grocery store. The AI driving system proceeds to make its way to the mall where the grocery store is located. Sensors of the self-driving car, including video cameras, radar, LIDAR, ultrasonic units, and the like are all collecting sensory info about the driving environment.

Within the onboard computer processors, the AI has been programmed to assess the data flowing in from the sensors. This data is examined to identify where the road is, where pedestrians are, and otherwise scope out the surroundings. After doing MSDF (Multi-Sensory Data Fusion), the AI updates a virtual model of the driving circumstances. This internal computational model is used to determine which roads to take and how to safely drive the vehicle.

The AI is sending electronic commands to the under-the-hood driving controls (the driving controls are not available to the passengers of the vehicle). While on neighborhood streets, the AI driving system is going slowly, abiding strictly by the speed limits. Upon reaching a highway, the AI driving system gets the car to speed-up and flow smoothly with the available traffic conditions.

Okay, things seem relatively normal and pretty much what you'd expect a self-driving car to do.

All of a sudden, the self-driving car makes a somewhat dramatic swerve.

The rider in this self-driving car gets tossed around a bit. They are wearing a seatbelt, which will still be required even in the safest of self-driving cars, and fortunately, the passenger wasn't harmed by the swerving action. It was though somewhat upsetting.

The flummoxed rider looks around to spot what triggered the self-driving car to make the acute swerve. There doesn't seem to be any debris in the roadway. There wasn't someone on a bicycle and nor was there an errant pedestrian nearby. By general inspection of the street scene, there seems to be no discernable basis for the out-of-the-blue swerving action by the AI driving system.

Let's do some quick forensics engineering on this incident.

It could be that the AI driving system detected something that the passenger did not see.

Perhaps there was debris laying on the roadway and from the vantage point of the rider, it could not be seen. Or maybe a car that was in the adjacent lane had made a slight move toward the self-driving car, enough to prompt the AI driving system to mathematically calculate a heightened risk of a potential collision.

All in all, there is presumably a reasonable explanation for why the AI driving system took the presumably evasive action. And, with all due respect to those developing the software for self-driving cars, there is always the chance too that there is some kind of software bug or issue that might have led to the AI undertaking the action.

Furthermore, there is the chance of things working as intended, though doing so by a kind of false premise. Envision a visual reflection off of a camera that might have produced a false positive could have prompted the AI driving system to make the maneuver, especially if the action was categorized as "better safe than sorry" in terms of the probability that it might not be needed versus that it could be performed as a safety precaution. Better to shake up a passenger rather than getting into a car crash that might have much worse outcomes for the rider.

Now, here's where things take a turn, an ugly one, as it were.

The passenger believes the self-driving car is jinxed.

This seems sensible to the rider because there is no other apparent reason for the swerving action.

As an aside, this brings up an important point that I've tried to repeatedly emphasize to the automakers and self-driving tech firms about the user interface for riders in self-driving cars. Many of the existing approaches do not inform the passenger about maneuvers and navigation during a driving journey (see my columns for numerous exhortations on this). Other than having gotten the destination from the rider, usually at the start of the journey, there is not much other interaction as yet by the AI driving systems with the passengers in the vehicle.

A prime example was a recent rider in a prominent brand self-driving car that said they were somewhat baffled as to why the self-driving car drove them in a seemingly circuitous route to their sought destination (as reported online). The AI seemed to select a route that the passenger, already familiar with the area, believed was unnecessarily longer than needed and seemed a quite puzzling choice.

It could be that there was roadwork on some of the more common paths to the destination and the AI driving system was trying to avoid the construction impediments. Another possibility is that the "normal" path went past a school ground, and the AI driving system was programmed to try and avoid such areas while on a driving journey, if feasible, purely for safety purposes. Etc.

But the AI driving system did not inform the passenger about the basis for the routing.

Nor was there an immediate means for the passenger to ask the AI what it was doing.

That being said, there was a provision for the passenger to alert a remote human agent, kind of OnStar-like, which could have potentially allowed the rider to ask why the routing was taken. The passenger did not avail themselves of that feature, somewhat understandably so since the routing was not particularly earthshattering as a matter at hand.

In any case, the side point here is that the AI driving systems and the Natural Language Processing (NLP) interactivity with passengers has to get further attention and inevitably will be a significant determiner of how people will choose the brand of a self-driving car to use. Right now, this is not a differentiator, but once self-driving cars are prevalent, the NLP interface will loom quite large.

Returning to the swerving scenario, the rider in that use case could likely activate a connection with the remote agents that are monitoring the fleet of self-driving cars. Some riders will do so, some will decide not to do so. We might guess that those that lean toward a belief in jinxes might be less likely to try and find out what logical explanation might be proffered for the swerving incident.

The passenger that incurred the "inexplicable" swerving is convinced that the self-driving car is jinxed.

So what?

Turns out this rider is a social media influencer that has zillions of followers. We all know what social media influencers are apt to do, namely make postings that will get them even more views. The rider then quickly sends out a posting and declares that this brand of self-driving cars is jinxed. Word spreads rapidly and the posting goes viral. It would certainly seem likely to do so, especially when pushed by the social media influencer.

Does this mean that indeed that specific brand of self-driving cars is jinxed?

A rather crazy assumption and abundantly scientifically unfair.

Surely the automaker or self-driving tech firm would refute the jinx labeling. You can just imagine the feverish pursuit internally as the AI developers trace the cause of the swerving action to ergo provide a perfectly sensible and rational explanation for why the AI self-driving system opted to make the radical maneuver.

Perhaps the unfair jinx tarnishing won't stick and people will not take the claim seriously.

Then again, some might assert that the jinx tag is justifiable and that any rationalized explanation is a cover-up of sorts. On top of that, there might be those that say the self-driving car is jinxed due to the act of the social influencer, irrespective of the swerving action. They contend that merely the aspect that someone says they are jinxed is a sure sign of being jinxed, and the initiating act that led to the jinx assertion is no longer relevant.

Circular logic that makes your eyes roll.

Conclusion

Some people believe in jinxes and some do not.

For those that do not, the branding of being jinxed is always real, no matter whether jinxes are real, and can carry a stigma that will be arduous to overcome.

Here's a handy trick to keep in mind.

It is said that by knocking on a piece of wood, you can cure or undo a jinx.

All self-driving cars ought to have a small block of wood somewhere inside the vehicle, something nicely lacquered and stylish looking, for which those riders that think there might be a jinx therein, all they need to do is knock on that conveniently provided piece of wood.

Then again, rather than relying on the passenger to do so, maybe outfit the AI driving system with a means to knock on the wood, and the AI could then be programmed to avert any jinxes by taking the wood knocking action as needed.

Let's just hope the AI wouldn't need to be doing this repeatedly during the driving journeys.

CHAPTER 8
BOULDERING AND SELF-DRIVING CARS

Have you ever been subjected to another driver doing the so-called *road bouldering* maneuver?

You undoubtedly have.

The driving technique is rather straightforward.

Envision yourself calmly driving on a multi-lane highway and you are using the fast lane to proceed along quite smoothly. All of a sudden, up ahead, a car moves into your lane and seems to be driving at a leisurely speed. It is readily apparent to you that this other car is going slower than you are and that you will soon catch-up and become blocked by the other driver.

They are road bouldering.

Actually, more specifically, they are road bouldering you.

This attempt at impeding your progress might be done by pure happenstance. The other driver is lollygagging and merely enjoying some treasured driving time on the highway. They aren't paying attention to the traffic. They rarely if ever use their rearview mirror to see what is behind them. When making a lane change, they just saunter over into the adjacent lane and assume anyone else will accommodate their intrusion.

On the other hand, it could be that the driver is purposely aiming to thwart your progress.

One reason might be that they believe you are unlawfully going over the speed limit and they imagine themselves as a kind of rolling highway patrol, a kind of superpower and try to find ways to ostensibly even things out and provide justice for us all. By getting in front of you, they intend to slow you down. This is certainly for the good of humanity and they are virtuous in their cause (so they believe).

Another possible reason is that they are upset that you are doing something they would like to do, and yet feel compelled to obey the law, therefore they are somewhat envious or jealous of your maverick actions. The purpose of stalling your progress is a revenge play. If they can't speed along, by gosh you should not be able to do so either.

There are plenty more reasons for intentionally performing a road bouldering effort.

For example, it could be that a few minutes earlier there was something that happened involving your car and their car. Maybe you veered toward their vehicle and they didn't like the menacing act, though whether you did so by design or by mistake is not necessarily known. In any case, the driver might speed-up quickly to get ahead of you, and then place themselves directly in front of your vehicle, and then slow down. This is a means of showing you that you aren't the boss and ought to be more deferential and civil in your driving activities.

Of course, those myriads of reasons are not of much good since the likely outcome is that the driver being blocked is not going to somehow learn a vital life lesson by the road bouldering stunt. It seems that the person doing the road bouldering, when consciously doing so, assumes that the other driver will be spurred into realizing the err of their ways. They will finally see the light, as it were. This will cause a form of repentance, and never again will that driver repeat whatever unpleasant or untoward driving action that started the road bouldering response, to begin with.

Good luck on that.

The reality is that the driver that was cut off is going to more than likely get irked. This irksome reaction can produce a series of consequential steps that are risky and possibly deadly for them and all other nearby cars. Also, the irked driver might decide they going to proceed outright into a full-on road rage mode and opt to drive in a madcap and evildoer way for the remainder of their driving journey.

The reaction to one road bouldering incident can produce a monstrous and long-lasting response.

Let's be clear, no one is doing the right thing in any of these scenarios.

The person performing the road bouldering might believe in their heart that they are doing the moral or decent thing by blocking others that are scofflaws or roadway driving bandits. Vigilante justice is seen as the only way to prevent those dastardly uncaring drivers from taking over the byways and highways of our land. Unfortunately, even if there is a heartfelt basis for doing road bouldering, the act is not only frowned upon, it likely is an illegal act in itself.

The effort to impede the flow of others, despite the belief that it is justified, can land the road bouldering implementer in the same or worse category of driving unlawfully and dangerously.

Admittedly, the driver being blocked could be indeed usurping the law as a driver. That's wrong too.

On the other hand, there is also the chance that the blocked driver is completely innocent in the matter. Sometimes a road bouldering action takes place by the purely mindless happenstance of the driver doing the blocking action. There is no awareness of their doing so. The driver being blocked did not undertake some transgression that led to the bouldering.

Furthermore, the driver doing the road bouldering might mistakenly pick the wrong target. Maybe there was a red colored car that stung them a few miles back. They have been watching for the red car in hopes of undertaking the road bouldering. They see a red car and assume it is the same one as before. The reality might be that it is someone else and thus are utterly absent of any prior entanglement.

Nonetheless, they get the road bouldering treatment.

The sad thing is that the driver that is blocked might then become triggered into doing adverse acts. In that case, a perfectly calm driver that was obeying the law and driving safely is transformed into a crazed driver. They didn't start their day by thinking they would go into a driving frenetic mode, but the road bouldering was a piece of straw on the camel's back that triggered them into a furious reaction.

Speaking of road bouldering, perhaps consider your own driving efforts. Without triggering you unduly right now, dare I say or suggest that you might have perchance performed a road bouldering action at some point in your lengthy driving tenure?

I'm sure that you have, we all have.

Anyone that solemnly swears they've never employed road bouldering can supposedly be the first to cast the driver's stone, as they say.

There are some relatively unique situations whereby a driver has never done road bouldering.

For example, newbie drivers can potentially attest to not having done road bouldering. Those teenagers that are just starting to drive are unlikely to have enough roadway miles under their belt to have performed the road bouldering. That being said, it won't be long before they will take such action. Again, it can occur by lack of awareness or via a purposeful motive.

Shifting gears, consider the future of cars and the act of driving.

Here is an interesting question: *Will AI-based self-driving cars be subjected to road bouldering by human drivers, and will self-driving cars opt to undertake road bouldering as a driving strategy?*

Let's unpack the matter and see.

Self-Driving Cars And Road Bouldering

For Level 4 and Level 5 true self-driving vehicles, there won't be a human driver involved in the driving task.

All occupants will be passengers.

The AI is doing the driving.

Guess what?

Human drivers are already doing the road bouldering stunt to self-driving cars. Yes, even though there aren't many self-driving cars as yet on our roadways, the ones that are being tested out are getting their fair share of road bouldering done to them.

As mentioned earlier, sometimes road bouldering is performed by a human driver that is clueless about their driving actions. In this instance, they get in front of a self-driving car, oftentimes not aware they are directly ahead of a self-driving car, and manage to bring forth a road bouldering activity. Innocently performed.

Not all such occasions are entirely innocent.

There are some human drivers that upon spying a self-driving car are eager to perform a road bouldering action.

Why so?

They usually think it is a "cute idea" to showcase what they think is a funny action toward a self-driving car. Take that, they are imagining in their minds, as though they are trying to demonstrate that human drivers are better than AI driving systems and the proof of the pudding is the ability to undertake a road bouldering activity.

I've repeatedly exhorted that human drivers that are trying to prank self-driving cars are wrong to do so. These bullying drivers are creating potentially dangerous situations and endangering them and everyone else nearby. You shouldn't road boulder a self-driving car, and nor should you do a road boulder to a human driver.

Excise that road bouldering from your driving repertoire, as in stop doing it.

Another mental concoction by some human drives involves the wonderment of what a self-driving car will do when confronted with a road bouldering action. For this kind of thinking, the human driver believes they are doing a service to mankind. Those darned AI driving system had better know how to handle a road bouldering circumstance, and it is up to this particular human driver to ferret out whether the AI can handle the driving or not.

Get off the road, you AI driver, if you can't take the heat.

Again, despite the appearance of presumably wanting to provide a service to humanity, doing road bouldering to a self-driving car is not to be done. Rest assured that there are enough everyday road bouldering events that occur by happenstance and there is no need to devise intentional ones.

Plus, the odds are that the AI driving system has already been exercised on-road bouldering possibilities due to the millions of simulated miles of driving that the automakers and self-driving tech firms do with their self-driving cars. There is also a solid chance that during closed track runs of the self-driving car, which involves non-public roads that are set aside for experimental use of self-driving cars, road bouldering has been practiced upon the self-driving cars.

This does bring up some added points worth considering.

First, what will an AI driving system do when it is impeded by a road bouldering action?

It all depends.

Numerous AI driving systems are being crafted, each with its own way of handling the driving chores. You cannot state universally that all self-driving cars will make use of the same driving techniques and perform the same way in all driving scenarios. By-and-large, they are all being programmed or crafted to drive legally, but this leaves a huge opening in terms of how to otherwise drive a car.

We all perform our driving within a vast latitude of driving practices. This is true even when constrained by the legal rules of the road. The laws do not pin down every iota of how you should drive. One person that is driving legally can be driving somewhat differently than another nearby person that is driving legally.

Back to the self-driving car and what the response would be to road bouldering, one possibility is that the self-driving car does essentially nothing about it. In other words, the AI driving system comes upon a car that is slowing progress, and the AI mathematically computes that this is generally okay, opting to slow down the self-driving car and try to maintain a proper driving distance from the other car.

Some AI driving systems are regrettably not yet at a high caliber of driving prowess.

This means that for example the self-driving car can be "convinced" to slow down and come to a stop, merely by a car ahead of it doing the road bouldering and progressively getting slower and slower, until coming to a halt. There are reported cases of allegedly this being done by police cars that wanted to slow down a Tesla that was on Autopilot and the human driver had (wrongly, dangerously) fallen asleep (be clear that Autopilot is not yet a true self-driving capability).

A problem with this somewhat blind-leading-the-blind of a self-driving car also referred to as follow-the-leader or the Piped Piper syndrome, is that we would not expect a human-driven car to fall for such a trick.

In some instances, it might make sense for a human driver to gradually be slowed down to a full stop when behind another car, but most of the time, this would seem nonsensical. The human driver being subjected to road bouldering would assess the driving situation and try to ascertain what is taking place and whether the vehicle should be slowing down to a halt or perhaps take some other driving action.

The point is that there are AI driving systems that are not well suited as yet to respond to the road bouldering and will merely comply by staying behind the vehicle that is deploying the driving act. There is no further assessment of the roadway scene and the driving circumstances by the AI system.

Gradually, and seemingly inevitable, the response to road bouldering will become more advanced. The AI ought to be examining the opportunities to avoid road bouldering. Perhaps change lanes or take some similar action.

You might be wondering whether the AI will react in the same manner that humans might, such as honking the horn or flashing the headlights. Right now, most of the AI driving systems are not programmed to do that kind of action, which is purposely being avoided since the use of the horn or the flashing of headlights is an unlikely way to produce a desirable result. Sure, sometimes this helps to alert a human driver that does not realize what they are doing, but at the same time, it can be a disturbing trigger that makes the human driver enraged.

Whereas it used to be that everyone "knew" that you would honk your horn or flash your headlights, doing so in today's world is quite risky business. Probably prudent to not have AI driving systems use that approach, though an argument can be made that it should have this available in its back pocket, as it were, ready to be used when assuredly useful.

The final twist on this topic is the question of whether a self-driving car should itself make use of road bouldering.

This is a tougher nut to crack since there are two avenues of thought, one being that a self-driving car by happenstance will get into a situation whereby it performs road bouldering (the act of the innocent, as indicated earlier about human drivers), and the other is the intentional use of road bouldering. When I refer to intentionality and an AI driving system, do not mistake that to imply that the AI is sentient. None of today's AI is anywhere close to sentience. I am referring to the notion that the AI is programmed to try and explicitly use a road bouldering tactic when the moment for such usage is computationally calculated as worthy of doing.

There is a somewhat third ground or muddling instance of an AI driving system that has used Machine Learning or Deep Learning and has settled onto a road bouldering technique using mathematical pattern matching. In essence, the AI computationally found a pattern in how people drive and has adopted that same pattern, which in this case is the road bouldering action.

Generally, the automakers and self-driving tech firms are not purposely having the AI use a road bouldering tactic.

At the same time, it is going to occur with great frequency for the simple reason that self-driving cars are being programmed to drive legally. In essence, by going the speed limit, the odds are pretty high that self-driving cars are going to be doing a kind of road bouldering. Human drivers that are accustomed to going faster than the speed limit are going to get upset at the road bouldering trend of self-driving cars.

Conclusion

Some people are elated that self-driving cars are going to be doing road bouldering, though they don't use that nomenclature to refer to the action.

The reason for this elation is that if self-driving cars are nearly always driving at or less than the speed limit, and if this causes human drivers to slow down from their speeding ways, this is an exalted outcome of self-driving cars. By forcing human drivers to go slower, the hope is that human drivers will get into fewer car crashes and when they do get into a car crash it will be less injurious due to being at a slower speed.

I'm not so sure that this is going to work out in the manner envisioned.

Is it realistic to assume that human drivers will abide by the "slower" moving self-driving cars, despite the legally correct aspect that the self-driving cars are merely obeying the law?

This seems immensely doubtful (some humans will, many will not).

Instead, what seems more realistic is that human drivers will get irked by self-driving cars that are doing these actions. This might cause human drivers to decide to take dangerous reactive courses of action. They will make those crazy lane changes and do all sorts of driving trickery. And, sadly, this might in turn lead to even more car crashes of human drivers. The odds are that more car crashes of human drivers will likely entangle self-driving cars into the car accidents morass too.

A vicious and disastrous cycle. One obvious solution is to have the AI driving system attempt to ascertain if they are doing a road bouldering act, whether by design or by happenstance. As much as possible, the AI driving system should try to avoid being a road boulder and get out of the way of other traffic.

For this way of thinking, many of today's AI driving systems are programmed to try and stay in the slow lane and not get into the fast lane unless absolutely necessary. But this is not much of a viable way to drive, and it would inevitably become obvious to passengers inside self-driving cars that they are being driven around in a manner that seems much less expeditious than human drivers. In that case, passengers might decide to use human-driven cars, such as ridesharing, over switching to the use of AI-based self-driving cars.

Some wonder whether road bouldering is that notable of a topic and deserving of any rapt attention. One thought is that sometimes, something that seems like a molehill is really in fact a mountain, and we ought to be aware of boulders that can cascade until we have an entire avalanche on our hands.

Watch out for those road bouldering moments and drive safely.

CHAPTER 9
DRIVERS SPEEDING AND SELF-DRIVING CARS

Let's take a close look at some crucial driving statistics from last year entailing everyday conventional driving.

The driving-related stats of last year are an eye-opening and quite revealing instance of what likely happens when a significant element of prevailing traffic conditions gets demonstratively altered.

Due to the pandemic, there was a lot less traffic last year, logically so. You would naturally assume that this would ergo suggest that there would be lowered number of car crash fatalities since there is much less traffic all told. Indeed, the count of car crash fatalities did decrease, though only by a slim difference of about 2% (not as much a decrease as might be expected).

Meanwhile, here's the twist to the statistical intrigue.

Despite the sizable drop in the volume of cars on the roadways and the modest drop in the count of related fatalities, the car crash fatality rate per miles driven rose by about 18% reaching a level of 1.25 car-related crash deaths per 100 million vehicle miles (it was approximately 1.06 the prior year).

In short, the frequency of getting into a death producing car crash was greatly enhanced.

That's bad.

That's real bad.

The stats almost seem like one of those oddball paradoxes. There was less overall traffic and fewer (somewhat) driving-related fatalities, and yet at the same time, there was a humongous jump in the frequency of car crash deaths per miles driven.

Why did this happen?

The explanation that seems most sensible is that for those drivers behind the steering wheel during the pandemic time period, it was readily feasible to drive at higher speeds due to the lessened traffic in their way.

Yes, that indubitably makes sense.

And by going faster, they tended to suffer mightily when getting into a car crash, which is a usual outcome of high speeds and the consequences of car accidents. There is also the added chances of actually getting into a car accident per se since there is less time to react and it becomes problematic to avoid being embroiled in a crash when such an emerging moment arises.

Some pundits have characterized the presumed phenomena as indictive that people will drive recklessly, including and especially speeding if they are given an opportunity to do so.

Intuitively this all makes sense, albeit a sad commentary on human behavior and the role of driving a car.

In a more Utopian world, it could have been that the drivers during the pandemic were keenly aware of the frailty of existence and therefore would drive extraordinarily safely and with extreme caution. They would undertake the driving task in an abundantly lawful and cautious way. No speeding. There presumably would be no need to speed since the roads were ostensibly more open and traffic flow was smoother and closer to allowable maximum speeds than is usually the case.

The reality seems to be that the reaction of some drivers was that the lessened traffic meant that the roadways were wide open for driving like a racecar driver. Put the pedal to the metal. Punch it and let those tires peel.

I don't want to appear to be saying that all drivers did this. Assuredly, some drivers undoubtedly drove safely, perhaps even more safely than normal. For those drivers, thanks for being a mindful user of the highways and byways.

For those drivers that seemed to abuse the advantage of less traffic, we'll divide them into two camps.

One group of such drivers would be those that drove faster by happenstance and were somewhat lulled into being a less safe driver. They found themselves going faster and faster, not aware of the potential consequences. The roads were open. Open roads allow for going fast. In fact, they might argue that they weren't aware of how fast they were going since there wasn't traffic that they were passing during the driving journey. We all know how easy it is to incur "highway hypnosis" whereby you become a mental zombie that becomes entrenched while at the driving controls.

In short, they didn't know any better.

The other group of drivers will be labeled herein as roadway aggressors (I'm being exceedingly polite and shall mildly note that cruder terminology characterizing these drivers is often used).

These are people that will exploit any traffic condition, regardless of packed lanes versus empty lanes. When the roads are jammed with cars, these drivers are nonetheless going to weave in and out of traffic and do whatever they can to make progress. Imagine their glee when there is less traffic on the roadway. You might as well have declared that NASCAR racing is now allowed on the nation's highways. Since they were no longer confined to their traffic congestion driving skills, the aggressors opted to employ freewheel driving acumen and relished the rabid excitement of doing so.

In short, they knew better but consciously chose to be exploitive.

Does it matter that there were two camps?

Somewhat, to the degree that it would be relatively easy to raise the awareness of the segment that didn't know any better and perhaps get them to tone things down and drive more cautiously. The aggressor group is seemingly immune to being told to slow down and take things more mindfully. Someone that has that in-your-face driving attitude is usually shaped only by getting caught red-handed, nailed by the police for speeding and driving recklessly. Of those that get caught, some won't even learn to adjust their driving and will instead try to find "better" ways to avoid getting nabbed.

Shifting gears, the future of cars involves the advent of self-driving cars.

An important consideration about the emergence of AI-based true self-driving cars is how human drivers will react or respond to having self-driving cars intermixing on the roadways with humanity. Few are putting much thought into the possible reactions by human drivers to driving next to and with nearby self-driving cars.

The driving stats about the pandemic showcase that humans alter their driving behaviors depending upon the traffic circumstances.

Here's an interesting question to ponder: *Will the advent of AI-based true self-driving cars prod or spur nearby human drivers to drive differently?*

Let's unpack the matter and see.

Self-Driving Cars And Nearby Human Drivers

For Level 4 and Level 5 true self-driving vehicles, there won't be a human driver involved in the driving task.

All occupants will be passengers.

The AI is doing the driving.

This bodes for exciting times.

The hope is that there will be a lot fewer car crashes due to the AI doing the driving. AI driving systems are not going to drink and drive. AI driving systems are not going to drive in a distracted manner. The focus entirely of the AI driving system is devoted to driving the car. Human drivers are apt to drive while intoxicated or drive while watching cat videos. Right now, there are about 40,000 car crash-related fatalities annually in the United States and an estimated 2.3 million related injuries to people.

Some believe that the number of fatalities will drop to zero because of self-driving cars, but I've debunked this claim and exhorted repeatedly that there is a zero chance of zero fatalities. The physics of a car and the driving task will inevitably lead to some amount of car crashes and deaths, even including the use of self-driving cars. That being said, the deaths and injuries will inevitably be significantly lessened (every life spared is decidedly notable), and the number of self-driving car specific crashes will be much lower than conventional driving.

One assumption that some people keep making is that there will be a magical overnight switcheroo of us driving conventional cars to suddenly having all and only self-driving cars on our roadways.

That's just not sensible.

The introduction of AI-based true self-driving cars is going to be quite gradual. It will take years upon years for the amount of traffic to shift toward being self-driving cars versus being undertaken by conventional human-driven cars. There are about 250 million conventional cars in the U.S. today and those cars are not going to simply disappear out of thin air. They will continue to be used and there will be an ongoing mix of both human-driven cars and self-driving cars on our roadways.

As an aside, there is a brewing controversy associated with the potential extinction of human driving.

If you believe that self-driving cars are going to radically reduce bad driving, and save lives, the natural assertion is that human-driven cars ought to be outlawed and banned from our roadways. This is an extreme viewpoint in certainly the short-term as it will take many years, likely decades, for enough self-driving cars to be produced and made available to meet our driving journey needs.

Some oppose the idea of banning human driving. This idea of disallowing human driving seems altogether Dystopian to them. Driving is considered a privilege, but many see it as a basic human right. There are passionate debates on this topic, including those that say you will only get them to give up their driving when you pry their cold dead hands from the steering wheel.

Putting aside that controversy for the moment, we'll focus herein on the reality that there will be an intermixing of self-driving cars and human-driven cars on our roadways, which will exist for quite a while.

Hopefully, we can all agree to that at face value.

You might be thinking that there is no difference between how humans drive today and how they will drive whence there are self-driving cars on the roadways, thus, mixing together self-driving cars and human-driven cars is a non-issue and without any semblance of hullabaloo.

I don't think such an assumption is fully thought through.

I'll explain why in a moment.

Before we get into the details, when referring to the mixture of self-driving cars and human-driven cars, keep in mind that the proportions are going to adjust over a moderated time period. For example, we might begin with less than 1% of the total cars on the roads being self-driving cars, and the rest of the 99% consists of human-driven cars. At some time thereafter, the proportion will shift and become (let's say) about 20% of self-driving cars and 80% of human-driven cars. This will continue adjusting, eventually reaching 50/50, then tipping toward more self-driving cars than there are self-driving cars.

On a somewhat finer technical point, the number of vehicles is not as vital as the number of miles driven. I say this because it is anticipated that self-driving cars might be operating 24x7, continually underway and only rarely not in motion, while a conventional human-driven car sits unused for about 95% or more of its available time. Rather than comparing the number of vehicles, it is usually preferred to compare based on miles driven, a more universal metric.

Okay, we will have self-driving cars on our roadways and they will gradually become more prominent and in a sense more dominant in terms of the likely volume of traffic activity.

How will those human drivers react?

If a self-driving car drove in precisely the same manner as a human driver, the easy answer is that there would presumably be no difference in how human drivers will be driving. The human drivers would ostensibly not even realize that the car ahead of them is a self-driving car (well, perhaps the sensory gear is a telltale sign, but even that is getting streamlined and all cars might eventually have the same overall appearance, both human-driven, and self-driving).

You would drive as you do today.

Most of the time, you know nothing whatsoever about the drivers in the other cars nearby to you. All that you know is that they are driving a car and the car is nearby. You attempt to infer what kind of a driver they are by observing their driving. You rarely observe them directly as a human being, and instead, you watch how their car moves and maneuvers. From the actions of their car, you might ascribe some beliefs to the type of person they are, though this is just a guess and based on the driving that you see, and not by having sat with them over a cup of coffee and discussed global politics and the like.

Overall, the point is that if self-driving cars could drive in exactly the same manner as human drivers, the human drivers on the roadways with self-driving cars would not have any apparent means to realize that there are some cars around them being driven by humans and some being driven by an AI driving system (all else being equal).

The thing is, at least right now, self-driving cars aren't driving exactly like humans.

For example, by-and-large the automakers and self-driving tech firms are programming their self-driving cars to always drive in a fully legal manner. This means that there is no speeding allowed. The AI driving system is supposed to adhere to whatever posted speed limit exists in any passage of roadway.

I ask you, do humans always abide by the speed limits?

Unless you've never been on the road, you would for sure acknowledge that human drivers are apt to go faster than the speed limit. Routinely so. This is true not only on highways and freeways, it happens in places you would think it absolutely ought to not occur, such as in school ground zones. Yes, people drive past the speed limit on all manner of occasions.

This lambasting of human drivers is not intended as a rebuke of human driving (though it certainly has that edge), and instead simply emphasizes that there is an already pronounced difference between today's self-driving cars and the nature of human drivers, namely, self-driving cars abide by the speed limit, while human drivers will often speed.

There are other ways in which self-driving cars are driving differently than human drivers, right now, but I won't belabor that point and merely establish that speeding is one of many such differences. Speeding is a big one since it is highly noticeable.

Here's what sometimes happens when a human driver encounters a self-driving car on today's roadways.

There is a self-driving car up ahead of a human driver. For human drivers that have already seen self-driving cars, they know that the self-driving car is going to strictly abide by the speed limit.

In theory, if you are behind a self-driving car that is going the speed limit, you ought to keep your proper driving distance and also be going the speed limit, matching whatever speed the self-driving car is doing. This would be the proper and sensible way for a human to drive.

Sure, some human drivers will do that.

Unfortunately, some human drivers won't tolerate those darned slow-poke self-driving cars. It is almost the same as coming up behind a car that has a bright sticker saying it is a student driver. You know that means the car is going to do the speed limit, stop at all stop signs, allow pedestrians to fully cross the road, etc. This can be infuriating to those drivers that prefer the more assertive style of driving.

What do such drivers do when encountering a driving school teenage driver?

Many of these aggressive drivers decide to take matters into their own hands. They realize that driving on the bumper of the novice driver won't do much good and only makes the student driver nervous, likely sparking them to go even more slowly. So, the "best" option would be to circumvent that driver. Drive around them. Furthermore, since the driver has caused you to suffer a delay, the odds are that when you drive around them, you are going to speed-up to compensate for the exasperating delay.

This is the same reaction that those aggressive drivers are having when coming upon a self-driving car.

The reaction involves consternation that they are perhaps once again stuck behind a strict law-abiding self-driving car. The human driver anticipates that the AI driving system will proceed purely at the speed limit and no more so, it will stop fully at stop signs, and so on. This is going to be a huge inconvenience and not to be tolerated.

Thus, aggressive drivers go around the self-driving car. They sometimes rocket past, wanting to make up for a lost time while having followed behind the self-driving car. The irony, of sorts, would be that these aggressive drivers are likely to speed, more than usual, based on their belief that they need to overcome the delay while having been behind the self-driving car.

Remember earlier the point made that human drivers would adjust their driving behavior depending upon the traffic conditions?

Well, a self-driving car is changing the driving conditions.

Currently, a self-driving car is driving in a legal manner that is generally unlike the driving of many human drivers. There are so few self-driving cars on the roadways that this is not especially evident as yet. Only those people that perchance live in an area where self-driving cars are being fielded would have experienced this phenomenon.

Also, the phenomenon is only "in the small" at this time since few self-driving cars are being used on the roadways. Imagine that once there is a significant proportion of self-driving cars on the roads, this would become a quite pronounced difference between the way that self-driving cars drive and the way that human drivers drive.

Presumably, there will be those human drivers that opt to cope with self-driving cars by doing all kinds of reckless driving and speeding too. Some of those human drivers will be like those mentioned earlier that are unaware of how they are reacting to self-driving cars. They will be doing so without the realization that is doing so. You'll also have the other camp. Those are the aggressive drivers that will be gunning for self-driving cars in the sense of the moment they spot one, they will go into their super-aggressive human driving mode.

One facet is that if an aggressive driver did something untoward related to another human-driven car, there is a chance that the other driver will react adversely. This happens quite frequently, at times leading to road rage.

Will a self-driving car be irked by these aggressive drivers and go into a road rage mode?

No, it seems highly unlikely.

This would be a possibility if programmed to react that way, though it seems hard to imagine that automakers and self-driving tech firms are going to include a road rage mode into their AI driving systems (a dicey idea).

Recall that I mentioned there are other differences between an AI driving system and human driving?

Believe it or not, the aspect that the AI won't go into road rage mode is yet another difference. A subtle one, for sure, but demonstrative. Human drivers that realize the self-driving car will not react to nearby bad driving or will react submissively, are more than happy to exploit this difference (spurring the humans toward further reckless driving acts).

Conclusion

What to do about this conundrum?

One reply is that this "proves" that human drivers have to be given the heave-ho. Get rid of human drivers and this problem is solved.

Another perspective is that self-driving cars should be programmed to be aggressive drivers and thus be more human-like in how the driving is taking place. If humans are speeding, by gosh, the AI driving systems should be doing the same. Mimic human driving and then all drivers will essentially be on the same playing field.

That's a quite abhorrent notion for many, since the concept of having self-driving cars drive as atrociously as human drivers send shivers up the spine and would seem to undercut the hoped-for benefits of having self-driving cars.

Time will tell.

Meanwhile, if you see a self-driving car coming down the street, be prepared for not what the self-driving car will do, but instead for what the human drivers nearby the self-driving car will do. Those pesky and inconsiderate human drivers will do what they do, including and especially when they come upon a self-driving car.

One day, if we reach achieving AI that is sentient, I'm sure the AI will roll its mechanical eyes and simply retort, that's humans for you.

CHAPTER 10
SNITCH ON DRIVERS AND SELF-DRIVING CARS

Are you familiar with the expression that someone is a fink or a no-good dirty rat?

Perhaps you might be more acquainted with other ways that this is commonly depicted such as those that are characterized as a weasel, a snitch, or a stoolie.

Let's add to the matter a vexing ethical question, namely whether someone can be considered a stool pigeon or a squealer even if they are reporting on something that was an illegal or unlawful act?

You would normally be tempted to assert that reporting a prohibited act is entirely appropriate and the tipster or whistleblower ought to be rewarded rather than ostracized as a tattler or snitch.

Okay, consider a real-world example and see how you do.

You are driving along on your daily journey to the office. There is a stop sign at an upcoming intersection. As you approach the intersection, you notice that there is no other traffic of any kind and there aren't any pedestrians in the vicinity. Being in a bit of a hurry that morning, you approach the stop sign and make a *rolling* stop.

To be clear, you nearly came to a full stop, but decided to just kind of ease your way forward and slowly, carefully, judiciously continue in motion. This was definitely not a blatant blasting past a stop sign. You were thoughtful and calculated that there would be no harm in gently observing the stop sign versus fully abiding by the stop sign.

There was no danger, so you took the shot, as it were (thanks goes to *Top Gun*).

How are you feeling so far about this?

Your action seems perfectly justifiable. You looked both ways. There weren't any other cars. No pedestrians were nearby. And, notably, you did bring the car nearly to a halt. Admittedly, you inched forward and did not technically make a full stop, but that seems like quite a technicality and not worthy of notable discussion or acrimonious debate.

Time to add a twist to the tale.

Turns out that a neighbor adjacent to the stop sign has set up an automatic camera that takes snapshots of any vehicles that roll through the stop sign. You might say they are doing this for the sake of safety, or maybe it is merely a hobby. In any case, the camera captures your kind-of stop that was really a rolling stop.

The neighbor upon reviewing their camera film realizes they got you, in a veritable sense of hook, line, and sinker. So, they opt to notify the police and turn you in.

Now how do you feel about this?

Maybe your first thought is that this person is a fink, a tattletale, a snitch.

They are making a molehill into a mountain. Your driving action was relatively innocent, and this sanctimonious do-gooder has turned this teensy tiny transgression into a full-blown crime. You know in your heart that no one was hurt by your driving action.

If there are any ongoing efforts to get illegal drivers, by gosh, you see plenty of scary and outrageously unlawful driving actions by zany drivers all the time. Go after those nutty drivers that truly put others into jeopardy by running red lights, speeding way beyond the speed limit, and that otherwise are a danger to society while being behind the wheel.

After calming down, perhaps you shift into a realization that the stoolie was trying to do the right thing.

You can entirely understand the motivation to catch those that brazenly brush past a stop sign. Of course, that's not what you did. You mull over whether you can convince a judge that you are a good driver, and this was a minuscule infraction that should be tossed out of court.

But as you think further on the topic, you start to get enraged again. What a waste of time and energy. It was one stinking stop sign in one stinking little neighborhood on your stinking way to work on one particular day. The neighbor that reported you is a stinking informer and should go after those that zip past the stop sign and leave alone those that were obviously being much more mindful about (somewhat) stopping.

I realize that some of you might be thinking that the neighbor was absolutely right and you ought to have gotten nabbed.

Perhaps your efforts were generally well-intended, but maybe you are gradually going on a slippery slope towards abject lawlessness. One day, you roll through a stop sign, and the next thing you know, it is possible you'll justify driving on sidewalks or ramming into other cars that you dislike. Thankfully, this conscientious busybody with their handy camera has stopped you before you lead a life of outright debauchery and criminal behavior.

I'd wager a guess that few of you are having those kinds of thoughts.

Consider a matter analogous to this stop sign saga.

We already know that as a society there is a great deal of controversy over simple things such as those intersection red-light cameras. The cameras are intended to catch those that opt to run the intersection when the light has gone red. This is decidedly a perilous driving action and often leads to car crashes. Those car crashes lead to people getting injured or killed.

Some believe that having a red-light camera to detect such scofflaws is more so a deterrent versus capturing those that run the red light. Yes, of course, the idea is to snap a photo of those that do indeed run the red and notify them, along with punishing them, which might awaken them to not do so ever again. The other notion is that just knowing that the camera exists will get people to second guess themselves about running the red light and they will consciously avert doing so. Thus, this is more so a deterrent rather than a focus on capture and punishment per se.

Having an all-seeing eyeball that you know will detect your driving transgression is presumably sufficient to cause people to drive more safely.

As an example of the quirkiness of human behavior, some locations that had a red-light camera have removed their red-light intersection cameras for the very reason that it was supposedly spurring drivers to rush the intersection. Here's why. Not wanting to get caught by the red-light camera, drivers would intentionally attempt to zip through the intersection. This led to apparently more dangerous driving situations and actually increased the chances of car crashes.

That's quite a dose of irony.

The adoption of something intended to reduce bad driving seemed to have an unanticipated adverse consequence of prodding people toward bad driving, including those that seemingly would not have been doing bad driving to start with.

Now, be aware, not everyone agrees with those kinds of utilization assessments of the red-light cameras, and there is a lot of research that falls on both sides of the good or bad merits thereof.

Anyway, why all this chattering about the act of tattle-telling?

Time to reveal the true plot at hand.

Allow me a moment to show my cards.

There will eventually be a widespread emergence of self-driving cars.

AI-based true self-driving cars are chockful of sensory devices that are used for navigating and driving the vehicle by the AI driving system. Electronic devices typically used include video cameras, radar, LIDAR, ultrasonic units, thermal imaging, and the like. The primary purpose of that state-of-the-art equipment is to serve as the eyes and ears of the AI driving system. Data is collected via those sensors and the AI tries to figure out the nature of the driving environment and then ascertain what driving actions can be safely undertaken.

There are though other potential uses of the suite of sensory devices on a self-driving car.

I've previously pointed out that those devices are a kind of "roving eye" that can potentially record whatever they see or detect during a driving journey. This can be handy for a multitude of purposes, such as being able to keep track of homes and real estate in a community and readily allow knowing what properties look like (if the data was posted online and made available for use).

Unfortunately, the same roving eye can have some quite scary outcomes.

Imagine that there are thousands upon thousands of self-driving cars that have been fielded and are weaving their way through your community as they provide ridesharing services. That's great and a huge convenience for wanting to get a lift. At the same time, those sensory devices are collecting in real-time the activities of whatever is happening in that community.

In theory, if one could aggregate the data, it would be feasible to generally track your activities. Early in the morning, you walk out of your house to take your dog for a walk. Around noon, you and a friend decide to eat lunch on your front patio. Later in the day, you get a lift to a downtown restaurant. Self-driving cars passing past the restaurant spot you going in, and likewise catch images of you as you are leaving the eatery.

The gist is that it would be technically possible to piece together the jigsaw of your everyday life outdoors via grabbing up the data collected from the numerous self-driving cars. Those self-driving cars are likely to be outfitted with OTA (Over-The-Air) electronic communications, allowing the vehicles to get downloaded patches to the AI driving system, and likewise being able to upload the roving eye data they collected throughout the day.

Once that data gets into the cloud, there is an open question as to what happens to it next.

Presumably, whoever owns the fleet of self-driving cars will want to monetize that data. How they do so and what the data is used for, well, that's something yet to be decided. Some believe that heavy regulations are going to be needed to protect us from an otherwise inevitable Big Brother situation.

We can add more fuel to that fire.

Returning to the initial tale of the neighbor that perchance set up a camera to monitor the stop sign nearby their home, we can rachet up this notion.

Rachet up a thousand-fold, exponentially so.

There will be human drivers driving their conventional cars and doing so amidst the advent of self-driving cars. Those self-driving cars will be watching the roadway, like a hawk, including spotting whatever any nearby human-driven cars are doing or undertake to do.

Here is the intriguing question to ponder: *Will AI-based true self-driving cars potentially snitch or fink upon human drivers nearby that bend or outright bust the driving laws?*

Let's unpack the matter and see.

Self-Driving Cars As Snitches

For Level 4 and Level 5 true self-driving vehicles, there won't be a human driver involved in the driving task.

All occupants will be passengers.

The AI is doing the driving.

As mentioned, the AI driving system includes a host of souped-up sensors. Those sensors are trying to identify anything within the sensory range of the self-driving car. Are there pedestrians nearby? Is there a car up ahead? Are there cars behind the self-driving car? And so on.

Here's what can occur.

You are driving adjacent to a self-driving car. There is nothing odd or out of the ordinary about this since there are numerous self-driving cars on the roadways (this is somewhat true today in specific locales, such that during a regular driving journey, you can encounter self-driving cars every few minutes, which has happened to me many times).

You and the adjacent self-driving car are approaching a stop sign that has two lanes. You are in the right lane and intend to make a stop at the stop sign, and then proceed to turn right. The self-driving car is in the left lane and presumably, will come to a stop and then proceed straight ahead.

Sure enough, the self-driving car comes to a full stop at the stop sign.

Meanwhile, perhaps in your haste, you slightly roll through the stop sign, failing to have come to a complete stop. You were only moving inches at a time. Furthermore, there weren't any pedestrians nearby. The only other car nearby was the self-driving car. You did nothing that endangered the self-driving car. All in all, you simply did a modest and seemingly immaterial roll through the stop sign and then made your right turn.

Nobody would ever know that you did a small oopsie on obeying the law.

Not so fast with that assumption.

The self-driving car was surveying the surrounding driving environment, as it customarily does, and therefore detected the presence of your car being adjacent. The sensors also captured the fact that you did not come to a full stop.

So what?

One possibility is that the self-driving car does nothing about your transgression. You did not harm or threaten the self-driving car. You did not hit any pedestrians. Overall, your act was inconsequential.

But, wait for a second, you broke the law. If a police officer was standing at the stop sign, they surely would flag you down and issue you a ticket. As a society, we seemingly want the police to take this action. Even though you ostensibly did not pose a danger, you are possibly the kind of driver that does this act all the time. Best to nip things in the bud, before you get out-of-hand.

The AI driving system in this everyday self-driving car is not a cop. It is not enforcing the driving laws (well, not as yet).

Unquestionably, it did detect someone breaking the law.

What do we want the AI to do?

Some would argue vehemently that it is none of the business of the AI. The AI driving system should keep its head down and focus on driving the darned car (that seems somewhat anthropomorphic, so let's just say that the AI wasn't programmed to do anything about the detection). Leave others alone.

And, especially leave human drivers alone.

Others would as equally fervently argue that this is a godsend of sorts. By having detected a bad driver, this should be reported right away to the police. Furthermore, there is abundant proof to support the contention that an illegal driving act occurred.

If a human driver perchance saw another human driver rolling through a stop sign, there is a temptation to report on that other driver. This though is rather problematic. Once you get to court, it will likely come down to your word versus the word of the other. Assuming that the other driver won't admit to the infraction, the whole thing ends up as a potential frustration and waste of time. How is the judge to decide which of you is telling the truth and which is lying?

In the case of the self-driving car, there is a plethora of sensory data that has nabbed you. This seems like pretty hard evidence to overturn. You can bet that clever lawyers will try to find a means to do so. They can argue that the sensory data was faked, as in the popular Deepfakes that we see commonly appearing today. They could argue that the data was real but has been edited by someone, perhaps a systems administrator that has access to the cloud data of the self-driving car fleet. Etc.

Yes, those are all potential legal angles and loopholes, but it will be quite an uphill battle.

Once we have our streets, highways, and byways filled with roaming self-driving cars, there will be a nearly endless supply of recorded detections involving human drivers that have bent or entirely busted the proper driving laws.

You can bet your bottom dollar on this.

Conclusion

Some people have worried that we are going to have more cameras set up like the one that a neighbor placed to spot the stop sign in their neighborhood. We have already seen that the doorbell cameras are capturing quite a lot of what happens in a neighborhood. Undoubtedly, the trend of using stationary cameras will continue.

I respectively submit that those kinds of static unmoving cameras will be a drop in the bucket.

The advent of self-driving cars is going to inevitably take off like wildfire.

People will crave the use of self-driving cars, partially due to the hoped-for lower cost of use versus a human-driven ridesharing capability, but also (more so) because it is anticipated that self-driving cars will have many fewer car crashes. There are about 40,000 human fatalities each year due to car crashes in the United States, and about 2.3 million injuries. The belief is that self-driving cars will not be drunk while driving, will not be distracted drivers, and therefore there will be a sizable reduction in the number of car crashes and thus a sizable reduction in the number of injuries and fatalities.

Meanwhile, the craving for self-driving cars will also produce the possibility of routinely and rather extensively catching nearby human-drivers that break the driving laws. We need to wrestle with the idea that self-driving cars can be a snitch, or if you will, an added pair of helpful eyes that can detect those humans that are driving in unlawful manners and promptly report those transgressors to the police.

Some are handwringing that we will become a police state.

At first, it will be the running of a stop sign, and the next thing you know it will be a pedestrian that tosses a candy wrapper on the ground. Others emphasize that maybe we could establish thresholds, such as if the act detected is considered inconsequential or a petty act, the AI won't be prompted to tattle.

One final twist to these twists.

We already know and acknowledge that perhaps human drivers reacted somewhat paradoxically to the red-light cameras, leading to a presumed unanticipated adverse consequence.

Would human-drivers react in "unforeseen" ways if they knew that self-driving cars were going to be the proverbial fink or weasel?

Maybe human drivers would do whatever they could to avoid getting within sensory range of self-driving cars. This could produce adverse driving beyond that which we already have. Envision that a human driver coming down a quiet street might suddenly make an illegal U-turn to avoid coming up upon a self-driving car (kind of what happens by some that perchance come upon a police car). For each scofflaw being detected by self-driving cars, there might be many more new untoward driving acts being generated by human drivers determined to avoid coming under the gaze of a self-driving car.

Or, perhaps humans will try other means to confuse the sensors or somehow mask their car from the sensory suite. Some savvy entrepreneurs will provide electronic "invisibility cloaks" to hide your human-driven vehicle from the detectable scope of the self-driving car sensors. And so on.

Where there is a will, there is a way.

If AI ever becomes sentient, it would certainly be interesting to see what the AI says about all of this, specifically whether the AI would believe it is doing the right thing as an alleged stoolie, or perhaps be upset that humans are fearing it because of the heavy burden of always being the tattletale.

It's a tough job being AI.

CHAPTER 11
REPROGRAMMING PEDESTRIANS AND SELF-DRIVING CARS

When growing up, most children are taught the rather simple but altogether life-saving idea that they should look both ways before crossing the street.

Why is there a need to teach such a safety precaution?

Because the streets are occupied by moving objects, including heavy ones that can knock the stuffing out of you. Cars coming down a street can ram into a person and the result is downright ugly. It is likely that the pedestrian struck by a car is going to suffer some number of injuries, ranging from mild scratches and a few broken bones to the sad and all too often loss-of-life entirely.

According to U.S. government statistics, the year 2019 had about 6,200 pedestrian fatalities and approximately 76,000 pedestrians were injured, which is generally the annual counts that occur year after year. Over the course of a decade, this translates into perhaps 62,000 deaths and 760,000 people injured, all due to the regrettable act of getting into a collision with a vehicle of one kind or another (this includes cars, trucks, motorcycles, bicycles, etc.).

Speaking of a decade, going back to 2009 it turns out that there were quite a lot fewer pedestrian fatalities at that time. Surprisingly, the count of ten years ago has increased by about 50% to today's much larger number. The point is that the number of pedestrian deaths has gone up, unnervingly so.

One explanation for this growth in pedestrian fatalities is that we are not paying attention to the roadways like we used to do so. The notion of looking both ways seems to have worn off. Another claimed explanation is that drivers are driving while distracted, trying to watch cat videos or text on their smartphones. The distracted driver isn't watching for pedestrians and thus more pedestrians are getting killed.

Of course, the aspect of being distracted is also leveled at pedestrians. The use of smartphones has not only distracted drivers, but it also tends to preoccupy pedestrians too. Wandering around a city while listening intently to a podcast on your smartphone or looking to see who just texted you have become familiar and every day common.

Okay, so it could be that we have a one-two punch occurring. We have pedestrians being less cautious, and we have drivers being less alert. That's bad for everyone. Some though prefer to try and pin the tail on just one donkey by contending that only drivers are at fault, or perhaps that only pedestrians are at fault. The logic seems to be that they both cannot be at fault and only one should be wearing the badge of shame.

You could certainly wag the accusatory finger at the drivers.

A driver ought to relish the privilege allowed of driving on our public roads. For that permissible act, they should set aside any distractions and focus exclusively on driving the vehicle that they are responsible for. Trying to pawn off the striking of a pedestrian as a driver is outrageous since the driver should have at all times been going at a speed sufficient to avoid a collision with a pedestrian.

End of story.

Not so fast, say those that represent drivers.

If a pedestrian suddenly darts into the middle of the street, there is not much a driver can do. Their car cannot sprout wings and fly over the top of the pedestrian (well, maybe someday we will finally have those vaunted and long-sought flying cars, but not yet). Even the most conscientious driver is going to get caught unawares when a jaywalker steps between two parked vehicles and magically appears like a rabbit out of a hat. The blame for pedestrians getting snagged is on the head and shoulders of the pedestrians themselves.

Whoa, so which is it, the driver or the pedestrian that carries the fault in this state of woe?

Trying to narrow the blame to only one of the parties seems a bit questionable and portrays the matter in a type of false dichotomy. There are instances of irresponsible drivers and the pedestrian was doing their best to keep from getting clobbered. There are instances of pedestrians that were irresponsible and the driver did their best to keep from clobbering the person. Lumping all of the circumstances into solely one bucket does not appear to be a helpful way to solve the problem.

Notably, this is a problem that is obviously worth solving.

How can we save pedestrians from the dangers of getting smacked or killed by moving cars?

The easy answer is to ensure that pedestrians and cars are never in the same place at the same time.

For example, some downtown areas are exploring (or have implemented) blocking off their downtown streets to prevent any vehicular traffic. In that case, pedestrians can roam freely and not worry about looking both ways. This is a wonderful potential solution but whether it is scalable is an open question. Can we really decide to eliminate vehicular traffic wherever pedestrians might be? Unlikely. The counterargument is that at least we can do so in the hotspots that have most of the adverse car-and-pedestrian encounters.

Another viewpoint is to essentially reduce demonstratively the amount of car traffic. Get people to stop driving cars and instead take mass transit. Fewer cars mean fewer chances of an adverse car-and-pedestrian mismatch.

Here's another idea for you to mull over.

Suppose we could devise cars that would not be subject to driver distraction. The car would presumably no longer be as endangering a beast. In that case, maybe we could let cars and pedestrians intermingle since we are assuming that the cars would be more sensitive to pedestrian activity and hopefully a lot less likely to ram into one.

Voila, some would exclaim, you have just described the hoped-for advent of AI-based true self-driving cars.

In theory, we ought to have fewer pedestrian smackdowns when an AI driving system is at the wheel of a car. The AI won't be drinking and driving. The AI won't be watching cat videos. All in all, the AI is expected to end up being as safe a driver as humans and in fact aiming to be a lot safer.

Sounds like a great future is ahead of us.

Meanwhile, consider a twist that maybe you didn't see coming.

Today's self-driving cars are not necessarily so adept at avoiding pedestrians. Turns out that detecting and figuring out what pedestrians are going to do is quite a conundrum.

Human drivers generally do so with relative ease, though obviously, human drivers falter at this task, but on the whole, it is somewhat notable that there aren't even more pedestrian fatalities and deaths in a country that has a population of around 330 million people. To clarify, every injury and every death of a pedestrian is horrific, make no mistake about that. The gist is that drivers are seemingly doing well much of the time, and likewise so are pedestrians, and we are fortunate that the numbers are not magnitudes higher.

Shift your attention momentarily to car accidents all told.

Cars get into an estimated 6.3 million car accidents per year in the U.S., and there are nearly 40,000 deaths and 2.5 million people injured. The belief is that self-driving cars are going to radically reduce those counts. Car upon car collisions is predicted to drop tremendously. Thus, the number of car-related crash deaths and injuries is similarly predicted to be reduced enormously.

In short, here's the rub.

Suppose that we can get self-driving cars underway at the soonest possibility, doing so under the belief that we are going to dramatically reduce the car accidents and the corresponding injuries and deaths, but meanwhile what if the car-and-pedestrian related incidents stays the same or possibly even rises. You could argue that we ought to not let self-driving cars onto our roadways until they are readied to handle the wayward ways of pedestrians. The counterargument is that any delay in getting self-driving cars onto the roadways means that you are "agreeing" to allow the existing carnage to continue and are not seeing the big picture by making a myopic decision on the matter.

Please be aware those are fighting words, for sure.

Anyway, some are suggesting that the way to cope with this dilemma involves the so-called "reprogramming" of human pedestrians to make them more aware of the difficulties that self-driving cars will presumably present to them. The thought is that if we can't get the self-driving cars out-the-gate to be proficient at avoiding wayward pedestrians, we can convince pedestrians to no longer be wayward.

The question then to be considered is this: *Does the advent of AI-based true self-driving cars necessitate having human pedestrians become "reprogrammed" about crossing the road?*

Let's unpack the topic and see.

Self-Driving Cars And Pedestrians

For Level 4 and Level 5 true self-driving vehicles, there won't be a human driver involved in the driving task.

All occupants will be passengers.

The AI is doing the driving.

Detecting other cars that are nearby to a self-driving car is somewhat straightforward for the AI driving system. Usually, other cars are relatively sizable, and a self-driving car can make use of its on-board video cameras, radar, LIDAR, ultrasonic units, and other sensory devices to pretty much figure out that a car is in the driving scene of interest.

That being said, the speed of other cars can mean that where they are and where they are going will happen very fast (plus, weather conditions and other factors come to play too). The intention of the human driver of a car can be quite mysterious. We all know that human drivers can do some crazy stunts and opt to make wild turns or swerve erratically. Thus, not only is the detection of other cars crucial, so too is predicting what those cars are going to do next.

Pedestrians can be quite difficult to detect.

A pedestrian might be standing behind a large pole and be masked from view. Or a pedestrian might be standing still and momentarily sandwiched between two parked cars and be obscured by the size and shape of those cars. Keep in mind that children are pedestrians too, thus the profile of a pedestrian includes toddlers that are barely visible and can easily be behind other objects. Pedestrians crowded together are hard to differentiate in terms of how many pedestrians are present.

Confounding the detection is that even if a pedestrian is seemingly spotted, the question remains as to what the pedestrian plans to do.

Assume that a pedestrian is completely visible and easily seen at the corner of a street. The person is standing perfectly still.

Will the pedestrian wait to cross the street until traffic has subsided and allows safe passage?

Maybe yes, maybe no.

If it is raining, it seems that pedestrians tend to dart across the street, trying to avoid getting wet, and yet at the same moment imperiling their lives by perilously crossing the roadway. You've undoubtedly experienced pedestrians that seem to be playing a game of Frogger, whereby they try to make their way into the active roadway and weave around the moving cars.

Anyway, the pedestrian that is standing perfectly still can suddenly and without any particular warning decide to come into the street.

A car that is going 35 miles per hour will usually require a stopping distance of around 130 feet. This suggests that if the pedestrian standing still decides to suddenly come into the street, and suppose that the self-driving car is arriving at that point, the pedestrian is going to get hit if the distance is less than about 130 feet or so.

See, the self-driving car might detect that the pedestrian has gone into the street and the AI might immediately invoke the brakes, yet the distance involved is a matter of physics. There isn't a magical way that the self-driving car is going to avoid hitting that pedestrian. I mention this important point because some are predicting that no pedestrian will ever get hit by a self-driving car. That is plain crazy talk.

Of course, you might try to argue that in the scenario that is being depicted that the self-driving car ought to swerve to avoid the pedestrian. Suppose though that there is oncoming traffic, and no viable option exists to swerve (this is often referred to as the Trolley Problem. Assume that braking is the only plausible alternative.

You might try to argue that the self-driving car should have predicted that the pedestrian was going to dart into the road. How can this be done? If the pedestrian was perfectly still, there is little clue to be utilized. Sure, if the pedestrian was antsy and seemed to be readying to dart, that is a different matter and in fact, many of the AI driving systems are getting better at trying to predict pedestrian behaviors.

Another common argument is that the self-driving car should not have been going 35 miles per hour. The stopping distance for a car going at 10 miles per hour is a mere 27 feet. If self-driving cars would go slowly, they would have more chance of avoiding hitting a pedestrian that leaps in the way (and, the forces at collision are a lot less damaging). This is partially why some of the self-driving cars are being outfitted for use in low-speed locales, such as a community that has restricted speeds and closed-off roads.

Unfortunately, the real-world of driving does not allow for always driving at 10 miles per hour. If all self-driving cars were forced to drive that slowly, it would seem unlikely that people would want to ride in them. Human-driven cars would remain a much greater attraction.

Perhaps we then should restrict self-driving cars to drive only wherever there aren't people walking around. Allow self-driving cars to drive on the freeways, for example, but insist that they aren't permitted to drive on city streets. Again, this is a rather stilted way of making use of self-driving cars and does not seem especially tenable.

Now that we've gone through those potential "solutions" to the problem, some have reached the reluctant conclusion that the prudent step requires getting pedestrians to be more careful when crossing the street.

Perhaps the pedestrian standing at the corner could use an added awareness about the dangers of stepping into the street, regardless of whether a self-driving car or even a human-driven car is approaching. A hefty campaign of reminding pedestrians to be careful might do the trick, some believe.

There is another reason often cited for this kind of educational effort.

Pedestrians are bound to at first assume that self-driving cars are safer drivers than human drivers, in which case, whereas a pedestrian would not take an outsized chance when a human driver is at the wheel, they might do so when the AI is at the wheel. In a sense, people might falsely believe that the AI is going to always stop for the human pedestrian.

To clarify, it is indeed the case that if the AI does detect a pedestrian, the odds are going to be higher than the self-driving car will be brought to a halt. AI driving systems are being programmed to do so. Human drivers are a different animal, one would say, in that human drivers might or might not choose to stop when they see a pedestrian.

Human drivers play a game with pedestrians, and likewise, pedestrians play a game with human drivers.

It is a high-stakes game of chicken.

Which will backdown first, the car driver or the pedestrian that is aiming to dart into the road?

We know for sure that the car ought to win, in that the pedestrian is normally at much greater risk of harm. Nonetheless, pedestrians seem to calculate mentally that the human driver doesn't especially want to deal with the aftermath of hitting a pedestrian and will more than likely avoid doing so. You see this kind of eyeball-to-eyeball game playing all the time in any busy downtown area.

One viewpoint about AI driving systems is that they ought to challenge pedestrians, in the same manner as human drivers. The underlying logic is that if pedestrians get used to AI driving systems that are essentially wimps, always allowing humans to jaywalk, this will cause pedestrians to become brazen. Not only will pedestrians take advantage of self-driving cars, but this will also spill over into their behavior towards human-driven cars and we will have quite a rampage on our hands.

Overall, it would seem beneficial to try and get pedestrians to be safe, and in some respects safer, about the crossing of our streets. This is a good practice to observe whether there are self-driving cars or not since the stats indicate that conventional car-to-pedestrian mashups are already increasing.

Some though question whether the effort to educate or "reprogram" human behavior will have much luck.

Human behavior can be quite stubborn. Changing the way that people act while in the capacity of a pedestrian is no easy feat. Will trying to teach pedestrians to be safer proffer sufficient results? What is the cost to try and bring about that kind of awareness?

Conclusion

Some are holding out for the use of V2P (vehicle-to-pedestrian) electronic communication.

The notion is that a pedestrian holding their smartphone can communicate electronically with nearby self-driving cars, and so too the self-driving cars can convey messages to the pedestrian. In this manner, an approaching self-driving car might send a message to the pedestrian at the street corner and ask them to remain still and not yet enter into the street.

This might help, but it certainly doesn't seem to be the panacea that some are betting on, including:

- Will a pedestrian getting such a message to be willing to abide by the instructions of the AI?

- Will a pedestrian attempt to get a self-driving car to stop by using the V2P, even when the self-driving car has the right of way?

- And, even though a lot of people have smartphones, how many pedestrians will have one, and that is ready to receive a V2P, and that will look at their smartphone to see what the V2P message is telling them?

A famous saying by Stephen Jay Gould, a noted evolutionary biologist, comes to mind: "The world, unfortunately, rarely matches our hopes and consistently refuses to behave in a reasonable manner."

That's something to keep in mind for both humans and AI.

CHAPTER 12
POINTS OF FAILURES AND SELF-DRIVING CARS

The recent multi-hour-long outage of Facebook, Instagram, WhatsApp, and Messenger that impacted perhaps billions of users has reportedly been attributed to a potential single point of failure (said to be triggered via a configuration change in a backbone router).

This brings up the inherent dangers or at least vulnerabilities that exist when a complex system is designed by intent or via happenstance to embody a single point of failure aspect. The lurking weakness can seemingly mysteriously arise and leave dreadful troubles in its wake. Plus, trying to overcome the failure can be problematic, including that if it is not fully remediated then the same condition will potentially recur. That's not good.

Speaking of single points of failure reminds me of something that you might not have previously considered as an illustrative example of how such matters can exist. The example has to do with a quite famous dog, perhaps you've heard of the wondrous canine named Lassie.

It seems that most people know the classic "Lassie saves the day" narrative.

Essentially, the beloved collie named Lassie is out on a wilderness romp with a human that happens to get trapped or somehow hurt, being unable to make their way back to civilization and safety. The person makes a plea for Lassie to rush home and alert the authorities. Lassie does exactly as requested, darts away on this grand quest, including heroically braving all sorts of troubles while seeking to get help.

Thankfully, Lassie ultimately reaches someone and guides them back to rescue the stranded person.

One gets teary-eyed at just thinking about this endearing and quite uplifting story.

Not wanting to cast aspersions on this revered tale, but suppose Lassie was unable to have gotten home and thus was unable to alert anyone about the woes of the doomed person?

That would have been a bad ending, for sure.

You might object to the premise since there doesn't seem to be any reason to believe that Lassie would not have done precisely as requested.

Well, just supposing, imagine that Lassie got lost during the trek homeward and never found home (I realize this seems nearly impossible, given the amazing intelligence of this venerated collie). Or maybe Lassie takes longer than expected, and by the time that rescuers are summoned and make their way to the marooned person, it is already too late. We can even envision that Lassie did find someone as a potential rescuer, but the stubborn-minded dolt does not grasp what Lassie is trying to do and fails to follow up. Even despite Lassie likely barking fervently and trying to lead the rescuer back into the wilderness, the rescue attempt is rebuffed.

The crux of this troubling version of the classic story is that the stranded person relied on only one form of rescue or survival, namely hoping and betting on Lassie being able to save the day.

This is known as committing to a single point of failure (a cherished one, in this case).

Sometimes you do something and do not realize that you have set up a Single Point Of Failure (SPOF) circumstance. You might be oblivious to the notion and therefore only become cognizant of the dilemma once you've gotten yourself into a tight predicament.

In other cases, you might have purposely devised an approach that entails a single point of failure and are entrusting that at least the worst-case scenario won't hopefully occur. You are betting that you will not get caught due to an adverse roll of the dice.

In the Lassie saga, perhaps the person stranded might have beforehand told others where to find them if they didn't return on a timely basis. In that case, there is the possibility of using Lassie as a lifeline (per the traditional story), plus there is the chance that even if Lassie can't make it home there will nonetheless be a search party sent out due to the prior agreed stipulation.

You could suggest that by establishing a dual path possibility, there is redundancy built into the situation. When a dire moment arises, there isn't just a single point of rescue, there are two, and thus it provides for a greater chance of being saved. That is the basis for devising or constructing approaches that have more than one means of continuing when one particular strand falters.

A tough question to always consider involves how much redundancy is enough.

In the variant of the Lassie tale, there are now two paths of rescue. A modern-day version might add a third path, perhaps the person has taken a satellite portable phone with them. Upon getting stuck in the woods, the person can try the portable phone, plus they can try sending Lassie on the grand quest, and they can hope that upon not returning that a search party will be sent to find them.

Is that safe enough?

Well, it is hard to say.

Suppose Lassie is unable to find the way to get home. Suppose that those informed beforehand about the trip are lax and do not on a timely basis undertake a search effort. And suppose that darned satellite phone cannot get a signal or maybe has gotten smashed on a rock when the person that is now hurt fell down a cliff.

What a downer.

There are presumably only so many ways you can try to set up a series of protective measures, especially as bounded by the potential cost or effort involved in doing so.

It is conceivable to argue that the cost of the multiple paths has to be weighed against the benefits of those paths, along with the risks or probabilities associated with the paths breaking down or failing. In theory, a prudently devised redundancy ought to imply that it would be a very rare chance of all of them failing at essentially the same time.

Of course, the greater the risk of relying upon a single point of failure, the greater there ought to be of divining appropriate redundant paths, and particularly seemingly robust ones.

By robust, the idea is that the redundant paths should not be so entangled that if one goes then the rest are also likely to be busted too. Imagine a bridge with lots of suspension lines. You've undoubtedly seen those horrifying scenes wherein one-line snaps, and all the other lines start snapping too. It could be that the loss of one of the alleged redundant paths serves to gut the other forms of redundancy, in which case, the true efficacy of the redundancy is ostensibly rather low or quite weak in value.

Shifting gears, stories of the past are about Lassie saving the day, while tales of the future are sometimes portrayed as self-driving cars saving the day (though, for clarification, Lassie is a much more heartwarming tale!).

When human passengers get into an AI-based true self-driving car, they are assuming that the AI driving system is going to work and do so in a fashion that averts a potential calamity due to any single point of failure. I'm not suggesting that riders in a self-driving car are fully aware of single points of failure. The gist is that they assume that whoever devised the self-driving car has already figured out where single points of failure are and have done something prudent about those weaknesses.

That brings up an interesting matter to mull over.

Specifically, here's the question to ponder: *What kinds of single points of failure might exist within an AI-based true self-driving car and how can those be dealt with?*

Let's unpack the matter and see.

Self-Driving Cars And SPOF

For Level 4 and Level 5 true self-driving vehicles, there won't be a human driver involved in the driving task.

All occupants will be passengers.

The AI is doing the driving.

Your first thought might be that there is nothing to worry about and you can simply trust that the AI won't go haywire and all will be perfectly operating at all times.

Recall that earlier it was mentioned that the risk of having a single point of failure is a crucial factor in ascertaining whether a SPOF is worthy of rapt attention. In the case of a self-driving car, keep in mind that the vehicle can readily go at high speeds, in fact, you want it to do so when driving on a freeway and similar open highways. At high speeds, the risk of the car getting out of control and crashing is something we all ought to be worried about. Thus, if a single point of failure could lead to such a disastrous outcome, we need to be alert for such a possibility.

Okay, put on your Sherlock Holmes cap, and let's take a look at the various ways that a single point of failure on a self-driving car ought to be dealt with.

First, we'll start with the sensory apparatus of the self-driving car.

For most self-driving cars, there are a bunch of specialized sensors such as video cameras, radar, LIDAR, ultrasonic units, and the like, all acting as the kind of eyes and ears for the AI driving system. Those sensors are collecting data about the surrounding environment and are fed into the AI system to try and ascertain the nature of the driving scene. For example, the cameras are providing visual images that can be examined to try and find where nearby cars are, and where pedestrians are standing, and so on.

Suppose a camera that is pointed forward and used to see the road ahead is suddenly unable to visually see the roadway.

How could that happen?

One means is that the camera lens gets smeared with say dust or mud, which is something I'd bet most of us have had happened to our own cameras. Another possibility is that the camera gets struck by a rock that got ricocheted off the street by a passing truck, and the lens is entirely cracked and no longer functioning. There is also the chance that the camera has just gone bad on its own, maybe it was defective to start with, or perhaps it has reached the end of its useful life, as it were.

The automaker or self-driving tech firm that has developed the AI driving system has presumably considered this kind of failure a possibility.

Without that forward-looking camera, the AI driving system could potentially be blinded as to what is happening in front of the vehicle. That's bad. That's real bad. The AI might not realize that a car has pulled in front of the self-driving car and that the two are about to ram into each other. Or maybe a pedestrian has opted to run across the street and assumes that the AI will bring the car to a stop.

Your first thought about the camera going out is that the self-driving car should immediately come to a screeching halt.

This can be more daring than it seems. If there are other cars immediately behind the self-driving car, let's say human-driven cars, and if the AI driving system merely jams on the brakes, this could start a cavalcade of car crashes.

In that case, maybe your refined way of thinking is that the self-driving car should gradually make its way to the side of the road, doing so cautiously and without disrupting other traffic. That is a seemingly better way to proceed, though the question arises as to how you can make your way to the side of the road and do so while completely blind to what is ahead of you. This seems like a tricky maneuver and one that even Houdini would shudder at trying to magically accomplish.

Astute designers and developers of self-driving cars are incorporating various precautions to try and cope with this potential single point of failure, doing so via the leveraging of redundancy.

For example, there might be more than just one camera that is pointing forward. Via having additional cameras, you can have the AI switchover to relying upon those other cameras, even when the mainstay camera goes amiss. Imagine similarly that you are driving a car and you suddenly get a fleck of something in your left eye. You would likely become attentive to now using just your right eye, and luckily have at the ready a built-in redundancy that allows you to do so.

Furthermore, part of the basis for having a multitude of sensor types is that it helps to detect the outside world in ways beyond only a visual mode. The radar can be used to gauge whether objects are in front of the vehicle. This is taking place throughout the course of a driving journey. If the forward cameras entirely went out, presumably if the radar is still working this would allow for some semblance of figuring out what is ahead of the vehicle (and allow for gradually getting over to the side of the road).

Realize though that the radar is not the same as the cameras, which means that you are not going to be gauging the driving scene in the same fuller way as you would with the cameras operating too. In that manner, the sensory capabilities of the AI driving system are sorely degraded and any further actions must incorporate the realization of that now limited facility.

An integral component of self-driving cars is the use of Multi-Sensory Data Fusion (MSDF). There is software within the AI driving system that is tasked with receiving the data from the sensory devices and then attempts to merge or align that data accordingly. The visual data from the cameras are compared in terms of what is spotted on the radar and to the LIDAR, and so on. A give-and-take must be devised since at times one form of the sensor is bound to be doing a better job at detection than another type of sensor.

Overall, you could say that the use of multiple types of sensors is a form of redundancy and a built-in means of trying to overcome any single point of failure.

There are though plenty of other avenues of single points of failure opportunities (or, more aptly stated, threats). Let's consider another one.

The AI driving system is software and it is running on onboard hardware within the self-driving car.

Suppose the hardware falters. It could be that the processor chips go bad, or maybe the computer memory has a hiccup. You've likely had a laptop that had the hardware decide to give up on you. If the hardware of the self-driving car perchance hits a snag, this could mean that the AI driving system software can no longer operate.

This is the unguided missile concern of any self-driving car maker.

To try and overcome this potential single point of failure, the hardware typically has redundancy to cope with any particular hardware component failing. There are bound to be multiple chips, and thus a switchover to one that still seems to be working properly.

Here's a tough question for you.

Is having two sets of onboard computing hardware setups sufficient as the needed redundancy to overcome a potential single point of failure?

It is tempting to perhaps indicate that this seems quite sufficient. On the other hand, there are lots of ways to undermine this redundancy. Suppose the hardware is positioned in nearly the same locale within the body of the vehicle. And, further, suppose the car gets hit by something that smashes that specific location. The redundancy of the hardware doesn't buy you much if it can be obliterated by one strike and takes them out altogether.

Okay, you respond, we ought to have a third set, perhaps positioned elsewhere within the vehicle, and thus reduce the odds of getting clobbered when the primary set is taken out. Sure, this can be done, and we can continue this logic by having a fourth set, a fifth set, etc.

Conclusion

This takes us back to the earlier point that there is a cost associated with trying to overcome a single point of failure. If a self-driving car is going to have a lot of hardware processing redundancy, there is an added cost to this capacity.

How much is sufficient?

The answer is somewhat amorphous.

You can try to estimate the risks and the probable outcomes, and then put in place an amount of hardware redundancy accordingly. Keep in mind that the "costs" involved include that of human lives and injuries.

Here's what will likely occur with self-driving cars.

At some future point in time, there will be a car crash involving a self-driving car. A legal case might arise. During that legal case, one argument to be proffered will be that the AI driving system was not devised with sufficient redundancy and ended up getting snagged by some points of failures that should have been better anticipated.

Mark my words, this will indeed happen.

Meanwhile, though not covered herein, there are many other aspects of the AI driving system that can potentially have points of failure, including the sensor fusion feature, the virtual world modeling elements, the driving controls commands issuance software, and a plethora of other facets. We are all assuming that the self-driving car tech and AI driving systems are being designed, developed, tested, and fielded in such a means that there is appropriate and sufficient redundancy.

I suppose that while riding in a self-driving car if it breaks down and you come to a safe stop, you hopefully had the presence of mind to bring Lassie with you, and away the collie would go, aiming to bring assistance to your stalled predicament (well, ignoring for sake of discussion the use of any on-board electronic communications, your cell phone, etc.).

Anyway, that's Lassie for you, always the hero.

CHAPTER 13
MINECRAFT
AND
SELF-DRIVING CARS

Minecraft is big business.

This quite revered and now over a decade old video game has reportedly attained more than 126 million monthly active players and has sold well beyond 200 million copies of the gaming software. Besides the game itself, there is plenty of merchandise to be had and lots of spin-offs that have been successfully catapulted off the backs of *Minecraft*.

What makes this particular game so enduring and endearing?

There are lots of theories that attempt to explain the popularity of this vaunted juggernaut.

One somewhat apparent aspect is that it is an exceedingly easy game to get started with. Unlike some online games that require gobs of hours invested before you can readily get underway and be productive in the game, the beauty of *Minecraft* could be said to be its simplicity at its core. Most people, young and old, can immediately start actively using the game upon the first login.

Some also say that another strong point is that you can take the game as far as you want to go. In other words, those that want to just meander and take a lackadaisical approach can do so, meanwhile, those that want to push the limits and make this into a nose grinding gut-wrenching "ordeal" (of the fun variety) are equally able to double down on that kind of a sports gaming experience.

Shifting gears, you might be surprised to know that there are some interesting parallels between aspects of self-driving cars and the game of *Minecraft*.

Say what?

This assertion might seem at first glance like trying to compare apples and oranges, or maybe more like comparing apples versus pickaxes, meaning that the two are not of the same species and therefore there is not a viable side-by-side comparison to be made.

In a moment, I'll walk you through various facets that can reveal some similarities, which might be pleasantly unexpected for those of you that already know self-driving cars but do not know *Minecraft*, and likewise intriguing for those of you that know *Minecraft* but do not know about self-driving cars.

For those of you that aren't familiar with the *Minecraft* game (or, nor self-driving cars), no worries, I'll make sure to explain the essence as I roll along on making the comparison.

Before jumping into the matter and mining for golden nuggets and some precious diamonds, let's start with some handy background about the nature of self-driving cars.

Self-Driving Cars And *Minecraft*

For Level 4 and Level 5 true self-driving vehicles, there won't be a human driver involved in the driving task.

All occupants will be passengers.

The AI is doing the driving.

From a *Minecraft* player perspective, having the AI do all the driving of a car is handy when you want to be able to play *Minecraft* during a driving journey. Of course, a human driver ought not to be playing the game while at the wheel of a car, and perhaps not even thinking about the game, since their attention should be entirely focused on safe driving. In any case, with AI doing the actual driving, human passengers can do as they wish while inside a self-driving car, including binging on playing *Minecraft* when doing a cross-country vacation road trip with the family.

As a sneak-peek for the future of self-driving cars, besides having gobs of connectivity and bandwidth while riding in a self-driving car, some designs involve lining the interior walls and windows of the vehicle with essentially LED screens. You can generally blot out the outside world, and become cocooned inside the self-driving car. Imagine the kind of immersion into playing Minecraft that this might allow.

When your self-driving car reaches the destination that you had specified, perhaps arriving at your office or maybe at the mall, envision how strange it will seem to disembark from your fully immersed *Minecraft* experience and be back in the real world.

Kind of a *The Matrix* type of moment, for sure.

Anyway, let's get back to the gist of things and consider what we can learn about comparing self-driving cars and the game of *Minecraft*.

Here are some interesting similarities worth contemplating.

The Sandbox Is A Crucial Metaphor

Let's start with a foundational aspect, namely that *Minecraft* is considered a sandbox video game.

Here's what that means.

When you enter into the game, you are ostensibly in a new world or environment that allows you to wander around. Somewhat akin to having played in a sandbox as a child, you can play around and have fun, making new things, trying out new stuff, and opt to rework the playground to some degree based on your imagination and wherewithal.

You can also explore without having to necessarily earn points per se or try to score a victory.

Some liken this to being a non-game game, implying that unlike traditional games, there is no need to be a winner and there is not a grand fear of being a "loser" (well, just to clarify, there are aspects involving health and food, and potential threats from various hostile creatures such as spiders and zombies, but by-and-large the notion is that you aren't in a pell-mell panic as might be commonly found in other more stressful games).

You can select various game modes, including survival mode, creative mode, adventure mode, and the like. This is what allows for ratcheting up from being an idle player that saunters around to instead deciding to strive for being a topnotch player and become known for your talent and versatility in navigating and succeeding at *Minecraft* in a highly competitive sporting fashion.

Let's revisit the sandbox notion in a different context.

When you think about a self-driving car and what it is intended to do, the core function involves taking a driving journey and doing so safely.

The AI driving system is not trying to score points or particularly win at something.

Human drivers sometimes conceive of driving a car as a type of sport wherein they desperately seek to outmaneuver other cars and beat the clock by speeding down roadways and rushing red lights. The assumption for self-driving cars is that they will be operating in a completely lawful manner, obeying the rules of the road, being civil drivers, and make sure to drive legally.

In that sense, the self-driving car is in the sandbox of our roadway infrastructure and intended to find its way from point A to point B. A passenger gets into a self-driving car, provides a destination, and the AI driving system tries to make sure that the vehicle safely reaches that destination. Normally, there is no race to do this. Sure, the self-driving car ought to be proceeding on a timely basis, and it ought to not dillydally, on the other hand, it is not attempting to score a win, other than reaching the destination and doing so without having gotten into a car crash or otherwise done something disturbing along the way.

I've predicted that we will eventually witness self-driving cars on actual racetracks in sporting competitions. Thus, the mild-mannered self-driving cars of today are going to also be those lean-and-mean race driving AI-based roadway speedsters (on closed tracks), showcasing the range of being able to "play" at driving (I use the word "play" cautiously since being at the wheel of a multi-ton vehicle is certainly not to be taken lightly and is a very serious and possibly deadly task).

The First-Person Perspective

While inside the *Minecraft* game as a player, you usually are inhabiting a character that walks, strides, swims or otherwise gets around in the sandbox environment. You can change up the character and also alter the appearance by applying what is considered customized "skins" or coverings on the character.

Typically, you are seeing the environment in a first-person mode, meaning that you see the surroundings as though you were walking around a wooded area or park of some kind. You see ahead of you some trees and bushes. Perhaps over to your right is a small lake. When you build something like a house or hut, you are watching as your limbs pick-up objects such as a pickaxe, a shovel, shears, and the like.

You can switch into a third-person perspective, as though omnipresent and able to see yourself from a distance, though much of the time it is relatively common to be in the first-person mode.

Let's see how this relates to self-driving cars.

An AI driving system makes use of a variety of sensors that are mounted onto or into the self-driving car, including video cameras, radar, LIDAR, ultrasonic units, thermal imaging devices, and so on. These are akin to the eyes and ears of the AI, providing data about the driving scene. By inspecting the data that is collected from the sensors, the AI attempts to figure out where nearby cars are, and where pedestrians are standing, etc.

Note that this construction of what the surroundings consist of will normally be done on a first-person kind of basis.

It is as though the AI is standing amidst the self-driving car and looking outward. The data showcases what is around the self-driving car. In that manner of perspective, the insider jargon is to refer to the self-driving car as the ego vehicle (the word "ego" meaning from the perspective of the vehicle that the rest of the world emanates from). As the vehicle moves along, the AI is recalibrating the surroundings based on looking outward from the self-driving car.

Human drivers are of course doing the same kind of first-person assessment of the driving scene. You let your eyes look forward and see what is ahead of the vehicle. You look over your shoulder to see what is behind you. All along, you are calculating the world based on where you are, and where everything else exists as related to where you are.

In your mind's eye, you can switch to a third-person perspective while driving a car. For example, you can try to imagine what a pedestrian standing at the street corner is seeing as your car makes the turn at the corner. They presumably see you at the wheel and watch as your car tightly makes the turn. I dare say that most of us do not do much third-person perspective thinking while driving, though it certainly crosses the mind from time to time.

For self-driving cars, the future is likely to add the ability to do a third-person perspective in several ways. One is that self-driving cars will be communicating with each other via V2V (vehicle-to-vehicle) electronic communications. This allows one self-driving car to send out a message to other nearby self-driving cars, perhaps warning that there is debris up ahead on the middle of the road. Other AI driving systems that get this message would be forewarned to be wary of the debris.

The same V2V can somewhat provide a third-person perspective to another AI driving system. Suppose a self-driving car observes that a self-driving car up ahead has a bicycle mounted on the rear bumper and the bike is poorly tied down, ready to fall off. The AI driving system of this trailing vehicle can send a V2V to the up ahead self-driving car and let it know that things are amiss. That would be a semblance of being able to construct a third-person perspective.

Even more so in the third-person is the anticipated use of drones.

It is likely that self-driving cars will come with an included drone. During a driving journey, the AI can launch the drone. This drone could then be flown further ahead, perhaps miles up ahead, and figure out what the traffic situation is. By using the drone, the AI can figure out what might be a prudent path to get to the desired destination.

It's A Blocks World

One of the most startling aspects for those that first see *Minecraft* is that it consists primarily of blocks, as in the notion of Lego-like blocks or somewhat relatively simple 3D computer-generated objects (these blocks are considered a cornerstone of the environment, malleable in many ways, and composed together into making overall structures and the like).

The reason that there is astonishment at the use of blocks is that in today's super-duper graphics and the ability to have even the cheapest computers portray photorealistic scenes, the aspect that this worldwide famous game is using the primitives of blocks seems like an outmoded and altogether outdated way of doing contemporary video or online games.

How can a blocks-based game be popular in an era when smooth graphics that can make computer-simulated worlds seem like the real world be something that people are willing and eager to engage in?

Just think of all the strenuous effort by those that have generally perfected computer graphics software that can make the hair on animated animals move as though it is the real thing, or that can have a faked bird fluttering around the sky, and you would swear it was a real hawk or eagle.

And yet, *Minecraft* is using blocks.

You could readily argue that this is what makes *Minecraft* so popular.

If the game attempted to portray a real-world setting, in all its true physical characteristics, you would likely no longer feel like you were in a playground or sandbox. All of that intrusive real-world stuff would prevent you from being immersed into a fantasyland atmosphere. The blocks too are an instantaneous harbinger of childhood and being able to play at will in a sandbox of one kind or another.

Before we go too far into the philosophical realm, let's get back to the self-driving car's side of things.

I earlier mentioned that the AI driving system is reliant upon a suite of sensors. Those sensors are collecting data and the AI has to analyze the data to try and turn the raw data into something intelligible about the driving scene. For example, a visual image captured by the forward-looking camera might indicate that there is a large object just ahead of the self-driving car.

What is this object?

What is the object doing?

The AI software uses various algorithms and potentially Machine Learning, a computational pattern matching capacity, to classify the object as a car. This identified car is ahead of the self-driving car. Based on multiple readings from the sensors, this car ahead of the self-driving car is moving, doing so at a speed of say 35 miles per hour.

To keep track of the surroundings, most AI driving systems have a type of special internal database or virtual world that is crafted and maintained during a driving journey.

This virtual world might indicate that there is a car ahead of the self-driving car. This identified car is labeled as a car and considered in front of the self-driving car. Furthermore, the object, this car, is listed as moving forward and doing so at an existing speed of 35 miles per hour. Realize that there is no need to have a picture per se of the car that is ahead of the self-driving car, at least not as needed in the virtual world. Instead, the virtual world has a denotation of an object, along with the so far identified characteristics.

What is the purpose of this self-driving car virtual world?

Assume that the AI driving system needs to make a right turn up ahead. Via the virtual world, the AI is also crafting an internally calculated map, or overlaying the virtual objects onto a preexisting provided map, and has to figure out what actions the self-driving car should take to make the right turn. If the road is a single lane, the other car ahead of the self-driving car has to be considered in the calculative efforts of when and how to make the right turn.

So what?

Well, guess what, this virtual world is akin to a block's world.

Yes, the AI driving system is using a type of block world to keep track of the real-world. Those houses at the side of the road are marked in the blocks world as houses, but there is no need to have pictures of them and nor keep track of their assorted details (such as whether the house is a two-story or one story, doesn't much matter during the driving of the vehicle).

In perhaps a twist of irony, Minecraft makes use of a blocks world to get away from the real-world, while an AI driving system uses a blocks world to try and rapidly and readily keep track of the real-world.

Mind blown.

Conclusion

There are quite a number of additional parallels that can be made between self-driving cars and *Minecraft* (I'll do more if this sparks interest by readers).

This starter list has hopefully provided a quick glimpse so that you can begin to see how they compare.

One might say that by playing *Minecraft*, you are indirectly getting ready to learn about self-driving cars. In fact, perhaps the children playing *Minecraft* today will grow up to become the AI developers and engineers that will push further forward on advances in AI-based true self-driving cars.

Yes, you can envision it already, those youngsters of today that will soon enough be punching out self-driving cars from the rudiments of extremely versatile redstone (that's a *Minecraft* insider quip, glad to say).

CHAPTER 14
ADD-ON OPTIONS AND SELF-DRIVING CARS

Cars always seem to come with available add-on options.

It is relatively easy to make a list of the customary add-ons that you can get with your car.

For example, one popular add-on encompasses getting an extensive infotainment package that provides a full surround sound experience in your vehicle and online access to the latest in popular videos and podcasts. Another obvious example is that you can get heated bucket seats, which also as a further bonus allows for cooling so that your bucket seats can be refreshingly chilled in the summer and toasty warm in the winter.

There are also under-the-hood add-ons, ones that you don't necessarily see with the naked eye but that is embodied into the vehicle for your use. This might include a souped-up engine proffering tremendously boosted horsepower. Most people do not look at the engine to witness the mechanics of how the bolstered speed will occur, and instead, merely experience the add-on when they jam down on the accelerator pedal and feel the exhilaration of being inside a rocket-propelled speedster.

The most expensive add-ons are much rarer, usually only available on so-called high-end or luxury cars, and not typically available on standard models of cars.

Consider the add-on of a center console housing compartment that you can gently rest a champagne bottle into, for which the unit will make sure to properly chill the (presumably) pricy champagne that you are carrying in your car (well, please, don't drink and drive). This would of course come with specially adapted cup holders in the vehicle that can snugly accommodate champagne flutes.

Do you have that champagne galore add-on in your existing car?

Probably not, but don't despair, one day it will probably become a standard feature.

You see, oftentimes an unusual or extraordinary add-on begins its life as seemingly outlandish or decadent, and then eventually there is a tide that turns toward everyone wanting that very same feature. The costs gradually come down, the availability goes up, and suddenly it seems that all cars have the same capability. If the feature is alluring enough, the odds are that it will ultimately be considered part-and-parcel of the mundane or required aspects of a modern vehicle.

Here's another add-on that perhaps seems a bit indulgent.

Are you ready?

Anti-paparazzi privacy curtains for the windows of your car.

These are specialized curtains that can be open or closed, depending upon whether you want to be seen or are trying to hide from those pushy photographers that are attempting to capture your every move and mood. We are all destined for our fifteen minutes of fame, so having those privacy curtains could be a worthwhile added investment. Make sure to get the ones that allow for being automatically opened or closed via the push of a button, otherwise you'll look quite ridiculous (and cheap) if you are trying to operate them by mere hand alone.

Shifting gears, consider that the future of cars involves the emergence of self-driving cars.

We are gradually going to witness the advent of AI-based true self-driving cars, whereby the vehicle is driven autonomously by an AI driving system and there isn't any human at the wheel of the car. Many are hopeful that the excising of humans from the driving act will demonstrably decrease the number of car crashes. This makes sense in that the AI won't be drinking and driving, and nor will the AI driving system be driving while distracted.

The focus today is on simply and somewhat miraculously getting a car to be driven by an AI driving system and do so with the appropriate capacity of safety during a driving journey. That's the heads-up aspiration and one that is extraordinarily daunting.

Assuming that the overarching goal of achieving a proper self-driving car is achievable, the attention can then go toward the bonus aspects beyond the "standard package" that we'll expect for a self-driving car.

What are the expected standard aspects?

You'd expect as a standard capability that there is a means to sit inside a self-driving car, such that suitable seats are provided. At first, the seats might be rather ordinary looking, akin to the usual seating of conventional cars, perhaps bench-style seating or maybe bucket seats.

Per various futuristic designs, many believe that the seats in a self-driving car might ultimately be swivel seats rather than the normal fixed-in-place seats. This makes sense in that there will no longer need to be a driver's seat in the fixed position at the dashboard of the vehicle, and thus the interior space of a car can be reimagined or opened up to new possibilities. People riding in a self-driving car might want to look this way and that way, watching the road up ahead or swiveling to watch the road that has just gone past, so swivel seats make indubitable sense.

Those swivel seats will likely morph into becoming fully reclinable seats, making them into a bed-like arrangement. This makes terrific sense since you won't need to pay attention to the driving and can get a quick nap on the way to work. Or maybe you'll take those cross-country driving trips and do so via sleeping in your car for much of the journey, letting the AI observe the road for you.

This seating progression then consists of having ordinary or conventional seats, progressing toward swivel seats, and incrementally being advanced to become a combination of swivel and bed-like seating. Thus, the notion is that there will be some initial "standard package" elements of the first iterations of self-driving cars, during which the newer and more experimental add-on variants will start to surface, and then those variants will likely become standards for the follow-on generation of the self-driving vehicles.

During that initial era, we will begin to subtly witness the add-ons for the next generation of self-driving cars.

Keep your eyes and ears open during that time.

Those bonus add-ons will eventually (maybe) become the standard fare. Not necessarily all of the add-ons will survive since there is bound to be a kind of Darwinian winnowing of which add-ons have long legs and which ones are a flash-in-the-pan and nobody really wants them for the long haul.

Here is an intriguing question to contemplate: *What kind of initial add-ons might be tried out in the first generation of AI-based true self-driving cars and then likely continue onward as expected capabilities for the standard fare of well-equipped next-gen self-driving cars?*

Let's unpack the matter and see.

Self-Driving Cars And Add-ons

For Level 4 and Level 5 true self-driving vehicles, there won't be a human driver involved in the driving task.

All occupants will be passengers.

The AI is doing the driving.

For the wealthiest self-driving cars, let's take a look at a chosen handful of add-ons that one might anticipate being made available in the initial era or epoch of self-driving cars.

These add-ons are likely to include somewhat impractical or unnecessary facets that are abstractly comparable to the champagne chiller mentioned earlier in conventional luxury cars (yes, I realize that some would argue the champagne capability is not impractical and not unnecessary, I hear you). While others of the add-ons are going to be of immense practical value and sensibly be included in all future self-driving cars.

Put on your seatbelt and get ready for those luxury add-ons of the first generation of self-driving cars.

Interior Wraparound LEDs

A conventional car allows you to see out the windows of the vehicle.

This is certainly prudent.

There is a human driver in the car and they have to see the driving scene to be able to appropriately drive the car. Some conventional cars provide a huge amount of window space, while others are a bit chintzier. In any case, the windows are mainly for the driver, one would naturally assert, and yet are handy for the passengers since they can also look at the world outside of the car too.

The AI driving system will be relying upon a suite of sensors that are mounted onto or sometimes into the body of the car, including the use of video cameras, radar, LIDAR, ultrasonic units, and the like. This means that the windows are of no consequence for the AI driving system. Any windows that exist will be purely for the benefit of the passengers and has nothing to do with the AI driving system per se.

In theory, self-driving cars can be made into bubbles that have absolutely no windows at all.

Many are doubtful that passengers will find that very alluring. People inside a self-driving car are going to want to look out the window, regardless of whether the AI needs such a facility or not. In short, windows will likely continue to exist on cars, including for self-driving cars.

That being said, there is a twist.

The glass in the windows can be potentially made of materials that will allow a transparent look or an opaque look. With a touch of a button, the windows will allow you to look out, and by touching the button again the windows will be cloudy or possibly entirely impenetrable. Even if the glass doesn't have this capacity, there can be specialized curtains (akin to the anti-paparazzi ones of today), which can be used to close off the windows when desired.

You might want to shut the windows, as it were, due to taking a nap while inside a self-driving car.

There is another basis for doing this. The interior of the vehicle might become your own drive-in (or, driving in motion) movie theatre.

The notion is that the entire interior is lined with LED screens. You can then play your favorite cat videos and be utterly surrounded by the playful cats, visually. Imagine that you have tilted your swivel seat into a reclining posture, and you are now watching the ceiling of the interior, upon which your cat video is being displayed. It is like being at your own Imax theatre.

For those that might find this somewhat claustrophobic, especially in versions whereby the car is indeed a bubble and the LEDs replace the windows altogether, there is a lifeline for you. The AI driving system can display what it sees via the cameras onto the interior LEDs. In a manner of speaking, this allows for the self-driving car to have simulated windows. You will look at the interior side panel LED, and you'll seemingly be looking outside "the window" (via the video images streaming from the actual camera mounted outside of the vehicle).

Trippy!

Drone Accompaniment

You get into a self-driving car and realize after the AI has driven you partway to your destination that you have left your wallet at home.

Sadness, madness, irksomeness.

Do you have the self-driving car drive you back home?

You could do so, but there's another way to solve this pickle.

Send out the self-driving car drone.

That's right, some self-driving cars will be outfitted with a paired drone. The drone can be launched from the self-driving car and sent on missions. In this example, you could have it fly home, have your loved one at home put your wallet into the drone, and the drone flies back to you.

Meanwhile, the self-driving car is still pushing along in traffic and aiming to reach your destination.

The drone will meet-up with wherever you and the self-driving car are. Perhaps the drone took flight when you were halfway to your destination. It was fast enough that it was able to fly to your home, get the wallet, and fly back to meet you while the self-driving car is now three-fourths of the way to your destination.

There is no need to stop the self-driving car for the launching and nor the landing of the drone.

If you don't like the example of getting your wallet, here's another example that is already being tried out.

The drone could deliver you some fast-food.

You are riding inside the self-driving car and the traffic on the freeways is slow going. You are getting hungry. If the self-driving car is told to get off at the next available exit that has a fast-food drive-thru, you'll lose time toward reaching your destination. So, the obvious and best alternative is to send your drone.

Or, if the eatery is suitably equipped, have them send their drone to your self-driving car, packed with that delicious hamburger and fries, ready cooked and drone-delivered to your eager hands (inside the self-driving car).

Exterior Electronic Skin

Today's conventional cars are generally bland when it comes to the exterior of the vehicle (no disrespect for the beautiful designs and shapes of today's cars).

By bland, I mean that they are usually painted a particular color and that's the likely look of the car for its lifetime. Sure, you might go to the trouble to take the car to a place that will paint it with a new color, but this is a sizable hassle and not many choose to do so.

Some conventional cars are outfitted with external LEDs that display messages on the rooftop or are mounted at the rear of the vehicle. This might include showcasing advertising or other kinds of signage.

Envision that a self-driving car is enshrouded in an electronic skin.

This would allow you to display whatever you'd like on the exterior of the vehicle. Maybe today you feel like going for a drive in a pink-colored car. Voila, you just tell the AI driving system to make the electronic skin look entirely pink in color. The next day, you change the color to blue. And so on.

One reason for having electronic skin is that it will help to make a self-driving car stand out when trying to pick-up someone. If self-driving cars of the same automaker or self-driving car firm are otherwise all looking alike, it will be hard to know which self-driving car is the one that you are supposed to be used when getting a lift. Via the electronic skin, the exterior could display an image or message that would make abundantly clear that the self-driving car is there to pick you up.

A big downside of these kinds of electronic skins is that they would be a distraction to human drivers. As such, until there is a preponderance of self-driving cars on the roadways, having these kinds of displays on the exterior will be problematic. You can also anticipate that there will be a lot of societal angst over what people can or shouldn't display on the exterior of their self-driving cars.

ODDs Selection

Level 4 self-driving cars are going to be based on Operational Design Domains (ODDs). This is industry parlance for the scope or nature of the driving environment and conditions that the AI driving system of the self-driving car can safely handle.

For example, some self-driving cars might only function properly in sunny weather and not be suitable for driving in heavy rain. That would be one instance of an ODD. There might be some self-driving cars that are capable of driving in the rain and sunshine but are not capable to handle nighttime driving. This would be another instance of an ODD.

Please be aware that those are simplistic examples, and the actual ODDs will be much more complex. In any case, the point being made is that depending upon which self-driving car you happen to use (of Level 4), it will have a designated ODD and thus it would be expected to only drive when those ODD conditions are met.

A type of add-on could be the variety of ODDs for your self-driving car.

In other words, the standard with the self-driving car is an ODD that allows for driving only during daylight, for example. And, for an added fee, you can get an ODD that will allow the vehicle to drive at nighttime.

I bring up this as an add-on to highlight an important point made earlier about add-ons, namely that sometimes an add-on starts as something considered extraordinary, and gradually becomes part of the standard.

You can likely expect that the ODDs will fit into that kind of progression.

Off-Roading Capability

Many people do not realize that the existing levels of self-driving cars do not encompass an off-roading capability (for my explanation, see **the link here**).

Off-roading is considered outside the scope of an everyday kind of self-driving car.

You can bet your bottom dollar that the automakers and self-driving tech firms will inevitably accommodate off-road driving into their AI driving systems.

Note that this is not a stated requirement to satisfactorily meet the levels of self-driving cars and would be done as a kind of add-on if you will.

Adult Provided With The Self-Driving Car

A final twist on the add-ons topic is the notion that an adult human being would come with the self-driving car.

That's a somewhat tongue-in-cheek way of depicting this aspect.

In short, I've predicted that there will be a type of nanny or butler (a new title will likely emerge), involving having a person that can be made available for a driving journey inside a self-driving car.

Why so?

Suppose you wanted to have a self-driving car pick-up your elderly grandmother and bring her to your house. You don't want her traveling alone in the self-driving car as she sometimes needs added attention. When scheduling the self-driving car, you also request that an adult be present that can aid your grandmother during the driving journey.

There will be a new niche of people that are hired to ride in self-driving cars and provide some assistance accordingly. It could simply be adult supervision, such as when you are having a bunch of kids rides in a self-driving car to a campground, wherein once they get to the campsite there is someone else there to receive them. During the car ride, you want to make sure an adult is inside the car and making sure the kids don't misbehave.

I realize that a human being is not an add-on per se.

No worries, since eventually those humans might get replaced by a walking-talking robot, in which case, you could then construe that the passenger robot is indeed an add-on (similar to the exemplar of a drone).

Conclusion

There you have it, a handful of potential add-ons that will appear in the first era of self-driving cars and then might become "standard fare" on future generations of self-driving cars.

In recap, here they are:

- Interior wraparound LEDs
- Drone accompaniment
- External electronic skins
- ODDs selection
- Off-roading capability
- Adult provided with the self-driving car

The good news is that all of those are relatively feasible and generally well within the realm of being made available. In essence, there is nothing about them that would seemingly preclude or make unlikely the technological chances of them becoming features for self-driving cars.

Now that you've had a chance to see the list of "reasonable" add-ons, get yourself ready for my next list.

The next set of potential add-ons are pretty outlandish and stretch the possibilities of what can be done, but one supposes that is what makes add-ons so delectable and desirable.

That list will be considered the uberwealthy or supremely indulgent self-driving car add-ons.

CHAPTER 15
CAR PILE-UPS AND SELF-DRIVING CARS

During the winter months, there is always a spate of massive car pileups that woefully take place and make rather noticeable and attention-getting headlines.

Recently, in Iowa, there was a forty-car pileup. This was especially eye-catching because two Iowa State Patrol cars were also enmeshed into the traffic cataclysm and ended up getting hit (thankfully, the officers were okay). In Japan, a mind-blowing pileup occurred that involved at least 134 vehicles, stranding about two hundred people, injuring seventeen, and miserably leading to one death.

Even though these somber events are often referred to as multi-car pileups, the more apt depiction is that they are ostensibly "multiple vehicle" pileups. This alternative naming is reflective of the fact that there are usually trucks involved in the car pileups and thus the calamity strikes not just cars but can encompass other vehicles too.

It seems that all drivers are subject to finding themselves getting embroiled in a chain reaction series of vehicle collisions.

The situation usually entails at least one vehicle that goes amiss, and then others ram into each other in a cascading cacophony. For example, envision that a car veers into the path of a large truck, the truck attempts to avoid a collision and goes into a jackknifed posture. Another car that is behind the truck makes a radical maneuver to avoid hitting the truck. This ploy then leads to a different car hitting the escaping car. Maybe they both then slide into the jackknifed truck.

The point is that the basis for the multiple vehicle calamity is that a series of cars and trucks find themselves getting into a dangerous dance of each trying to avoid the other. In a sense, the avoidance draws other vehicles into the morass. Everyone is doing something to avoid others, and yet they invariably ram into each other.

It is possible that some of those vehicles might luckily be unscathed and able to avoid striking anyone else. This seeming miracle can be short-lived since some other wayward vehicle might suddenly ram into them, as though an afterthought and the hand of fate deciding that all the vehicles are going to be damaged by the chain reaction. You'd have to really be relying upon your lucky rabbits' foot to be in the midst of a multiple vehicle collision and truly avert getting dinged or banged-up by the experience (if you are that fortunate, probably wise to thereafter go and buy a lottery ticket and test that luck for the furtherance of good fortune).

Not all of the drivers are necessarily on the ball and seeking to avoid the other vehicles that are enmeshed in the quagmire of collisions.

It could be that the event unfolds so quickly that some of the drivers do not have sufficient time to react. They are merely carried into the collisions by the physics involved. Imagine swimming in the ocean and getting carried by a large wave. There might not be much that you can do to cope with the overwhelming forces entailed.

Some drivers do react and yet might try to respond in a manner that makes things worse. Ironically, if they had done nothing in terms of attempting to steer out of the abyss, they might have come out with less damage. Instead, they try frantically to get out of the impending doom and find themselves confounding other drivers accordingly. This makes for a much wider array of confusion and extends the number of vehicles caught up in the adversity.

Time is usually a key factor.

The collisions happen so fast that there is very little time to make profound mental calculations and ascertain what is the best course of driving action to take. Furthermore, all those other drivers are making mental calculations that are somewhat unpredictable as to what they might be thinking of doing.

In that sense, probabilities are also crucial.

Assuming you have at least some available time to make a driving decision, you are no longer in a rather static traffic situation. When traffic is routinely taking place, you pretty much can anticipate what other drivers are going to do. There is a very high probability that the car next to you will continue forward and similarly it is highly unlikely they will opt to veer unexpectedly into your lane.

All bets are off when a multiple-vehicle pileup ensues.

The car driver to your left might think it is best to come into your lane. You might be thinking that the neighboring car ought to head into the emergency lane, but it seems this is not going to be the case. All of your normal assumptions about driver behaviors can get tossed into the air and become quite scrambled.

You've got some drivers that are trying to self-optimize and minimize their chances of getting hit. Some drivers are trying to minimize their chances of hitting other cars. And some drivers aren't doing any mental contortions and are being drawn into the evolving event without any direct effort of avoidance.

This is somewhat like a chess game that has gone amok.

You cannot assume that the other drivers are still playing the car driving game of chess by the proper rules. It has become every player for themselves in a do-or-die gambit. Worse still, some of the players are bad at this kind of chess game, namely one involving a multiple vehicles collisions scenario. Plus, there are those playing the game that is essentially asleep at the wheel, which doesn't mean they were actually dozing, and only suggests they maybe aren't paying attention or are stuck in a situation for which they are mentally freezing up and don't know what to do.

I earlier pointed out that these pileups seem to happen

predominantly during the winter months.

In theory, the advent of multiple vehicle collisions could happen at any time of the year. There are instances of these events happening during the summer months, especially when a lot of vehicles are on the roads and traveling at high speeds. Nonetheless, the winter is a particularly high chance of having such multi-car catastrophes.

Why so?

The obvious aspect is that the weather provides the "perfect storm" of stoking the elements underlying a large-scale pileup.

Once the freeway has become icy, the ability to control a vehicle diminishes. Add snow flurries to the equation and you get reduced visibility and ergo can no longer see the road as clearly. The driving scene turns into a problematic scenario.

The matchstick that can ignite the pileup consists of driving at unsafe speeds for the driving conditions involved.

First, let's conceive of the idealized setting that won't lead to chain reaction results.

Imagine an icy freeway that is encountering snow squalls. All the traffic consists of vehicles driving at super-duper slow speeds, cautiously crawling along. Each driver is carefully monitoring the distance between them and the vehicle ahead of their car. At all times, the drivers in this scenario are aware of the impending danger of a multiple vehicle smasher and so are conscientiously driving with great aplomb and rapt attention.

If one of the vehicles starts sliding precariously, the closest vehicles to this prospective pileup starter can react proficiently and avoid hitting the igniter of potential disarray. Or maybe they do lightly strike the vehicle, but at a slow speed that entails almost no demonstrative damages or injuries. Meanwhile, the other vehicles nearby have all reacted quickly and come to a stop, preventing a cascading chain reaction.

Your normal everyday commute probably is similar to the aforementioned scenario.

There are somewhat singular or unitary car crashes that happen daily on freeways and highways (I mean when two cars collide), yet they do not turn into massive car pileups. This avoidance is typically due to other nearby drivers able to react sufficiently to prevent the cascading impacts. Sure, it could be that a lot of the cars have to hit their brakes suddenly and tires are squealing, but fortunately, this happens in a manner that fewer slip-or-slides occur around and into other surrounding traffic.

It is like setting up a bunch of dominos.

When you place dominos stacked one after another, close to each other, you can readily get them all to fall down by simply starting the process at the start of the line. Touching the first domino and getting it to fall will strike the next one, which strikes the next one, and so on.

We've all done that before.

If there is a gap between one domino and another, when the one ahead of it falls backward, the chain is essentially broken such that the next in sequence domino does not fall. In a sense, that is what happens when drivers are paying attention and driving at safer speeds in the conditions of the roadway.

One aspect of multiple car pileups that you might not be aware of involves the possibility of human injuries and death. We already can visualize the car damage to fenders being bent and crumpled car doors. What doesn't necessarily come to mind is the human costs too.

The insidious aspect is that you can get hit not just once, but potentially a multitude of times. Perhaps the car behind you rams into your car. That's one blow. A car behind that other car rams into the car that just hit you and the forces carry once again into your car. On top of this, your airbag may have already deployed. This means that for the subsequent blows, your airbag is no longer especially useful since it is already deployed and now is partially deflated.

I don't want to linger on these dreadful aspects and will merely also point out that it can be hard to extricate yourself from your mangled vehicle. There is also the chance that gasoline leaks will occur, and the spilled fuel could be ignited by nearby sparks or flames. Into this horrid convergence is the other nightmarish aspect that the ambulances and paramedics might not be able to rapidly reach the vehicles since the whole entanglement is somewhat impenetrable.

One shudders at the whole predicament.

A massive pileup is assuredly a beast of a different kind and one that you never want to get ensnared in.

Shifting gears, the future of cars involves the emergence of self-driving cars. Some have asserted that the advantage of self-driving cars is that they will never get stuck in a massive car pileup. The logic of this contention is that the AI driving systems will be astute enough to avoid any such mishap.

That's quite a bold claim.

Here then is a vital question to consider: *Will the advent of AI-based true self-driving cars ensure that there will never be any multiple vehicle pileups?*

Let's unpack the matter and see.

Self-Driving Cars And Roadway Pileups

For Level 4 and Level 5 true self-driving vehicles, there won't be a human driver involved in the driving task.

All occupants will be passengers.

The AI is doing the driving.

Let's start this discussion with an important point that might get some pundits into a real tizzy.

Self-driving cars can get embroiled in a massive car pileup.

Yikes, that seems sacrosanct and goes against the prevailing wisdom about the revered safety aspects of self-driving cars. It seems like an impossible possibility.

We can quickly dispense with the false belief that self-driving cars will never get stuck in a multi-car or multi-vehicle pileup.

Here's how it can happen.

A self-driving car is driving along on a freeway. A human-driven car up ahead comes to a sudden stop, perhaps trying to avoid ramming into a truck that has just jackknifed. We will give a benefit of the doubt to the self-driving car that it was maintaining a proper stopping distance and thus can come to a halt before running into the up ahead human-driven car (I'll be taking back this assumption in a moment, but let's go with it for the time being, for sake of discussion).

Wonderful, you say, the AI driving system has saved the day and not hit the car that has come to a surprising stop.

Whoa, hold your horses.

The human-driven car behind the self-driving car is caught off-guard by the sudden stop of the self-driving car. It then rams into the self-driving car. This shoves the self-driving forward, and the self-driving car now rams into the car that stopped when trying to avoid the jackknifed truck.

Meanwhile, other cars and trucks behind this mess are all ramming into each other, doing so in the usual and unfortunate traffic dominos fashion.

Could this scenario happen in the real-world?

Of course.

There isn't anything about this scenario that is somehow rigged against the self-driving car. We are assuming that the self-driving car was driving in a perfectly legal manner, and it was dutifully trying to keep its distance from the traffic ahead. The self-driving car came to a prompt stop. The sensors detected that the car ahead was halting and the AI driving system did a tremendous job of bringing the self-driving car to a halt.

Yet, despite all this, the self-driving car was nonetheless enmeshed into the multi-car pileup.

I assure you, this can and will happen, whence we have a prevalence of self-driving cars on our roadways. Right now, there are so few self-driving cars that the odds of getting stuck into this kind of a situation are rather low. Envision that once there are thousands upon thousands of self-driving cars, and they are roaming all the time, likely 24x7, the chances of finding them perchance trapped into this circumstance is a lot higher than it is today.

Okay, so I hope this dispels the myth of the invincible self-driving car.

I realize that some pundits will be instantly up in arms and argue that this scenario is "unfair" because it presumes that there are human-driven cars in the traffic setting. In the minds of these pundits, they are envisioning a world of only self-driving cars, such that all human-driven cars are banned from the roadways.

That alone is quite a dreamy vision. First of all, there are 250 million conventional cars in the United States alone, and those cars are not going to overnight be junked merely to be instantaneously replaced by self-driving cars. The reality is that we are going to have many years of a mixture of both human-driven cars and self-driving cars, likely for decades to come.

Some have suggested that we ought to have roads that are dedicated solely to self-driving cars, thus avoiding having to come in contact with human-driven cars, but this is also a quite questionable proposition (it might be done in very narrow contexts, but this doesn't seem economically feasible on any largescale).

All in all, you have to assume realistically that self-driving cars and human-driven cars will be on our roadways together, at times being best buddies and at other times finding themselves at odds with each other.

Now that we've covered the "proof of existence" that there will be self-driving cars that get embroiled in massive car pile-ups, we can turn our attention to other related facets.

One point worth making as to why self-driving cars will *rarely* be involved in such pileups is that the self-driving cars might not even be on the roads at the time and place wherein these pileups happen.

Here's the story.

For the Level 4 self-driving cars, the automaker and self-driving car firms are supposed to define the Operational Design Domain (ODD) for their cars.

The ODD refers to the conditions under which the self-driving car will operate or be driven by the AI driving system. For example, an ODD might indicate that automaker XYZ has decided that their self-driving cars can only operate when the weather is sunny or maybe under light rain, but that once there is snow or heavy rain, the AI driving system will refuse to drive the car. This is for safety considerations in that the developers or the fleet operator have predetermined that the sensors and the AI driving system are not proficient in those kinds of adverse conditions.

Indubitably, this makes good sense.

The ramification is that when you hear or see these news stories of massive pileups that happen in those icy and snowstorm conditions, the chances are that a Level 4 self-driving car won't be there, simply due to the aspect that the conditions were outside the defined ODD and the self-driving car "refused" to drive in such conditions (when I say that it refused, this is not a mysterious form of AI sentience, instead, the AI is connected to weather forecasts and has been programmed to not get underway in circumstances outside its ODD, or that if it is underway then it pulls over to a safe spot and waits for the conditions to become drivable, etc.).

In short, the self-driving car never got on the road to start with, and therefore it didn't get ensnared into the pileup.

You might liken this to a human driver that looks outside the window of their house, sees that it is snowing, and proclaims they are not going to go driving since the roadway conditions are going to be rotten.

If a domino is not in the set of dominos that are stacked up to fall, it won't be part of the cascading series.

Conclusion

You might be tempted to think that this showcases that those self-driving cars are going to be more astutely run since they will not be on the roads when the chances of pileups are highest.

Yes, and no.

When those trucks and cars get stuck in a pileup, is your first thought that all of those drivers, each and everyone, was completely foolhardy and out of their minds to be on the roadways?

It seems doubtful that this is the case. There are drivers in that setting that chose the inherent dangers of being on the roads versus the needed basis for being in their cars. Perhaps some were heading to work and had to choose between getting to work and losing their job if they didn't drive in those conditions.

Many of those drivers likely had compelling reasons to take a chance and be on the roads.

The point is that if the car itself refuses to drive (again, based on programmatic facets), this does not particularly solve the problem.

This would imply that those humans that believed they had a bona fide basis for getting on the roadways would no longer be able to do so, assuming that they were fully reliant on only using self-driving cars.

This is quite a conundrum.

Who shall decide that it is safe to be on the roads?

Is this a question to be ascertained by the individual human driver, or by some overarching system or process that decides this matter? You could argue that the government routinely will close roads or urge people to not drive, and thus a means to ensure this decree would be to prevent cars from getting on the roads at all, rather than relying on humans to individually decide to abide or not abide by such cautionary aspects.

A counterargument is that if this kind of driving the decision is going to be made by a collective, you will have human drivers that are going to categorically clamor that they will never give up their driving.

They will vehemently say that the act of driving is a decision for the individual. You will take away their driving only when their cold dead hands are pried from the steering wheel.

Anyway, returning to the multi-vehicle pileups overall, one small point to be made is that one intriguing aspect of having self-driving cars enmeshed in pileups is that they will be handy "eyewitnesses" due to their sensors and sensory collected data.

Oftentimes, it is very difficult to reconstruct what occurred in a massive pileup and figure out the sequence that led to the chaos. Via inspecting the data from the self-driving cars, it might be a lot easier to discern how things went awry.

Whether this detective-like facility is endearing would likely depend upon whether you were a human driver that wanted to prove your innocence or was trying to avoid getting nabbed as the troublemaker that knocked down the first domino.

AI as a tattletale will be good for some, and a form of angst for others.

Please watch out for those pileups and I hope none of you get entangled in one.

CHAPTER 16
CROSSING GUARDS AND SELF-DRIVING CARS

A video went viral that showcased a school crossing guard heroically saving a child from crossing into the path of an oncoming car.

The mother of the child was standing across the street and watched in abject horror when her offspring began to dart forward and appeared completely unaware of the impending danger. With quick reflexes, the crossing guard waved his arm to block the child from further crossing, letting the car then skirt forward and go past the two of them.

Mother and child were then reunited, and the school crossing guard was hailed as a hero.

What do you call this?

Answer: Just another day in the life of a school crossing guard.

You see, being a school crossing guard is pretty much a sacred duty and filled daily with these kinds of rescues and heroic acts.

It is all quite a big deal when you think about it. A school crossing guard is entrusted to help guide young school children across the street. This act includes getting cars to come to a stop, thus letting the boisterous and joyful kids safely skip and hop their way over to the other side of the street, blissfully so.

Keep in mind that a car is a multi-ton vehicle that can readily overpower any human, young or old, and readily smack into and harm anyone within its path. Drivers of cars have at their hands the ability to knock people over, and yet drivers oftentimes treat the driving task carelessly, chatting while on their cellphone, watching cat videos, or pruning themselves for the day ahead.

The only means a crossing guard has to compel or more like persuade cars to come to a halt is a sign they are carrying and for which it says something akin to stop or halt.

You prominently hold-up the sign, usually made visible by being mounted on the end of a long stick, and presumably, the drivers of nearby cars will see and obey the signage. That's the hope. That's the dreamy notion that is supposed to work, presumably all of the time and without fail.

To garner additional attention, some crossing guards also wave their other arm or do a bit of a dance to be noticeable. They might also whistle or yell out to the drivers. Most crossing guards also wear some form of garb that makes them stand out, such as bright red colors and reflective strips or shiny buttons.

Of course, the crossing guard might enter into the street to make things plainly clear that it is time for cars to come to a halt. When standing up on the curb, it seems that some drivers perceive the waving of the sign as merely a warning and do not strictly believe they need to come to a stop. Only until the crossing guard is firmly implanted into the street will such drivers begin to believe that the crossing guard is really serious about wanting to have traffic come to a halt.

Even after moving into the street, this still might not be a sufficient indication for some stubborn or wanton drivers in their strident driving efforts and so they treat the crossing guard as an obstruction to maneuver around. Yes, that's right, some drivers seem to think that the crossing guard is merely a kind of statue or object that perchance is in the way of driving. If you can get behind the crossing guard or pass in front of the passing guard, that's perfectly fine (in the minds of these flighty drivers), as long as you don't directly strike the crossing guard you are okay to proceed.

According to stats published by the New Jersey State League of Municipalities (NJLM), the accident rate for school crossing guards has sadly and dangerously increased by about 65% over the last decade or so.

Yikes!

That takes us back to the earlier point about the revered duty of a school crossing guard. Not only are they trying to save the lives of children, but they are also putting their own lives at risk too.

You probably are shocked to think that school crossing guards ever get run down or smacked by a car, since you would never imagine hitting one, but regrettably, some drivers do this dastardly act. Some drivers do so by happenstance, in the sense that they didn't see the crossing guard and therefore plowed into the person without realizing what they were doing. Other drivers are more intentional, playing a kind of game with the crossing guard.

Do you remember the game of chicken that you might have played when you were young? You stare blankly at someone else. They are staring at you too. Whichever one of you looks away or maybe blinks first is the loser of the game. As a form of child's play, this is simple enough and usually a safe thing to do.

The same game of chicken can occur between a crossing guard and a driver of a car that is trying to shove its ways forward and disobey the crossing guard.

The crossing guard is waving frantically to get the car to stop. The driver is staring at the crossing guard and essentially mouthing that the interloper had better get out of the way. In this one-on-one battle, neither side wants to back down. Of course, the car and the driver are heavily favored since a human being is not able to singlehandedly physically stop a car (only superheroes in the comic books can do that).

Here's a curious and mind-bending facet about school crossings that dovetails into the matter of crossing guards and the potential for injuries or fatalities of these vaunted guardians.

The percentage of children that walk or bike to school has dropped precipitously from when we were youngsters. Reportedly per the NJLM, about 50% of kids used to walk or bike (that was thirty years ago), and now only around 15% do so.

Why care about this stat?

Your first thought is that this means a lot fewer kids are trying to cross the street. If there are a lot fewer kids seeking to cross the street, this would seem to suggest that the odds of any one of them getting struck by a passing car is lessened. Apparently, that is not quite the case, and in fact, the opposite seems to be occurring.

The missing factor is to include into your mental equation the vast numbers of kids that *aren't* walking or biking are being driven to school. Those children have to get to school somehow. They are being driven. This means more drivers and more cars are converging upon a school during the most active moments when children would be crossing the street.

More cars mean more chances for a crossing child to get hit (i.e., more cars per capita of children crossing). Children are in a bizarre sense the proverbial sitting duck for all those maddeningly wayward-driven cars.

You betcha that those drivers are undoubtedly in a frenetic mode.

You've certainly seen this if you've ever driven nearby a school when it is opening in the morning or when the kids are being let out of school in the afternoon. These are crazed drivers. They weave into the traffic without much thought. Their focus is getting their kid, and being overly concerned about other children is not on their list of things to care about. It is a dog-eat-dog world, and this is the time to be a fighter.

The cars are in a fierce battle with each other. The kids on the street and the sidewalks are merely window dressing for the real head-to-head struggle that is taking place among the amazing machines called cars. One car driver notices that another driver has pulled ahead. That's not right! So, the offended driver tries to jam into the line of cars. Sure, there might be children walking all around these vehicles, but that's not important. What is important is ensuring the pecking order of the cars.

Into this ferocious morass steps the school crossing guard.

It would be like putting yourself into the midst of a herd of elephants, seemingly angry and rampaging elephants. Do you have an elephant gun to try and stop them? No, you have a thin stick with a shiny sign on the top of it. Not especially empowering. Human drivers will decide for themselves whether they want to abide by the crossing guard or not.

Very few crossing guards have any kind of policing capability per se.

They often are not legally empowered to issue tickets. They cannot bolster their actions by indicating that they have the full force of the law standing with them. Some drivers take a dim view of crossing guards for this very same reason. If the crossing guard is not an official arm of the law, this implies that the crossing guard is simply an optional roadway indicator and not someone or something of a mandatory requirement.

Many drivers are unaware that their state driver licensing code usually contains a provision that you are required to abide by the actions of a formal crossing guard. In theory, if you disobey a properly conveyed instruction about your driving action, you could be subject to getting a ticket and potentially losing your driver's license. This is an aspect that few drivers take into account and summarily do not know or patently don't believe is enforceable.

These same drivers would likely obey a stop sign at an intersection.

But the stop sign being held aloft by the crossing guard is given short shrift in comparison. This is why sometimes a crossing guard will wear an outlandish outfit, hopeful that maybe the mirth of the outfit will shock such drivers into a willingness to play along. If those drivers won't accede to a normally attired crossing guard, perhaps one wearing oddball clothing will garner their attention and make them think twice about disobeying the instructions being issued.

Perhaps one of the biggest kickers to this whole situation is that many school crossing guards are not getting paid a dime.

In other words, they are out there trying to protect our children on a pure volunteer basis, meanwhile putting themselves at grave risk, and yet they do so solely for the heartwarming reason of helping others and not due to the pay involved. To clarify, even those getting paid are also equally performing an uplifting duty. The pay involved is oftentimes minuscule and only amounts to a few hours of work per day and thus not much-accumulated earnings during a school year. You can take a look at the U.S. Bureau of Labor Statistics (BLS) website at section 33-9091 on the topic of occupational employment and wages of crossing guards if you'd like to see a breakdown on the annual pay and hours of crossing guards.

By the way, though the focus herein has been school crossing guards, please note that there are lots of other crossing guards that daily aid in stopping cars and letting people cross the street. There are crossing guards at downtown intersections, and construction sites, and the mall, and so on. Note too that all these crossing guards are not just protecting children, they also help protect adult pedestrians too.

I'm sure that some adults are insulted at the notion of a crossing guard trying to protect them.

Shouldn't all adults be responsible enough on their own to know when to cross the street? This same kind of thinking will often surface when an adult is wanting to urgently cross the street and believes that the judgment of the crossing guard is wrong or overly delayed. The viewpoint seems to be that the crossing guard might be for those other "idiots" waiting to cross, but not for those that are of their own mind and can make their own darned judgments.

Returning to the discussion on school crossing guards, it was noted that more cars than ever are congregating into a tight space-time continuum when it comes to arriving at a school for picking up or dropping off their kids. This makes the school crossing guard role even more vital, and more harried, and riskier.

Keep your eye on the cars, that's the crux of the entire matter.

If there were no cars, there would by-and-large be no worry about children crossing the street (one supposes that bikes and other threats might persist, though this would be less menacing overall than cars). Until we all have jetpacks, you might as well assume that cars will prevail. Of course, the hope would be that mass transit might be used in place of cars, but that's a different discussion for another day.

Assume that cars are here to stay.

The future of cars includes the advent of self-driving cars. These are cars that are being driven by an AI driving system and not being driven by a human driver.

Here's the intriguing question to consider: *Will self-driving cars do a better job of abiding by school crossing guards and are school crossing guards going to be better off by the emergence of self-driving cars?*

Let's unpack the matter and see..

Self-Driving Cars And Crossing Guards

For Level 4 and Level 5 true self-driving vehicles, there won't be a human driver involved in the driving task.

All occupants will be passengers.

The AI is doing the driving.

A touted benefit of AI driving systems is that they won't be driving while drunk, and they won't be watching cat videos or otherwise distracted while driving. As such, the current and heartwrenching statistic that there are about 40,000 car crash-related fatalities annually in the U.S. and around 2.5 million related injuries is predicted to drop tremendously.

Some assert that the number of fatalities will reach zero. I've repeatedly exhorted that there is a zero chance of reaching zero. The physics belie the likelihood of achieving a zero count of fatalities.

Here's what I mean.

A child is standing between two parked cars. The child cannot be seen and is essentially hidden from view by the large-sized parked automobiles. A self-driving car is coming down the street at the posted speed limit of say 35 miles per hour. Suddenly, the child darts into the street, directly in front of the self-driving car. The distance between the self-driving car and the child is now about 10 feet.

Let's assume that the self-driving car instantaneously detects the child, and the AI driving system immediately jams on the brakes. The stopping distance depending upon the situation (weather conditions, type of brakes, etc.), probably is around 50 to 75 feet.

Compute the math, and you'll realize the child is going to get hit by the self-driving car.

My point is that despite all the super-duper tech of a self-driving car, and assuming it is working at peak performance, there are still nonetheless going to be car crashes and there will (sadly) be human deaths and injuries.

Put the zero out of your mind and be relieved and eager that we will at least be reducing demonstrably the number of car crashes. The logic on that assumption is that if self-driving cars do not drink and drive, and they aren't driving while distracted, and if they drive as safely as humans normally do today, this would right away cut out around 30% to 50% of existing car crashes (or more). That's a lot of saved lives and averted injuries.

Back to the topic of the school crossing guards.

The expectation is that AI driving systems are going to drive in a strictly legal manner. They will abide stridently by the posted speed limit. They will always come to a full stop at stop signs. They will never run a red light. To the degree feasible, the AI driving systems will be programmed to be the most law-abiding driver that you can envision.

Okay, this suggests that the AI driving systems will certainly obey a school crossing guard.

If only the world was that easy and straightforward!

First, the AI driving system has to detect that a school crossing guard is present. This detection is a lot harder than you might imagine. Humans can easily scan a driving scene and spot a crossing guard. Getting the AI systems to do so, even using the latest in Machine Learning and Deep Learning, can be quite challenging.

If the school crossing guard is indeed spotted, the next difficulty is trying to figure out what the school crossing guard is doing and what their actions signify.

For example, suppose there aren't any children nearby and thus the crossing guard is standing at the curb, leaning casually somewhat while waiting for kids to arrive. The long pole with the sign is being held in the hand of the crossing guard. The stop indication is clearly visible.

Suppose the sensors of the self-driving car have detected the presence of the crossing guard. The mathematical analysis of the video images show that this is a seemingly bona fide crossing guard, and they are holding a sign, and the sign indicates the word Stop. The AI driving system has been programmed to always obey the school crossing guard.

Thus, the self-driving car comes to an immediate stop.

Yay, it has done what we want it to do.

But, has it?

In this use case, the crossing guard is not trying to stop traffic. They are merely holding the sign gingerly and not attempting to thrust it or proclaim it upon the passing cars.

The AI driving system is going to have a tough time trying to discern when the crossing guard is actively using the sign and desirous of stopping traffic versus when the school crossing guard is waiting for the right moment to do so. Human capabilities at surveying a driving scene, analyzing the elements of the scene, ascertaining the meaning of those elements, and then taking an aligned driving action is a lot more complicated than we give due credit for.

Also, a school crossing guard is a potential moving object. And, each crossing guard is unique in the sense that they each look different from each other. Sure, there is a commonality in that they are likely adults, they are likely attired in something that we assume signifies a crossing guard, and they are likely carrying a sign.

All of those factors add further complexity to the matter at hand.

Got a novel twist for you.

A local sandwich shop is trying to attract customers. They put outside their shop and stationed at the curb a person in a colorful outfit that is holding a sign aloft. The sign says "Stop for Joe's" and looks akin to a stop sign.

This could easily be mistaken as a crossing guard that is holding a sign to stop traffic.

Humans would be less likely fooled since they would assess the context of the setting, namely, the person is standing near a sandwich shop and we've seen this kind of promotional or marketing effort before. When comparing the situation to that of a normal crossing guard, there are apparent mismatches and thus the human would ascertain this is not a crossing guard instance.

Getting an AI system to be able to undertake that same kind of mental contortions is not easy. Also, for clarity, there isn't any AI that is yet sentient, and we are not going to likely have sentient AI for a long time to come (if ever, some would assert). So don't be betting on magical sentience to save the day toward achieving robust AI driving systems.

Conclusion

The assumption that a self-driving car will always abide by a school crossing guard is accurate in the theory of wanting to have that occur, but the practical reality of programming the AI and getting it to do so is much more complex and not readily out-of-the-box viable.

In short, this is a hard problem.

The automakers and self-driving tech firms are working on coping with school crossing guards, but it is pretty much still a nascent capability and subject to faltering and not doing what you would hope would occur. Some AI developers have put this onto an edge or corner case list, meaning that it is something they will get done at a later time, but it isn't a particularly high priority right now.

Getting the AI to do the everyday driving, safely so, consumes their attention right now.

One could argue that perhaps it is rare to come upon a school crossing guard. You have to be driving nearby to a school, usually, and you have to be driving at a time of day that a school crossing guard would be on duty. Yet, for any daily commute or even driving to the grocery store, this seems a lot higher odds than one might initially assume. Furthermore, the importance of the school crossing guard cannot be understated, for which if they aren't properly detected and aren't obeyed, puts children at heightened risk.

Those developing and fielding self-driving cars need to keep their nose to the grind and continue to improve and enhance the AI-based capabilities coping with school crossing guards.

There is also the upcoming hope that via the widespread adoption of V2P (vehicle-to-pedestrian) electronic communications, a school crossing guard could via their smartphone inform the AI about what to do. That will be advantageous, but even this electronic wizardry is insufficient in that the AI still ought to be able to gauge the school crossing guard, just in case the person is not equipped with a smartphone or otherwise unable to communicate electronically with the vehicle.

It takes two to tango, and in the case of self-driving cars and school crossing guards, they will need to coordinate and act in unison, ensuring that those precious and precocious children are able to safely get across the street.

The next time that you see a school crossing guard, I hope that you will think about all that they do to protect all of us.

I'm sure that if AI does become sentient, it would tell those school crossing guards a hearty thank you for their heroic efforts.

CHAPTER 17
DRIVING ROBOTS AND SELF-DRIVING CARS

Those driving robots.

What's that?

I've previously described that one approach to achieving a self-driving or driverless car would be to make a robot that could drive a conventional human-driven car (see my discussion at **this link here**).

Thus, rather than building the driving capabilities directly into a car, the notion is that a robot would be able to get into a normal everyday car and drive the vehicle, akin to having a human being be able to get into a car and do the driving. This kind of exploratory activity is taking place in some research labs, but generally is a long way afield of being practical.

In the near term, the only viable route to a true self-driving car is going to involve infusing the self-driving tech into the vehicle itself.

But just because something is not immediately or near-term achievable doesn't mean that it should not be pursued. Those having a longer-term time horizon can readily envision a future that would have robots for driving cars, and for trucks, and for busses, and so on.

Doing the hard work on that kind of AI-based breakthrough is perfectly fine and indeed quite laudable.

It would be easy to toss in the towel at this juncture and assume that all self-driving cars will consist of built-in mechanizations. Some might even exhort that the driving robot is a fool's errand or that the world will be entirely self-driving cars by the time that a driving robot is achieved. I don't agree with that assessment and have proffered a rebuttal in my prior discussion of this topic.

For those researchers pursuing the driving robot, keep up the noble work and do not be deterred in your valiant pursuits.

As they say, keep on truckin'.

You might be wondering why it would be advantageous to have a robot that could drive a car. In other words, it might seem that it wouldn't make a whit of difference whether the car drove itself via built-in capabilities or whether a robot got into the vehicle and did the driving.

In my prior coverage, I identified several key benefits for having a robot that could drive a conventional human-driven car, including these notable advantages:

- Any conventional car could instantly become a so-called self-driving car, albeit being driven by a robot, but at least not requiring a human driver, and do so by simply having the driving robot get into the vehicle and perform the entirety of the driving act.

- You could presumably easily switch the driving robot from one conventional car to another. This means that any car at any time can immediately become a self-driving car (i.e., non-human driven).

- The driver of the car would be readily seen. This is a somewhat less obvious downside about the upcoming self-driving cars, namely that with the built-in driving capabilities there isn't a driver in the driver's seat. Worries abound that when human drivers in other cars attempt to look at the driver of a self-driving car, they will not have any cues about the driving acts, and likewise, pedestrians will lack such cues too. Various add-ons might be needed for self-driving cars to overcome this qualm.

- The cost of having a self-driving car goes towards the driving robot rather than the car itself. In brief, one concern about true self-driving cars is that they might be exceedingly pricy and unaffordable, perhaps becoming something only the wealthy can afford. A driving robot would drive an everyday car, meaning that the car itself is still the same price regardless of whether the robot is driving it or a human is driving it.

- A driving robot could be more readily shared around and used on a widespread basis. A true self-driving car with built-in capabilities is merely one car. A driving robot could drive any conventional car. As such, the driving robot has greater utility, plus the cost of the driving robot can be spread amongst a multitude of users or owners in a more versatile way than could a singular self-driving car.

- A driving robot might provide additional uses. A true self-driving car has just one purpose, ostensibly it is a car that drives and that is all that it does (though, notably, this is a darned impressive act!). A driving robot might be able to perform other tasks, such as being able to get out of the car and carry a delivery package to the door of a house. Note that this is not a requirement per se and merely identifiable as potential added use that might be devised.

There are also various *disadvantages* of using a driving robot versus aiming to utilize or craft a true self-driving car, which I won't delineate those shortcomings here. I urge you to take a look at my earlier article on the topic to see the articulated list of downsides or drawbacks. The only reason I am not listing the disadvantages herein is merely due to the amount of ink space that it would consume and want to instead focus on some additional elements on the topic of driving robots.

Meanwhile, please do know that there are disadvantages to driving robots and I trust that you are aware that a driving robot is not all roses and can also contain prickly thorns.

One other quick point. Do not fall into the classic mental trap of thinking that these two approaches have to be mutually exclusive of each other. That's a false dichotomy. We can have true self-driving cars that have all the AI guts built-in directly into the vehicle, and we can also have driving robots.

This might seem puzzling.

Wouldn't we only need one or the other, and not need both?

In the United States alone there are about 250 million conventional cars. Some pundits are dreamers that espouse that somehow, magically, overnight all of those conventional cars will disappear or evaporate into thin air, once we have viable self-driving cars. This doesn't make economic sense and the reality is that it will be many years, likely decades before we gradually see a predominant prevalence of self-driving cars and the winnowing of conventional cars on our roadways.

As such, it makes perfectly good sense that you might have some portion of cars on the highways and byways that are true self-driving cars, and simultaneously have conventional cars that are being driven by driving robots. Doing both such approaches is absolutely sensible and certainly doable, assuming that self-driving cars are achievable and those driving robots are achievable.

One final comment before getting into the meat of this discussion and covering more details about driving robots, none of this says anything about forcing human drivers out of the driver's seat. All told, you could be on any given freeway, highway, or street, and witness next to you a true self-driving car, and a driving robot in a conventional car, and a human-driven car nearby too.

They would all co-exist on our roadways.

This is a bit of a disappointment for some that want to excise or make extinct the act of human driving. Their sentiment is certainly in the right place due to the hope of forever doing away with drunk driving, distracted driving, and the other foibles of human drivers. The U.S. has about 40,000 car crash fatalities annually and about 2.5 million injuries due to car crashes, of which much is due to human driving shortcomings. In that frame of reference, the less there is of human driving, and assuming that true self-driving cars and robot drivers are as safe or safer than human driving, the better off we all are.

A sticking point is that whether doing away with human driving is a societally feasible option remains an open question. Essentially, even if you could scale-up the self-driving cars and the driving robots, thus imagining that no human driving was needed, would we indeed forbid or ban all human driving on our public roadways?

Right now, some people would argue stridently that the only way you'll stop them from driving is when you remove their cold dead hands from the steering wheel.

Shifting gears, let's get back to those driving robots.

Here is today's intriguing focus: *What kind of ground rules ought there be about those driving robots?*

Let's unpack the matter and see.

Cars And Those Driving Robots

I'd like to identify some ground rules about driving robots.

Upon making such a bold statement, let's be abundantly clear that a driving robot can be crafted in whatever way anyone wants to do so. Assuming that the driving robot is able to perform the task of driving, and furthermore assuming it abides with any rules or lawful regulations, the design, and other facets can be whatever you want.

As an aside, you can bet your bottom dollar that if we do reach a point of having driving robots, this will raise all sorts of interesting questions about how to ensure they are proficient and properly-being permitted to drive a car. Just as humans have to undergo various requirements to get a valid driver's license, so too would those precious driving robots.

Envision, if you will, a driving robot that is standing in line at your local DMV (Department of Motor Vehicles), waiting to take the driver's test.

Of course, that's a bit of a ridiculous form of theatre and not likely how the regulating and certifying of driving robots would occur. There would undoubtedly be all sorts of vital checks-and-balances underlying the deployment and use of driving robots. We certainly don't want to end-up replacing human drivers with something worse that causes more harm than good.

Anyway, if you mull over the notion of a driving robot, some handy ground rules might come to mind. Rather than having you start that list from scratch, I've put together my own list that can provide fodder for discussion on the topic.

Each of the ground rules is "reasonable" in the sense that there is a rational basis for proposing the ground rule. I can only cover so much of the underlying logical basis herein, plus I'll try to briefly explain what makes the ground rule worthwhile for consideration. I'm sure you'll come up with even more ground rules to be added to the list, and in which case, that's wonderful, and the more the merrier.

Here you go.

1. The driving robot must be mobile in its own right.

This ground rule is that the robot must be able to enter into and exit from the car, doing so on its own, without any human assistance. If it required a human to get it into place, my qualm is that this would severely limit the utility of the thing. Just as a human can usually get into and out of a car on their own, so should the driving robot. This also allows then for a human to readily take over the driving, when so desired, by simply asking the robot to get out of the way. It also means that a human can presumably tell the robot to get into the car and start driving. No need to deal with picking up the beast or otherwise lifting a finger to get it to become the car driver.

2. The driving robot must be able to fit within the normal driver's space.

For this ground rule, the notion is that the robot cannot be larger than the usual amount of space set aside in a car for a driver to sit and drive the car. If the robot was oversized, it would then not be able to drive in most cars. Furthermore, suppose it took up the space of say two people, well, there aren't many cars these days that would have a front bench-style seat to accommodate this. The driving robot has to be able to sit in a normal-sized driver's bucket seat and cannot use up any space beyond that of a rotund human.

3. The driving robot must be able to drive the car entirely on its own.

In this ground rule, the point is that the driving robot cannot "cheat" and somehow require someone or something else to aid it in doing the driving. For example, imagine if a human needed to do the steering, meanwhile the driving robot did everything else. I reject that idea. The driving robot has to be good enough that no other adult driver is needed in the car. This means that the driving robot can completely undertake the driving task when there isn't an adult present, and indeed can drive on its own when no human passengers are on-board either.

4. The driving robot must use the existing human-based driving controls.

This ground rule is that the driving robot must be able to use the conventional steering wheel, brake pedal, and accelerator pedal, along with being able to access and use all of the other conventional operational driving elements in the car. You might be tempted to suggest that the driving robot could merely plug-into some specialized port of the car, and issue electronic driving commands. Yes, that's fine as a bonus, but this also assumes that a conventional car has such a provision. Almost none do, and you would need to convince the automakers to start changing their cars to allow for this possibility. Nope, the car is a car, and the driving robot has to drive it as it exists, just as humans drive the car. That is a core requirement.

5. The driving robot can plug into the car for power, but only conventionally so.

I going to somewhat carve out a kind of an exception to the prior ground rule, allowing for the driving robot to potentially plug-in and draw electrical power from the car. But don't get too excited about this. The restriction is that the driving robot can only plug-in and get power in the same manner that you could plug-in any other electrical accessory. In that sense, the car doesn't need to be outfitted with anything special to provide power for the driving robot (it will undoubtedly need its own source of power). In short, this willingness to have the driving robot use the power of the car is not that big a deal, since it is restricted to what one can do with any car already, and likely will not especially solve any power consumption design problems for those devising a driving robot. This won't make things much easier in that regard, sorry.

6. The driving robot cannot depend upon any kind of ADAS that exists for the car.

This ground rule is similar to the earlier rule that the driving robot must be able to drive the car on its own. Some cars have almost no semblance of ADAS, and as such, the driving robot has to be able to drive those kinds of cars. That being said, if a car does have various ADAS, the driving robot is welcome to use the ADAS, similar to how any human driver might do so. Keep in mind that the driving robot is still responsible for the driving (in a technological sense, not necessarily a "legal" meaning), and it cannot rely on the ADAS any more than a human might. The ADAS cannot become a needed crutch for the driving robot to be able to undertake the driving task.

7. The driving robot must be able to interact with passengers, doing so normally.

This is a somewhat trickier ground rule. For a true self-driving car, the automakers and self-driving tech firms are still figuring out how to enable the passengers to interact with the AI driving system. In some instances, you convey your destination via say a smartphone, and that's about it. The future is supposed to entail having the AI driving system using Natural Language Processing (NLP), thus the passenger can converse with the AI driving system to indicate preferences like swinging through a drive-thru burger joint amid a driving journey. For a driving robot, there have to be some viable means to have passengers communicate with it, else the driving robot would be a rather stilted driver and the driving act would be a lot less valuable.

8. The driving robot must be reliable, safe, secure, trustworthy, etc.

This ground rule is the usual kind of table stakes for any robotic system that might be interacting with humans and that is performing a truly life-or-death type of task. If the driving robot sometimes hiccups and is going to freeze-up with a blue screen of death, well, that's certainly not the kind of driving system anyone would want. Any and all driving robots that are going to be at the wheel of a car must be reliable, safe, secure, trustworthy, etc., and imbue a slew of such vital and absolutely required traits. Unlike humans that might decide to take a drive when they are out-of-touch or out of their gourd, the driving robot must not drive if it isn't fully ready, capable, and able to drive. Enough said.

9. The driving robot can do bonus aspects but must at least do the minimum set.

This ground rule involves the notion that the driving robot must be able to do all of the normal activities that a human driver would or could do as it relates to the driving task. That is the bare minimum. On top of that, additional icing can be placed on top of this cake. Can a driving robot also be your personal chef and make the world's greatest souffle? Sure, but not at the expense of somehow being unable to fully and properly drive a car. The car driving chore is the forte and raison d'etre. Anything else that the driving robot can do is a nice plus, and welcomed, assuming it is civil, proper, lawful, and sensible.

Conclusion

You might have realized that the key underlying theme is that the driving robot is essentially supposed to be backward compatible with the conventions of human drivers.

In the computer field, we refer to backward compatibility as the proviso that any new hardware is fully compatible with prior hardware (that's a quick definition). For the driving robot, the widest possible usability would be that the thing would be able to slide easily into the driver's seat of any car that a normal human could drive, start the engine, and drive away, just like a human.

Not one iota or ounce of a change needs to be made to the car itself. Admittedly, this is a bit of a dreamy vision. There would likely be some exceptions. The exceptions though should not become the rule. Robust and popular mechanization would ensure that the driving robot would be able to be a driver whenever you needed to have one.

For self-driving cars, you need to find a self-driving car before you can use it. In the case of a driving robot, as long as you have a driving robot near you or accompanying you, any car will do.

You don't need to know how to drive. You don't need to tell the driving robot how to drive. You can entrust the driving robot to do the driving. The driving robot can drive without any instruction. The driving robot can even drive when the car is otherwise entirely empty and has no human passengers at all.

As a smarmy aside, I'm sure that someone will ask what would a driving robot do if it got into a true self-driving car? Nothing.

That's a bit of a quippy answer, it would be a passenger and do whatever any passenger might do (well, probably, some human passengers are going to try and offer driving advice to self-driving cars, so one supposes maybe a driving robot might be tempted to do the same).

Overall, if I have whetted your appetite for a driving robot, I'd suggest you band together with those that are trying to pull off a miracle and craft a driving robot and get to work with them (of the ilk described herein, which is a tall order, I assure you).

CHAPTER 18
RAIN DRIVING AND SELF-DRIVING CARS

I'm singing and dancing in the rain.

Well, I'd so while on the sidewalk and walking along as a pedestrian, but assuredly I would not be doing any "singing and dancing" while at the wheel of a car that is being drenched by a savage rainstorm.

All around me are other cars that are struggling to make their way through the rain barrage. Traffic has become as slow as molasses. Everyone is late to wherever they are trying to drive. It is a colossal rain-soaked mess. In short, driving in the rain is rarely a frivolity and decidedly not a proverbial picnic in the park.

An astute driver is on their toes while driving in the rain.

Visibility can be radically reduced, so you need to strain to see what is up ahead. The windshield wipers are doing their best to whisk away the blurry coating of rainwater, but this does not entirely solve the problem of being able to see clearly and without any kind of obstructed view.

The roads are super slick and there are deep puddles to be dealt with. There is bound to be flooding somewhere along your driving journey. Perhaps the roadway was poorly designed and fails to ensure that the rainwater cascades off the roadway surface. Or maybe a storm drain is jammed up and won't let the accumulating mass of water get out of the street.

All in all, the roadway infrastructure plays a big part in whatever happens while undertaking the driving chore.

There is another major factor that has to be taken into account.

Drivers and their wacky ways of driving.

Yes, besides contending with the roadway ramifications due to torrents of rain, a whole other beast arises when dealing with our fellow human drivers.

In a sense, our daily driving in ordinary weather conditions that lack rain is tantamount to a form of equilibrium. Drivers do what they do. Some drivers tend to drive faster than they should. Some drivers drive slower than the rest of us prefer. On the balance, there is a kind of status quo that develops. During a normal day of relative sunshine or even cloudiness, the cars come and go. The drivers have gotten used to each other. An occasional nutty driver will shake things up, but this is a tiny perturbation. Their antics as a driver are like a small pebble causing a barely noticeable ripple in a large pond or lake.

When the rain comes along, all bets are off.

The equilibrium established for an ordinary day of driving is knocked on its head. People that once drove fast, might decide to start driving extraordinarily slowly. The regularly slow driving drivers might opt to now drive overly fast. It is hard to know how people will react to the rain.

To some degree, the driving task changes because of the rainy conditions, and the reaction of the drivers is altered too. In theory, if we all agreed to drive in a "reasonable" manner during the rain, the difficulties of driving in the rain would be a lot less problematic.

Unfortunately, the world is a dog-eat-dog struggle, and this is demonstrated fully while driving in the rain.

Drivers won't let you get ahead of them. Whereas taking cuts in line while on a freeway or highway was somewhat okay before, the civil arrangements of roadway etiquette are verboten now amidst the rain. Most drivers are on edge. They are edgy about their own driving. They are edgy about the driving of everyone else.

There is a boiling pot of driver angst when driving in the rain.

One slightly good piece of news is that the rain alteration can inevitably lead to a new status quo, effectively producing a new kind of equilibrium. For people that live in rainy climates, the rain is not a surprise or shock to the system. Drivers have their accustomed mode to rain driving and they employ it accordingly.

Localities that rarely get rain are the ones that seem to have the greatest overall challenge of driving in the rain. People have either forgotten how to adjust to rain-related driving, or they never learned how to cope with it, to begin with. They are somewhat in awe that this water appears to be dropping from the sky above, and perhaps are more focused on the act of raining versus the act of driving.

You might have heard of the famous saying that drivers in California do not know how to drive in the rain (ostensibly due to the relative rarity of annual rainfall). This is somewhat apt for parts of California, though you would find some areas that are more acclimated to rain-related driving.

In any case, one of the interesting twists is that you'll find people complaining incessantly about other drivers and their lack of rain driving prowess while insisting that they know what they are doing. Thus, it seems that by-and-large no one will fess up to being a lousy driver in the rain. This creates a conundrum, it would seem. If everyone is really good at driving in the rain, this creates a bit of a mystery or riddle about why everyone else complains about everyone else.

Simulations of driving behaviors help to showcase an intriguing element about driving in the rain.

The rainy conditions spur some drivers to go slower than usual.

This seems quite prudent as a sensible reaction to the driving environment. Since your visibility is hampered, and the car traction is bound to be reduced, it makes perfectly good sense to drive more slowly. Take your time. Be extra careful on those tricky turns. Ensure that you can stop in time for a red light and that the tires will not slip-and-slide on a layer of rainwater. And so on.

Here's the twist.

Other drivers that might normally drive at a customary speed are frustrated at the enormous abundance of these slower moving cars. Rather than deciding to go with the same flow, these exasperated drivers will turn toward the other end of the spectrum, namely, they will drive faster than they usually do. This is their reaction to the driving environment becoming *plagued* with slower driving drivers.

The logic for going faster is that you need to make up for the now added delays by these abundant slower driving drivers. Add to this circumstance that there are likely roadways that are closed due to the rain or that must be slowly driven due to the pools of water, and there is a one-two punch that the impatient driver is responding to.

These faster driving drivers are having to make up for the lost time due to the infrastructure issues caused by the rain, and make-up for the lost time due to the "slower drivers" that now inhabit the roadways in a much larger volume than during an ordinary driving setting.

One might politely suggest that such drivers should merely allow for more time in their driving journey, ergo leaving from their point of origin earlier than usual, but I digress and those are surely fighting words for some (I can't get away sooner, some lament, and am on-the-clock such that there is no choice but to go into a higher gear during the rain).

In any case, the kicker is that as these faster driving drivers get into pickles, they tend to inspire many other drivers to go even slower, doing so out of an abundance of caution at witnessing the fevered driver.

In turn, this stoking of driving slower will spur the fast drivers to drive even faster.

Around and around the cycle goes. One might even be tempted to say that when it rains, it pours (but that would be a rather misty-eyed pun).

Why do people drive overly fast in the rain?

That classic question can be generally answered by the aspect that since many drivers are driving more slowly than normal, other drivers believe that the correct response is to drive faster. This presumably will allow them to make up for the lost time.

Of course, driving faster in rainy conditions and among other more careful drivers is not a prudent driving strategy. You might at first believe that you are making good time and that those other drivers are all sheep that do not realize the fox is among them.

Regrettably, the faster moving driver can generate all sorts of added problems. Besides the obvious aspect of themselves getting into a car crash or collision, they can spark others to do so. There is seemingly nothing more infuriating as a driver than to see a crazed driver that manages to confound a more careful driver, and for which those other drivers might end-up in a collision, while the grinning driver scoots away by the skin of their teeth.

There is another somewhat oddball aspect that can arise too.

When some drivers see another driver that is driving fast, while amidst the delayed and rainy conditions, they are turned from being the benevolent driver into the frenzied driver. This can happen because they are thinking that if someone else is getting away with the wild driving, they might as well do so too.

Another mental concoction is that if it is "safe" for the other driver to be driving fast, this is some form of "proof" that driving fast is fine and quite acceptable.

In short, similar to a social media posting that can rapidly spread from one person to another, the act of driving too fast in rainy conditions can spread virally among human drivers.

Well, perhaps this discussion has opened your eyes to the complexities of driving while in the rain. On the other hand, maybe you already assumed the aforementioned aspects and knew in your heart or your head that this is the typical phenomenon of what happens in rain-related driving.

Shifting gears, the future of cars and of driving consists of self-driving cars.

Here is today's interesting question: *Will AI-based true self-driving cars be able to cope with rain-related driving and if so, what will they do?*

Let's unpack the matter and see.

Self-Driving Cars And Rain Driving

For Level 4 and Level 5 true self-driving vehicles, there won't be a human driver involved in the driving task.

All occupants will be passengers.

The AI is doing the driving.

Some pundits suggest that the beauty of having self-driving cars will be that the AI driving systems will drive in a quite rational way and will not drive in an oddball manner that humans drive. AI driving systems will drive in a lawful manner. They will be programmed to drive within the posted speed limit. They will be coded to be courteous to other cars on the roadways. Etc.

How does that parlay into rain-related driving?

In theory, if the only cars on the roadways were all self-driving cars, the AI driving systems would be civil towards each other and drive in a careful manner appropriate to the rainy conditions (when I refer to aspects such as being civil, do not misinterpret this to imply that AI is sentient, and instead realize it is due to the programming of the AI that this behavior arises; do not anthropomorphize the AI).

Keep in mind that the AI driving systems are not collectively collaborating with each other in some kind of cohesive interconnected way (that's not how things are currently being devised). Right now, the AI driving system on-board a self-driving car is focused on the driving of that car. It does not particularly know or care what the other AI driving systems are doing, other than how those other nearby self-driving cars are driving.

The AI of one self-driving car is using its sensors such as video cameras, radar, LIDAR, ultrasonic units, and the like, and detecting other nearby objects. Those nearby objects include other cars. Those other cars are at times self-driving cars and at other times human-driven cars. The AI driving system is attempting to track and predict what those other cars are going to do, regardless of whether being driven by AI or being driven by a human driver.

An added plus for AI driving systems is going to be the use of V2V (vehicle-to-vehicle) electronic communications. This feature allows an AI driving system to send an electronic message to other nearby self-driving cars. For example, suppose the AI driving system has detected a big pothole in the road that is hidden by a muddy pool of water, the AI can use the V2V to forewarn other self-driving cars about the roadway issue.

Okay, so if we had only self-driving cars on our highways and streets, they would presumably be careful and cautious around each other.

They would all equally by-and-large opt to take the slower approach to drive as a proper response to the diminished driving conditions. This would happen not by some Wizard of Oz command that went across all the self-driving cars, and instead would be due to each AI driving system reacting (as programmed) toward the compromised driving environment.

I want to be very careful here and continue to emphasize that this notion of the self-driving cars all seemingly in unison being able to accommodate the rainy conditions is not axiomatic and nor is it as a result of some kind of sentience. Furthermore, each automaker and self-driving car tech firm will programmatically be injecting their own preferred approach into the AI driving systems. Thus, the driving actions of self-driving cars by the XYZ firm can certainly be reacting differently than those of the ABC firm.

But let's assume generally that if we did have only self-driving cars on the roadways that they would likely end-up driving more cautiously overall in the rain, and they would defer to other nearby self-driving cars in a somewhat neutral dance of sharing the roadway in a balanced manner.

The thing is, this notion of having only self-driving cars on our roadways is rather dreamy and an unlikely scenario. We currently have over 250 million conventional cars in the United States alone, and those vehicles are not going to overnight be replaced by self-driving cars. It will take many years for self-driving cars to ramp up in terms of production and being brought onto the roadways. All told, it is presumably decades before we could consider having solely self-driving cars on the roads.

And some insist anyway that you will never take away their human driving privileges, other than when you remove their cold dead hands from the steering wheel.

The upshot is that self-driving cars are going to be mixing it up with human-driven cars. This includes the scenario of a rain-soaked real-world environment that has a fouled-up roadway infrastructure due to the rain, and that has the usual human antics of aberrant driving behaviors while driving in the rain.

Can self-driving cars deal with this changed equilibrium from an ordinary driving environment?

If you were ever wondering why a lot of the public roadway testing of self-driving cars is taking place in locales such as sunny California or Florida or Arizona, you now have your answer. Part of the reason is due to the "easy" weather conditions. Getting an AI driving system to drive safely and properly from point A to point B is arduous in the simplest of roadway conditions, thus adding the rain is a much tougher added condition.

Yes, there are lots and lots of simulations being done for the preparing of the AI driving systems to cope with rainy conditions. These are computer-based simulations wherein the cars are simulated on various kinds of roadway infrastructures. Amongst the simulated conditions are aspects such as adding rain, adding snow, and so on. This does help to get the AI driving ready for real-world settings.

Also, there are special closed tracks that are being used. This can be undertaken in areas that have inclement weather. They can also take place in locales wherein various weather conditions can be created on-demand, such as using a sprinkler system to sprinkle out water as though it is raining.

The other approach consists of having the self-driving cars operate on public roadways in places that do get rain.

One thought that you might have is that self-driving cars should proceed to be like those slower and cautious human drivers. This would seem the best approach. In other words, do not have self-driving cars act like those fast driving humans that seem to drive with disdain for their fellow human drivers. Instead, make sure that all self-driving cars take the proper care and move slowly accordingly (to clarify, slowly is meant to convey the relative difference between when driving in ordinary driving conditions versus those of rain-soaked setting).

Allow the crazy antics of human drivers to take place, essentially ignoring those antics, and just keep plowing ahead as though the mainstay is to deal with the rain and the adverse roadway status. No matter what else the humans are doing, at least the self-driving cars can be counted on to drive in a manner suitable to the diminished driving environment.

That does seem to make indubitable sense.

Conclusion

Unfortunately, what might seem sensible at first glance can have inadvertent and adverse consequences. Remember that earlier it was indicated that human drivers often react to those around them that are driving slowly by opting to drive fast. Here's the rub.

If self-driving cars are prevalent in a given area, and it is raining, and if those self-driving cars tend toward driving more slowly to accommodate the rain, what will the human drivers do?

You guessed it, the human drivers (some of them) will tend toward driving faster and faster, trying to make up for what they perceive as the slowed-down driving taking place around them. Ironically, the effort of the AI driving systems to essentially make the driving safer can spur human drivers into driving more recklessly. Yikes!

Some would argue that this is yet another reason to get rid of human drivers. The sooner we can have only self-driving cars as our means of car transportation, the better off we will be, since those insidious human drivers are going to mess-up anything and be doing so while behind the wheel of a car.

Another reaction to this mental riddle, and an altogether opposite one of the sorts, consists of wanting the self-driving cars to essentially fight fire-with-fire, opting to drive faster, just like the human drivers do. This is a rather hard pill to swallow and has quite alarming downsides.

There is one thing that seems to absolutely be the case, which is that trying to figure out how to get self-driving cars to drive in the rain is a complicated problem. Dealing with the rain and the changes that occur to the roadway are one aspect of that problem. Ascertaining how to cope with human drivers and the alterations in the overarching driving equilibrium is yet another part of that problem.

CHAPTER 19
STOP SIGNS AND SELF-DRIVING CARS

That driver must have been as blind as a bat.

Those are the first thoughts that you might have upon witnessing a driver that blows through a stop sign. In that same instant, you probably are also thankful that no one got hurt. Whenever a driver opts to ignore or omit stopping at a stop sign, the chances of a calamity are pretty high. The kind of ultimate tragedy that comes to mind involves the shameful driver striking a pedestrian or ramming into another vehicle.

Government statistics suggest that perhaps 20% of all traffic fatalities are annually due to running a stop sign (considered a failure-to-stop, or possibly a failure-to-yield).

Take a moment to give that some serious and somber thought. Stop signs are important and whenever you are near one, you have to be wary of what other drivers might do, or what they might fail to do.

A research study estimated that around 700,000 car crashes each year take place at stop signs, though this number might be higher since those are just the crashes reported to the police (presumably, the bulk would be so reported). By-and-large, the crashes studied involved angular collisions. This makes sense since the odds are that the car running the stop sign is likely to broadside another car that is already in the intersection or the street wherein the stop sign was preventing traffic from immediately flowing.

I'm focusing herein on car drivers that completely run a stop sign and thus don't even try to come to a halt.

Perhaps just as deadly are those drivers that do a rolling stop, sometimes also referred to as a California stop.

These drivers will come upon a stop sign and somewhat slow down, though not come to a complete halt. They then roll through the stop itself and continue brashly on their path. In their minds, they believe that since they gave a kind of wink and a nod to the stop sign, slowing down a tad, this constitutes a "reasonable" kind of stopping action. Tell it to the judge when you get ticketed for this unlawful act.

The types of rolling stops can vary in degree.

Sometimes the driver nearly comes to a halt, meanwhile crawling forward at a minuscule speed and not using the brakes entirely, but at least lightly pumping them. Maybe this is a delicate or gingerly done form of navigating a stop sign and the driver figures that no cop would ticket them for such a seemingly minuscule infraction. Of course, this is nonetheless still an illegal driving action.

The brazen driver that opts for a rolling stop does a proverbial head fake about the stop sign. They marginally slow down their car. They act like nobody can see them as though their car is invisible. The result is swift streaming past the stop without any demonstrative degradation in their speed.

Finally, the whoppers of the stop sign violators are the ones that do not reduce their speed by a single ounce. These lawbreakers don't lift a finger to come to a stop. They proceed through the stop without any hesitation.

One supposes the worst of the worst whoppers are those that decide to accelerate as they run the stop. Presumably, they must be thinking that if they are going to do something egregious, they might as well go all in. Maybe too they are thinking that the faster speed will lessen the time involved in the committing of the atrocious act. I can scoot past this stop sign and slip under-the-wire, as it were, with nobody being the wiser, seems to be their mantra.

Quick question for you.

Can you name the top 10 states that have the highest percentage of drivers that fail to stop at a stop sign or a red light?

Note that the question doesn't ask which states have the highest counts of those incidents, and instead refers to the percentages involved. This is because the states vary dramatically in terms of the number of drivers, thus the presumed answer on counts alone would likely involve the states with the highest number of drivers and be ostensibly obvious (well, one supposes this is not necessarily the case since perhaps drivers in such states could potentially be more law-abiding in their driving).

Anyway, to try and even things out, the question entails the percentage of drivers in that particular state.

Studies seem to indicate that the highest percentage as ranked #1 (not the kind of top pole position any state would wish to attain) to the lowest of the top 10 is:

1) Delaware
2) New York
3) Hawaii
4) Wyoming
5) Virginia
6) Oregon
7) Florida
8) Iowa
9) Illinois
10) California

If your state is not listed, the absence is no cause for celebration. It only means that your state didn't perchance land on the top 10 list. You still can have a slew of drivers that are running your stop signs. You can still be in danger whenever you approach a stop sign and meanwhile another car is approaching too.

Starkly stated, you are still going to either die or be injured when a callous driver blows through a stop sign and rams into your car.

Why do drivers opt to entirely run a stop sign?

One of the most common claims is that they did not see the stop sign and so were utterly unaware of the need to come to a stop. In that sense, it was an unintentional mistake.

Maybe the stop sign was hidden by an overhanging tree. Perhaps the stop sign was marred by graffiti and rather unreadable. The stop sign might have been bent and chopped up, no longer fully resembling a pristine looking stop sign. These are seemingly plausible claims.

There are counterarguments to be made.

Did the driver dismiss the aspect that though the stop sign was partially obscured, they ought to have nonetheless driven more cautiously under the assumption that a stop sign might be present? Was there a painted line to demark the stop and if so, did the driver ignore or dismiss that indication too? Has the driver ever driven at that location before, such that they would already have known that there is a stop sign there, even if it is now obscured?

And so on.

Another variant of an unintentional mistake could be that the driver was distracted while watching cat videos on their smartphone. This stretches the notion of intentionality since the driver was intentionally not watching the roadway and therefore you could argue that the alleged "unintentional mistake" was caused by a form of intentionality.

Yet another claim includes the straight out "I didn't see it" assertion.

The driver might agree that upon hindsight that the stop sign was clearly identifiable. For some inexplicable reason, the driver just failed to notice the stop sign. They weren't watching any videos. They were looking intently at the road. Somehow, the stop sign did not get included in their gaze or they were mentally preoccupied and failed to visually recognize and react to the stop sign.

This brings up those drivers that sometimes run the stop sign and then abruptly after-the-fact come to a full stop, doing so in the middle of an intersection or street. It is a kind of delayed reaction. They just realized they ran a stop sign, oops. To try and make up for the blunder, they decide that perhaps coming to an immediate halt will showcase their remorse. Of course, this might be handy as a driving action, or it could make things worse, depending upon where they decide to suddenly come to a screeching halt.

Besides those that unintentionally blow through a stop, there are the drivers that intentionally do so.

Some drivers assume that if they don't see any other cross-traffic, there isn't a need to come to a stop. The stop sign is apparently an optional form of traffic control. For all intents and purposes, a stop sign is the same as a yield sign. If there are other cars to be contended with, well, in that case, the stop sign might be of use. Otherwise, the stop sign really is a waste of time and attention.

Among those emboldened drivers are the ones that believe stop signs are meant for the sheep and not for the fox. You are the sheep since you legally come to a stop. The fox does not need to come to a stop. When approaching a stop sign, they believe that the stop is there to aid them in their progressing unabated. It was planted there to stop those other drivers that ought to get out of their way.

Whew, that is some impertinence.

Consider some other variations involving running stop signs.

We might have some sympathy for those that intentionally blow through a stop and are doing so for some understandable reason. A driver is rushing to the hospital and has a family member in the car that has suffered a heart attack and desperately needs medical care. That seems like a quite compelling basis for zipping past a stop sign.

The problem though is that if the urgency of this driver overrides the utility of the stop sign, suppose the anxious driver rams into and kills others in a car that was legally driving along where the stop sign was. It would seem erroneous to excuse the flagrant transgression of the stop sign if it endangers the lives of others.

The running of a stop sign can also occur by someone fleeing or escaping from a crime they have already committed. A driver that has just robbed a convenience store or a bank might decide that stopping at stop signs is going to slow down their absconding from the crime scene. There is some notable irony that oftentimes a crook is caught by the act of ignoring a stop sign. A police car perchance witnesses the stop sign infraction, pulls over the transgressing vehicle, and ends up capturing the suspects for the other crime that they had just committed.

Perhaps the golden rule is to always come to a full stop at all stop signs.

Our society tries to ensure that we all do indeed come to a stop at stop signs by usually making the act of not stopping into a criminal act. If you are nabbed running a stop sign, the usual penalty is a financial fee, along with added adverse points on your driving record. You might need to also go to traffic school or possibly incur some other stipulated repentant action. Your driver's license could be revoked and the odds are that your car insurance rates will go up.

All in all, though these are important ways to threaten or browbeat drivers into complying with stopping, none of these methods are one hundred percent certain to stop someone from blowing through a stop sign.

Give that unsettling statement some added contemplation.

A stop sign does not have some magical powers that can force a car to come to a halt. The actions of the car are entirely on the shoulders of the driver. The driver can choose to stop or choose to not come to a stop. There won't be a metal fence that suddenly pops up and prevents the vehicle from proceeding. There isn't an underground magnet that can stop the vehicle in its tracks.

A stop sign is overwhelmingly a purely voluntary indicator and has no direct and no immediate enforcement to get a driver to bring their car to a halt.

All of us are betting that other drivers will realize a stop sign exists, they will observe the stop sign and proceed to properly come to a stop, they will remain at the stop for a sufficient amount of time to ensure that it is safe to proceed (some argue that there are a three seconds rule-of-thumb, namely you should wait for at least three seconds, but this is a slippery slope and the real answer is that you should wait for however long is needed to ensure proper safety), and they will then cautiously continue to drive ahead.

That is a mouthful and something that we all stake our lives on, daily, during the course of each and every driving journey.

Shifting gears, the future of cars entails the advent of self-driving cars.

These are cars that are being driven by an AI driving system and do not involve a human driver. We generally take for granted that self-driving cars will drive legally at all times. This implies that whenever a stop sign is encountered, a self-driving car will dutifully come to a full stop.

Even if that is the case (which we'll examine further in a moment), there are still those darned human drivers that are driving around and opting to roll through or entirely blow through stop signs. That is a harsh reality that needs to be included in the calculations and computations of any semblance of a viable AI driving system.

Here is today's intriguing question: *What should an AI-based self-driving car be doing to contend with human drivers that blow through a stop sign?*

Let's unpack the matter and see.

Self-Driving Cars And Stop Signs

For Level 4 and Level 5 true self-driving vehicles, there won't be a human driver involved in the driving task.

All occupants will be passengers.

The AI is doing the driving.

If an AI driving system has been programmatically devised to always stop at stop signs, this is some reassurance that the self-driving car will in fact be stopping at stop signs. The assumption is that unlike human drivers that might choose to abide by a stop sign, the AI is going to always bring the self-driving car to a halt at each and every stop sign.

Please realize that this is a somewhat arguable contention.

The AI might be programmed to come to a stop at a stop sign, but there are various means by which this might not get properly performed. For example, suppose that the sensors of the self-driving car do not detect a stop sign. Similar to how humans can contend that a stop sign was not fully visible, the same problems can impact the AI driving system.

The sensors on the self-driving car will typically include video cameras, radar, LIDAR, ultrasonic units, and the like. These sensors might detect a stop sign, or they might not. Furthermore, a stop sign might be somewhat detected, as in the system assigning a probability, and the question arises as to whether the AI ought to bring the car to a halt depending upon the assessed probability (obviously, this is helped mightily by having predefined maps of an area, though this can have its omissions too if a new stop sign has been set up since the map was last refreshed).

Imagine that the probability estimate was that a stop sign exists up ahead is at 10%. Is that sufficiently high enough to warrant the AI bringing the self-driving car to a stop? Your first answer is that it must do so, based on the belief that it is safer to stop than to not stop.

Aha, suppose that there isn't a stop sign there, and meanwhile, there are cars directly behind the self-driving car. The self-driving car suddenly opts to come to a stop, yet the human drivers see no explicable reason for the self-driving car to do so. The human drivers are caught entirely by surprise, perhaps ramming into the rear of the self-driving car.

So, you see, summarily coming to a stop is not necessarily the always right answer.

One reaction to that scenario is that it "proves" that human drivers ought to be banned from driving. If we had only self-driving cars on our roadways, the aforementioned rear-end crash would presumably not occur. A self-driving car could use V2V (vehicle-to-vehicle) electronic communications to forewarn other nearby self-driving cars that a believed stop sign exists and thus the self-driving car is going to execute a full stop. All other nearby self-driving cars would ergo respond accordingly.

Yes, that's a nice idea and it is a perhaps dreamy world of some far off future. Currently, there are about 250 million conventional cars in the United States alone, and they aren't going to miraculously be replaced with self-driving cars overnight. It will likely take decades to gradually witness the advent of self-driving cars and the winnowing of conventional human-driven cars. On top of that, some say they will never give up their human privilege of driving, other than when you pry their cold dead hands from the steering wheel.

Setting aside the question of self-driving cars coming to a stop at stop signs, let's assume for sake of discussion that they will do so, and shift our attention toward the other cars that are approaching a stop sign.

If a self-driving car detects a car approaching a stop sign, for which the AI driving system is expecting that the other car will come to a stop (let's say it is a four-way stop and the self-driving car is now at one of those stop signs), what happens next?

Your first thought might be that the self-driving car should assume the other car will indeed come to a stop. But that flies in the face of the earlier discussion about the nature and frequency of human drivers that disobey a stop sign.

In short, the AI driving system has to take the posture that the other car might not stop.

As a human driver, if you are quite cautious, you do the same. You wait patiently to see if the other car is going to come to a halt. Does it seem to be slowing down? Does the driver of that car seem to realize a stop sign is there? Is the driver still in motion as though they are going to roll through the stop?

There is that shocking moment when you realize that the driver is going to entirely blow through the stop sign. It takes your breath away, that's for sure.

Anyway, the AI driving system cannot simply be detecting that the other car has stopped. Similar to a human formulation, the AI should be detecting and tracking the other car as it approaches the stop sign. A vehicle that is approaching a stop sign should be reducing speed. If the speed is not being sufficiently reduced, it is a reasonable predictor that the car is likely not going to come to a full stop.

This requires the AI driving system to do anticipatory detection, tracking, and planning.

Rather than simply waiting to see if the other car comes to a halt, there is a need to anticipate what might happen. The AI driving system then needs to figure out the best strategy and tactics for the self-driving car to take accordingly.

Conclusion

You might be tempted to say that if the self-driving car can ascertain that the other car is also a self-driving car, the AI can essentially let down its guard and assume that the other self-driving car will come to a proper stop.

Nope, this would still entail a trust but verify kind of calculation.

Let the physics decide what the reality consists of.

AI driving systems are entering into a dog-eat-dog world of driving. Human drivers are susceptible to not obeying a stop sign. Fatal car crashes and terrible injuries can result from this human driving "foible" or lack of responsiveness.

Some pundits have argued that a future feature on cars, encompassing especially conventional human-driven cars, ought to be an electronic stopping switch that is activated electronically by a stop sign. All stop signs would be outfitted with an Internet of Things (IoT) electronic transmitter with a beacon that is continuously broadcasting a signal telling cars to come to a stop (known generally as V2I, vehicle-to-infrastructure devices).

All cars would be programmed to automatically come to a halt upon receiving the stop signal. A human driver could not override the stopping action.

Do we need to go that far in terms of forcing human drivers to stop at stop signs?

There are some that worry this would be a bridge too far. Suppose too if the automatic feature went awry and suddenly stopped human-driven cars when there wasn't a stop sign present. And so on.

One last thought.

Many of the AI driving systems are being trained to drive via the likes of Machine Learning and Deep Learning, which are computational pattern matching techniques. Imagine if an AI driving system has been given driving data that contains examples of human-driven cars that blew through stop signs.

Would the AI "learn" that this is an acceptable driving action?

It would be an odd twist of fate to envision human drivers being wary of self-driving cars because you just never know when that zany AI is going to opt to run a stop sign.

Bad AI, bad?

CHAPTER 20
CLOUD AND AUTONOMOUS VEHICLES

There continues to be avid and growing adoption of the cloud for those involved in autonomous vehicles and the coming transformation of mobility and transportation.

Why so?

Simply stated, the advent of autonomous vehicles is fueled by the use of the cloud.

The other side of that same coin is that the pace and viability of autonomous vehicles could be inadvertently dampened or hampered without utilizing cloud-based capabilities.

As readers of my column are aware, I've frequently covered various cloud-related facets in the arena of self-driving cars, a particular type of autonomous vehicle. In addition to self-driving cars, we will all be gradually witnessing the emergence of self-driving trucks, self-driving drones, self-driving planes, self-driving submersibles, self-driving surface ships, and so on.

That is a veritable boatload of self-driving vehicles and they all require gobs of online storage, tons of online computing power, and stridently need real-time accessibility at all times in all places.

The answer to providing that plethora of computing resources is found via harnessing the cloud.

Throughout my years as a global top executive and CIO/CTO, I've lived through the origins of cloud services and undertaken many enterprisewide conversions from internal and proprietary computing storage and computational processing cycles to embrace both public and private cloud facilities. At first, many companies suffered the pangs of a great hesitation to give up the perceived warmth of holding tightly onto their own purchased hardware and directly licensed software. This eventually gave way to the realization that the scalability of the cloud, and numerous other benefits, were hard to beat.

To clarify, don't assume that migrating to the cloud is necessarily a breeze since there are a lot of organizational changes and technological adjustments that are needed. Akin to any large-scale systems effort, the shift to the cloud requires thinking strategically about the overall portfolio of systems and how to sensibly and seamlessly make the substantive transition. This requires close collaboration between all parts of the business and cannot be summarily handed-off as a background chore to the already harried technologists in your firm.

Interestingly, some companies that contain separate divisions or subunits devoted to autonomous vehicles are at times experiencing the so-called "odd man out" syndrome.

Here's what that means.

Consider two somewhat comparably vexing scenarios:

1. The rest of the company is on the cloud, but the AV units are not
2. The AV units are in the cloud, but the rest of the company is not

Let's unpack those conundrums.

AV Outside, Aiming To Be Inside

In some instances, the rest of the company other than the portion incorporating the AV units is already on the cloud and the autonomous vehicle units are not.

This phenomenon is often due to the belief that the AV groups are technologically proficient of their own accord and ought to be making whatever choices they need to make for the betterment of achieving the AV realization. Yes, this seems sensible at first glance, namely do not mess with the perceived gilded goose that can lay the golden egg.

Unfortunately, left to their own heads-down preferences, sometimes those in the AV arena are prone to not thinking ahead toward the bigger picture. They are so focused on the day-to-day scramble of trying to devise the AI-based systems for autonomous vehicles, their attention is diverted from considering the overarching down-the-road needs and scalability that will be required.

Essentially, if you are tasked with getting something up and running, you are tempted to take whatever shortcuts and technological trickery that you can get away with. Included in this bag of tricks are the lack of documenting what you are doing, shoving quality assurance and other cornerstone principles under the rug, and basically tossing wildly everything and the kitchen sink at the problems trying to be solved.

This all-out scramble to get a pilot or prototype achieved is certainly valiant, but the obligation of ultimately paying the piper is going to come due. An autonomous vehicle experimental pilot that can in an illusionary way showcase the autonomous features is potentially more misleading than it is constructive since the assumption by others will be that it can be supercharged and fielded, right away.

This is going to become a whale of a quandary when reality hits that the one-off cannot be ratcheted up readily.

In that sense, if the rest of the company is using the cloud, it is worthwhile to gently inspire the AV units to consider doing likewise. Notice the operative word there revolves around gently or gingerly doing so.

Hammering the autonomous vehicle developers with a cloud-haranguing is not particularly advisable. Some top execs attempt to utilize edicts from high above as a change agent, but this generally doesn't work out very well. Merely dropping a discordant monkey wrench into the painstaking work of the AV developers is bound to gum up their efforts, will likely slow down the AV progress, and altogether irk the AV members toward leaving or otherwise feeling deflated in their herculean efforts.

The prudent approach involves methodically stepping through how a cloud migration could be undertaken and do so while averting undercutting the ongoing progress of the AV efforts. Indeed, the chances are that the analysis underlying shifting to the cloud will reveal existing unmet needs that were on the back burner, and for which by getting into the cloud can be given refreshed priority and attention.

And there is the important and at times hidden consideration that there are lots of intersecting aspects between the AV units and the rest of the firm. The limelight goes accordingly to the AV development activities, but this is all done within the milieu of running a business, meaning that there is payroll to be generated, inventory to be tracked, and so on. If those business-oriented systems are already in the cloud, it makes synergistic sense to bring the AV units into the cloud, encompassing the intersecting elements and additionally those specialized elements that are specific to the technological realm of crafting self-driving vehicles.

Okay, that covers the instance or use case of the AV being the "odd man out" as it were and realizing that the synergy of bringing them into the cloud is worthwhile for pursuing.

AV Inside, Inspiring More Inside

Turning to the other commonly experienced situation, consider a scenario involving an AV unit that is cloud immersed, and meanwhile, the rest of the company has yet to make that same shift.

As might be obvious from the preceding variant scenario, it could be that there are intersecting business elements that are loose ends and could be appropriately connected by having the rest of the firm enter into the cloud too. In that sense, the AV units have done the pioneering work and perhaps set the stage for the rest of the firm to undertake a similar cloud-focused adoption.

Aha, some are prone to exhorting, the AV unit might have had an advantage in that they started with a blank slate and were able to get underway at the get-go with a cloud approach. Yes, this often is decidedly the case, namely that the AV area is a newer part of an already established company, either having been started anew organically or possibly purchased by grabbing up an AV startup.

When the AV unit first got off the ground, the founders selected the use of the cloud. Maybe they did so since they could not otherwise afford the purchase of their own hardware and systems, or perhaps they realized that if they wanted to accommodate their expected high-growth trajectory that the only viable path would be via using the cloud. Or they might have all grown-up using the cloud, coming from other firms that were cloud-based, and thus it was a natural choice.

No need to reinvent the wheel and might as well use what they know and had already been proven.

In short, sure, the AV units might have had an easier journey toward going with the cloud, though this does not somehow alter the reality that the cloud provides key advantages. Furthermore, there are lessons aplenty to be learned by closely looking at how the AV units are utilizing the cloud. Those tidbits of internal machinations are likely to offer stellar insights into how the rest of the firm can successfully adopt the cloud.

There is an intriguing twist on that point too.

Sometimes the rest of the firm looks at the AV units as the future, which makes sense since the nature of self-driving is a futuristic vision and one that will dramatically alter how we make our way throughout the world. You've likely seen me repeatedly emphasize the mobility-for-all mantra that it is hoped will arise via widespread AVs.

The point is that the rest of the firm can be enamored of what the AV units are accomplishing, and in that admiration are looking for how they too can somehow share in that future. This can be demonstratively empowering when trying to get the rest of the firm to adopt the cloud. In short, if the AV units are doing it, by gosh, the rest of us ought to be doing the same.

Do not undervalue that kind of inspirational aura.

When getting a firm to change from legacy approaches to modern ones, there is a tsunami of resistance usually encountered. Rather than trying to solely and ruthlessly push such changes into and across the organization, a wiser approach seeks to get the organization to seek out the change. For whatever goodwill that the AV units might have, it makes for a handy change catalyst to aid in motivating the rest of the firm to proceed with open arms.

Another somewhat peculiar twist can also arise.

One viewpoint at times expressed is that the AV units needed the cloud for the advanced use of AI capabilities such as Machine Learning and Deep Learning (ML/DL), Natural Language Processing (NLP), and the like, and thus their cloud needs are relatively unique and unlike the rest of the firm.

Using that logic, the belief is that it might have made sense for the AV developers to adopt the cloud, but the rest of the firm is another animal and ergo the uniqueness of the AV unit does not apply to any of the rest of the firm.

That undoubtedly seems like a compelling argument, until given additional scrutiny.

First, there is little doubt that the AV units and their likely uses of the cloud could be construed in many ways as specific to the nature of autonomous vehicles.

Consider these aspects:

- Self-driving cars are going to need software patches and other updates that can be downloaded into the on-board vehicle systems, thus doing so from the cloud is abundantly pragmatic (using OTA or Over-The-Air updates).

- The self-driving cars of a fleet are going to upload their collected data about the roadway travels, allowing the use of ML/DL to assess the performance of the AVs and crunch through the data to generate improved driving capacities that can be transmitted back down into the on-board processing. Once again, more OTA is involved, along with cloud storage and cloud-based computing.

- Roadway infrastructure devices using edge computing are going to be put in place and allow for V2I (vehicle-to-infrastructure) electronic communications. The odds are that the V2I collected data will also be uploaded into the cloud of the AV units. This can be examined for patterns of roadway infrastructure issues and be included subsequently into the online navigational maps that are downloaded into the autonomous vehicles.

- In my columns I've repeatedly mentioned that self-driving cars are going to have a "roving eye" capability, being able to for example indicate the status of real estate in a locality such as homes for sale. The AV unit can leverage the data being collected by their AVs and turn that into an additional form of monetization.

- Etc.

If you mindfully ponder the future, you begin to realize that many of these same AI-infused advances are going to occur in other areas of industrial use too.

The odds are pretty high that if you look at the rest of the firm, you'll realize that many of these AV efforts are going to inexorably occur in all facets of a business.

If a firm is primarily a manufacturer, the chances are that the manufacturing plants and the automation therein are going to gradually become "autonomous" and will require the same kinds of systems needs as those of the self-driving realm. They might not necessarily entail "vehicles" as in autonomous vehicles, but they will be machinery that is operating autonomously via AI infusion and they will have similar autonomous needs as those of AVs (thus requiring cloud access, cloud storage, cloud computing, and more).

Looking even wider, access to AI tools and capabilities via the cloud will be warranted for all parts of the business.

Indeed, in case you didn't already notice, AI is being infused into conventional applications such as AI-empowered apps and chatbots within the functional areas of human resources, accounting, finance, marketing, and so on. Though ML/DL might seem only suited for the "extremes" such as autonomous vehicles, rest assured that the same technologies are going to be injected into all kinds of applications and be utilized throughout the enterprise.

It just so happens that autonomous vehicles are somewhat leading the charge.

This is admittedly a bit arguable because other areas are equally infusing autonomy into their wares, but they do not seem to get the same vaunted attention as those of the AV penchant. In any case, the point is that the AV side of the business, even if only looking at the specifics of the AV particulars, provides a visible and early-on heads-up of what the rest of the business will likely find themselves doing.

If you've been watching the news about AVs and the cloud, you've certainly noticed the ongoing announcements by Amazon AWS, Microsoft Azure, Google GCP, and others that are joining hand-in-hand with AV firms, encompassing the autonomous vehicle biggies and newbie startups alike.

AV entities realize they need the cloud.

Cloud providers realize they can provide needed capabilities to AVs, along with positioning for a future in which AVs will be a humongous business and will gradually become one of the most sizable cloud consumers imaginable. It is going to be an ample bonanza, and the time is ripe to get in when the nascent efforts are underway, planting the seeds for future growth.

There are additional compelling reasons for cloud providers to pursue the AV realm.

It is said by many experts that the aspirational attainment of truly autonomous vehicles is tantamount to a moonshot effort, akin in some respects to the first forays of having mankind step onto the moon. In that viewpoint, consider the pride amongst those within a cloud provider that had an integral role in achieving self-driving vehicles. Of the myriad of cloud services and clients that a provider might engage with, the notion of doing so with AVs and thus serving as a vital contributor to a mobility expansive future rings poignantly and can resoundingly motivate employees accordingly.

This same embrace for a stretch-goal of technological innovation in the sphere of autonomous vehicles can have an afterglow associated with the cloud provider too. If the cloud capabilities could aid toward the achievement of self-driving, this suggests that the use of the cloud can presumably shine in other avenues too.

Conclusion

Sometimes I get asked whether the cloud is the tail wagging the dog of autonomous vehicles, or whether autonomous vehicles are the tail wagging the cloud.

Sorry, but all this tail-wagging seems a bit confounding and misleading.

They are two peas in a pod (how's that for an alternative metaphor).

The cloud provides benefits for the AV and all of its constituent parts, given the realization that the AV exists within the environment of a business and can leverage the cloud in particular for the AV and as a sustainable business operation.

Mutually beneficial is the watchword here.

In many respects, this might be likened to a match made in heaven, interlinking the intricacies of autonomous vehicles and the cloud. That being said, it still takes a lot of legwork, careful insight, and prudence to make sure that the heavenly match is a sound one.

It just goes to show, there isn't a free lunch, even with especially well-suited matches.

CHAPTER 21
OPPOSITION TO SELF-DRIVING CARS

The headlines proclaiming the emergence of self-driving cars are usually soaked in high praise for the advent of these technological marvels.

This heralding of such wonderment in innovation is certainly understandable.

Getting a car to be driven entirely by automation and altogether absent of human hand at the wheel is an enormous feat, let there be no doubt or question on that account. Other than dreamy portrayals in sci-fi novels and movies, the notion that a car could safely and sufficiently make its own way on our public roads is a stretch goal, some assert it is a moonshot-like aspiration, and one that has alluded inventors and systems developers since the automobile itself was first rolled out for human use.

If you are looking for reasons to want self-driving cars, a boatload exists.

Pundits are anticipating that we might find ourselves entering into an age of mobility-for-all.

The idea behind this mantra is that the availability of self-driving cars will dramatically increase access to transportation. Self-driving cars will be continually on-the-go, 24 hours per day and seven days per week, roaming our streets and highways so that they are nearest to you when a lift is requested. Unlike human-driven cars that require a human operator at the driving controls, a self-driving car does not need any rest breaks per se and can just keep on trucking, as they say.

The hope too is that the cost of using self-driving cars will be substantially less than the cost of using human-driven automobiles.

By subtracting out the labor involved in driving a car, the assumption is that the use of these AI-driven cars will be a lot less costly per mile. People today that are unable to afford the use of a car, such as existing ridesharing services, will find themselves readily able to pay the much lower cost of a ridesharing self-driving car (not everyone agrees on this cost aspect, including qualms that self-driving cars might be overly expensive and only for the rich or famous.

With the huge upside of self-driving cars, the celebratory welcoming of self-driving cars is indubitably sensible and deserving of outsized headlines.

That being said, some have expressed and continue to express deep concerns about the arrival of self-driving cars all told.

We all seemingly realize that with any new innovation there are going to be positives and also likely negatives. Any realistic real-world invention that touches mightily upon society has got to have rough edges and downsides. There is no free lunch in this world, and that certainly includes self-driving cars.

It is easy to dismiss out-of-hand some of the objections raised against the introduction of self-driving cars.

For example, sometimes the objectors proffer nothing other than vacuous statements that land as hollow accusations without any substantive foundation. Anyone merely touting that self-driving cars are "bad" and yet does not provide a basis for such a boisterous claim, well, this kind of empty argument does little and regrettably gives the more reasoned naysayers a bad name.

Another set of oppositional arguments drift toward sci-fi possibilities.

This includes the postulated future of AI becoming sentient and then opting to use self-driving cars against humanity. AI is not sentient at this time. We don't know that AI of the kind that we are devising will ever be sentient. The AI driving systems that are being put in place today are absolutely and abundantly not sentient, and there is no miracle breakthrough seemingly required for reaching sentience in order to adequately drive a car.

These aforementioned ways of trying to warn us about self-driving cars are not particularly successful in their meaning and nor merits.

Despite those shortcomings, we ought to not let that cloud our thinking on this quite important topic.

In short, there are assuredly bona fide reasons and a poignant rationale for those that seriously and sincerely have doubts about the benefits of self-driving cars versus the "costs" of self-driving cars (I've put the word costs into quotes since this is not just a dollars and cents consideration, as there are downsides or disadvantages that are not immediately relatable in monetary terms alone).

Perhaps I've now whetted your appetite to find out about the more rigorous arguments in opposition to self-driving cars.

They are coming up next, I promise, but first, some added and crucial contextual milieu.

These are arguments that can each of their own accord can be separately debated and in some ways separately discounted (a classic divide-and-conquer form of unraveling an argument).

Tackling each of the arguments individually or on a standalone basis is an easier way to undercut their total argumentative power or sway. As such, it might be instructive to try and weigh together the entire set of arguments.

Out of this final weigh-up, the scales can ergo be more notably claimed to tilt toward not unleashing self-driving cars, so some proclaim.

Take a reflective moment about that somewhat startling assertion.

Essentially, the claim is being made that there are a core set of fundamentals that inform as to not permitting self-driving cars to proceed at all. The declaration is straightforward and directly grasped: Do not let self-driving cars get underway now, and ostensibly not in any foreseeable future. Don't let self-driving cars be dribbled out. Don't let them gain any grassroots.

That undoubtedly seems a bit of an extreme and nearly counterintuitive posture.

This relatively stark viewpoint that self-driving cars ought to not be made available is quite a far cry from stating that before self-driving cars are put into use that certain steps or mitigations ought to be established. As you will see, the counterargument is that it makes no sense to start something that opens essentially a Pandora's box.

Once you've let the genie out of the bottle, it isn't going back in, and turning back is nearly impossible. In that frame of mind, consider this collection of reasons to not let self-driving cars proceed as not just a red flag, but instead, a permanent stop sign that shall never be passed (of course, "never" is a long time, and maybe we'll all change our minds in some distant future).

Before leaping into the arguments, one aspect to clarify involves the definitional aspects of what it means to refer to a self-driving car.

Let's unpack the self-driving car definition first, and then get into the guts of the arguments for fundamentally preventing them from being placed into use.

Self-Driving Cars And Why Don't Proceed

For Level 4 and Level 5 true self-driving vehicles, there won't be a human driver involved in the driving task.

All occupants will be passengers.

The AI is doing the driving.

The crux of the basis for not wanting self-driving cars is due to the AI doing the driving (as I early exhorted, this is not because the AI possesses sentience or is omniscient, so please do not anthropomorphize today's AI capabilities).

The primary source of concern is that a human won't be doing the driving and that instead, a form of automata will be doing so (a form of automation that is devised by humans, will be overseen by humans, will be managed by humans, and so on).

I mention this to also help clarify that a self-driving car is still a car.

In other words, the automobile itself is not particularly different than a conventional car. Sure, a self-driving car has a suite of specialized sensors such as video cameras, radar, LIDAR, ultrasonic units, and the like, but that isn't especially unlike a regular car. Indeed, the first wave of self-driving cars is almost certainly going to be conventional cars that have been retrofitted with the sensors and the computing processing units needed to enable the on-board AI driving system to function.

Furthermore, even once we begin to see new kinds of cars that are devised from the ground-up as "pure" self-driving cars, those will still nonetheless be cars. They will have four wheels, they will have an engine, they will pretty much be the same as conventional cars are today. Sure, the interior of self-driving cars is likely to be reimagined, allowing for riders to swivel while seated in a self-driving car and also recline for catching a few winks while the AI is undertaking the driving chore. This is still the essence of a car.

The point is that there is no need to look at the car (as an automobile) for being the culprit or gotcha in not wanting to have self-driving cars.

Look at the AI driving system, that's where the thorny problems ensue, as will be discussed now.

Strap on your seatbelt and get ready for a heck of a ride.

Arguing About The Lives Lost Or Saved

For those that *favor* the advent of self-driving cars, there is a simple and commonly declared reason for wanting self-driving cars, namely the saving of lives.

Here's the logic, and then we'll see how the side that oppositionally *disfavors* self-driving cars offers an intriguing retort.

Currently, in the United States alone, there are annually about 40,000 car crash-related human-fatalities and around 2.5 million injuries due to car crashes. A sizable portion of those car crashes is due to human drivers that are drunk while driving. Another sizable portion is attributed to human drivers that are distracted from the driving task. An AI driving system is not going to be a drunk driver. An AI driving system is not going to be a distracted driver.

The assumption is that the use of self-driving cars will significantly reduce the number of car crashes, thus saving lives and foregoing the concomitant injuries. No more human drivers that are drunk while driving. No more human drivers that are watching cat videos while driving. And so on.

That does make sense.

But there are those in the favoring camp that take this a bridge too far and say that we will have zero deaths and zero injuries because (allegedly) self-driving cars will never get into car crashes of any kind.

For various reasons that I've carefully articulated, this zeroing mantra has a zero chance of occurring. The notion of zero crashes is certainly alluring, though it also presents utterly false expectations. There will irrefutably be some amount of self-driving car crashes, beyond zero, though we don't know how many and how frequently it might occur.

Okay, so if you'll agree that there will be some amount of self-driving car involved car crashes and related human fatalities and injuries, which is the likely and realistic scenario, this is where the disfavoring arises.

Those that fundamentally oppose self-driving cars would argue that any deaths of humans at the hands of an AI driving system is one too many. AI should never be allowed to kill a human, as per the classic Asimov's rules of robotics. Until an AI driving system can be guaranteed on an ironclad basis that it will never ever get into a car crash, and thus would fatality harm a human, such AI driving systems should not be allowed on our public roadways.

That is a showstopper.

Why so?

A child is standing between two parked cars and cannot be seen from the active roadway. A car is coming along at the posted speed limit. The child suddenly darts into the street. No matter how responsive the car is, the child in this scenario is going to get run over and sadly become a fatality, even if the car immediately applies the brakes.

Suppose this was a self-driving car. That is undeniably a self-driving car that has killed someone.

Case seemingly closed.

Of course, a human driver could equally be in the same quandary and have produced the same result.

The assertion by those that disfavor self-driving cars would be that though the result might be the same, the apparent fact that an AI driving system was at the wheel is intrinsically wrong and showcases that the AI driving system is undertaking the sacred duty that should be reserved exclusively for humans and human decision making. This gets the other camp in arms since they point out that the net benefit of the number of lives lost will be likely tremendously reduced. In other words, the AI driving systems will save lives. It might not prevent all lives from being lost, and yet any lives saved are precious and ought to outweigh the fact that self-driving cars can nonetheless still be attributable to some lives lost.

For those that believe that even one life lost due to an AI-based self-driving car is too much, albeit that perhaps many lives will have been saved, this is a key cornerstone for disfavoring or outright opposing self-driving cars.

There is a quagmire of ethical considerations amidst all of this (see my columns for further details).

We'll move to the next argument for now.

Arguing About The Extinction of Human Driving

At first, there is going to be a mixture of human-driven conventional cars amidst the advent of self-driving cars (there are about 250 million conventional cars in the U.S. today). Gradually, the number of self-driving cars would be increased and thus the proportion of human-driven cars versus self-driving cars would shift accordingly.

Some have urged that we ought to curtail all human driving on our public roadways and enforce that only self-driving cars could use the publicly shared highways, streets, and byways. The logic is similar to the foregoing discussion about the dangers of drunk drivers, distracted drivers, etc. Remove all human drivers and all of those untoward driving actions would presumably no longer exist.

Assume that indeed human driving becomes summarily banned (well, maybe with some exceptions, such as driving allowed on private property or for old-fashioned human-driven car races).

If that ban occurred, in many respects this would be the extinction of human driving.

No one would be driving a car (setting aside the small exceptions).

The bulk of society would no longer know how to drive, either forgetting how to drive or never having learned to drive since there was no need to do so. In any case, driving a car on public roadways would generally be considered an illegal act, subject to criminal prosecution and incarceration, one presumes.

The disfavoring camp emphasizes that this is a denial of what some would characterize as a foundational right for mankind, namely the act of driving a car (even though, admittedly, it is currently classified as a privilege, and not an inherent right). Some have suggested that the day you'll take away their driving is the day that you pry their cold dead hands from the steering wheel.

As a counterargument, it is said that we don't know that such a ban will occur.

Meanwhile, the counter to the counterargument is that it is a likely slippery slope and an obvious insidious outcome of the advent of self-driving cars.

Arguing About The Dependency On Machines

Envision that nearly all use of cars involves self-driving cars.

Imagine that very few if any cars remain that are able to be driven by humans. The days of conventional cars that contain a steering wheel and pedals have faded into history. For all practical purposes, using a car entails having an AI driving system do the driving task.

This is similar to the prior discussion about banning human driving, but we don't have to go that far. Just assume that there aren't many cars with driving controls, thus, even if a human wanted to go for a drive, there aren't any cars around to do so. You don't particularly need to ban humans from driving if by default there isn't an available means to do the driving.

This can be claimed as supporting the disfavoring case, here's why.

Want to go for a drive on a whim and go wherever you want to go?

Since you can't do the driving, you'll need to tell the AI driving system where you want to go.

Change your mind during a driving journey and want to take the next exit to see something interesting that caught your eye. You can't opt to do so. That being said, yes, you can tell, or might accurately ask the AI to take that next exit for you.

Humans will become dependent upon machines, the AI driving systems, and self-driving cars, and will no longer be in charge of their own driving pursuits and interests.

Tying this point to the prior one, this also bodes for the problem that if human driving is extinct, and we somehow suddenly need to be able to drive because the machines aren't or won't (this is somewhat inching onto the sci-fi quicksand, but not entirely so), humans won't be ready to do so.

The decay in driving skills or the absence of driving skills cannot necessarily overnight be overcome.

Arguing About The Traceability

Today, you get into your car and drive to the store, then over to the neighborhood park, and then head back home. Nobody other than you is aware of your travels.

With AI driving systems, the odds are that they are going to be keeping track of every ride and every inch that is being driven. This data will then be uploaded to the cloud of the fleet operator. You are going to be tracked to a degree that boggles the mind.

Do we want that kind of traceability of every driving journey and personal choices of where we go, when we go there, etc.?

That seems like a quite compelling argument for the disfavoring camp.

A counterargument is that if you use ridesharing today, this same kind of tracking occurs.

Aha, the counter to the counterargument is that the preponderance of driving in the United States today is not ridesharing, which is a drop in the bucket. By-and-large, our driving currently is done via our individual and relatively untraced personally owned cars.

It is likely that self-driving cars, regardless of ridesharing use or personal use, are going to always be tracking their every activity and driving effort.

Arguing About Collective Control

You decide to drive up to the mountains where you have a vacation home. Along the way, you hear on the radio that a forest fire is underway in that area. Though you know there is risk involved, you drive there anyway, for reasons of wanting to protect your property and reach some beloved animals being kept there.

In an era of self-driving cars, here's what might happen.

The government decides that it is too dangerous for people to be going into the mountains that have forest fires. Contact is made with the major self-driving car operators that have the largest fleets of self-driving cars. They are told to command the self-driving cars to stay out of those now-restricted areas. Electronic missives are transmitted to the self-driving cars and the AI driving systems are informed to not drive in those restricted areas.

Your choice of going up to the mountains has been summarily taken away from you.

Whereas in a conventional car, you could make that choice, the AI driving system as instructed by the fleet operator is not going to proceed there.

This particular example allows for easy debate about whether the government is making a prudent choice and perhaps saving lives by enforcing such an edict. Suppose though that the government in other circumstances started restricting where you could go and did so on not quite such an apparent lifesaving basis. There might be no end in sight for where you could no longer go, and for which there won't be much you can do about it (assuming that there aren't human-driven cars available and that you cannot override the AI driving system instructions).

The advent of AI-based true self-driving cars can potentially produce a form of centralized control over driving that is nearly unimaginable today. It might seem laughable by today's standards, but if you look closely at what some major state-actors are considering doing with self-driving cars, this kind of emergent centralized control is decidedly not a farfetched notion (see my column for examples).

Arguing About Societal Downgrading

In interests of saving ink, I'll lump together a bunch of additional disfavoring arguments into this one category of societal downgrading or downfall aspects.

Here they are in rapid succession:

- Learning to drive a car is considered a societal rite of passage, but that won't happen anymore in an era of self-driving cars. That is ostensibly a societal downgrade or downfall that could be construed as an indirect adverse consequence of self-driving cars.

- No more sense of independence comes with being able to drive a car and go where your heart desires.

- We might undermine some of our cognitive skills by no longer learning to drive and carrying out the act of driving.

- The same might be said of the accompanying fine motor skills of handling the driving controls.

- Some believe we might become lazy, using self-driving cars when we ought to be walking or riding a bike.

- You can readily sleep while inside a self-driving car, thus, perhaps we'll become more sloth-like.

- You can easily go for a drive yourself via a self-driving car. No driver's license is needed and no one else is required to drive the car for you. This might splinter us into becoming more alone.

- Children can be driven around by a self-driving car. No need to have a parent do this. Some wonder if this might undermine the family bonding that normally entails the act of using a car for family activities.

- People might eschew using mass transit and flock exclusively to self-driving cars, thus undermining and likely ultimately decimating existing mass transit and the future of such transportation.

There are lots of these kinds of societal ramifications that no one knows whether they will arise or not.

Conclusion

Another facet to keep in mind is the possibility of bad actors that are somehow able to overtake the cloud of a fleet operator or that can manage to implant unsavory code into the AI driving systems. This is yet another disfavoring point that can be added to the mounting heap of such foundational objections.

Conventional cars of today are currently relatively untouched by this kind of viral attack. That being said, even conventional cars are gradually adding interconnectivity and tons of on-board processing, such that they too are going to have these kinds of potential vulnerabilities.

Overall, now that you've gotten a ton of bricks dropped on top of that outright joyous glee over self-driving cars, does that crush those ambitions, and should we bring things to a Luddite-like halt?

My take is that the future will be what we make of it. These disfavoring assertions are worthy of our rapt attention, now and later on, and we ought to not undervalue or avoid the difficult questions that have to be properly addressed.

The glass is half-full, but it is also half-empty, and we need to be cognizant accordingly.

CHAPTER 22
NEOPHYTE TESTIMONIALS AND SELF-DRIVING CARS

A smooth ride.

Really enjoyed taking a short nap while getting a lift to the grocery.

Those comments might seem like everyday remarks by someone that has recently undergone a typical ridesharing journey and subsequently was asked how the ride experience went.

Add this next comment to the bunch and see how it somewhat changes the picture: *Was fascinated by the empty driver's seat and the fact that no one was at the wheel during the entire trip.*

That type of remark is a bit more surprising, namely that there wasn't a human driver at the wheel of the ridesharing car.

Sure enough, various rider testimonials are now increasingly being used to promote the ride experience related to taking a journey in a self-driving car that is being used on our public roadways. To clarify, for true self-driving cars there isn't a human driver at the wheel and instead, an AI-based driving system is undertaking the entirety of the driving chore.

These alleged off-the-cuff testimonials are usually by first-time riders in self-driving cars.

Why care about this?

From an industry perspective, the public roadway tryouts of self-driving cars are occurring at a very formative time.

So far, the general public and regulators have not taken an outsized interest in these self-driving car efforts, as long as nobody seems to be getting hurt and there aren't significant calamities or complaints (exceptions apply). It would seem that as long as those ostensibly stable conditions seem to remain relatively calm and are otherwise below the radar of mass media attention, self-driving cars will continue to get their initial footing established.

The thing is, being too far below the radar is also unattractive, at least for the advent of self-driving cars all told. By not sufficiently getting the word out-and-about that self-driving cars are presumably becoming proficient at navigating our roadways, doing so without car crashes and car mishaps, these moonshot-like efforts are nearly invisible to the public at large.

And, this also tends to suggest that there isn't a reservoir of goodwill being gradually accumulated.

The need for goodwill is going to be more pronounced once these nascent tryouts want to expand further and go both deep and wide in rolling out self-driving cars. It is one thing to do such tryouts when there aren't many of the vehicles and they are gingerly being used in very narrow ways, meaning that the chances of something going awry is less likely. Whence self-driving cars are more largely put onto our roadways, the odds are that there will be untoward moments.

How will the public and regulators react to such untoward moments arising?

Probably not very well.

The assumption is that if sufficient goodwill has already filled the public sentiment reservoir there will be a cushion to cope with the anticipated backlash. Ergo, the belief is that any bad apple instances won't ruin the entire barrel.

At least that's part of the thinking behind promulgating these testimonials.

Of course, another factor involves wanting to get investors interested in and excited about investing in self-driving cars.

Trying to keep the attention and funding by antsy investors can be challenging when the payoff is years upon years in the future. Whereas there were earlier "false expectations" about self-driving cars as being viable on day one, most prudently now seem to realize that the development and fielding of self-driving cars is a lot harder and a lot longer to ferment, thus requiring a form of investor patience seldom seen by those that want a quick payoff.

Okay, so a lack of calamities is wonderful, but then how can you otherwise generate positive interest and overall awareness that self-driving cars are getting underway?

Some of the automakers and self-driving tech firms have been posting online videos that showcase their self-driving cars roaming around a town or city. These videos are meant to reflect that these AI-driven cars are doing just fine, thank you very much, and they are able to do day-to-day driving. Most of the video running time is devoted to watching as the vehicle makes turns here and there, stopping cautiously and correctly at all red lights and stop signs, and pretty much demonstrate the same driving prowess that you might expect any newbie driver to perform.

I've previously pointed out that these videos are handy but can also be somewhat misleading, depending upon how they are recorded, and how they are sometimes edited, and I have put together a list of handy ways to scrutinize such videos for their veracity in reflecting the truth about how self-driving cars are coming along.

Beyond the posting of videos, another means of publicizing self-driving car tryouts consists of posting testimonials by riders.

For much of the self-driving car tryouts to-date, the only riders consisted of trained back-up drivers that rode in the vehicle and had to be prepared to take over the driving controls if so needed (for the skinny on back-up drivers). Getting the reaction of back-up drivers to being in a self-driving car is not especially noteworthy since they are being paid to serve as hired-gun safety drivers. Usually, they are not allowed to say anything about the job, other than occasionally releasing carefully scripted comments.

In a sense, it would seem to be the equivalent of asking a ridesharing driver (a human one) about their efforts of driving a car for ridesharing purposes. The odds are they would provide a glowing account of how tremendous the driving ability is. It seems doubtful that they would fess-up to nearly having bumped into a pedestrian or openly talk about tires screeching when precariously traversing some street corners.

In any case, the general public would be decidedly less impressed by what a paid-for back-up driver might have to say than what an everyday person might have to say about riding in a self-driving car, doing so on a non-paid basis and solely in the capacity as a passenger.

In short, people would likely want to know what other ordinary riders have to say.

This helps to then establish whether self-driving cars seem safe enough and are real enough to be taken seriously. We already all seem to be fascinated and convinced by testimonials about toothpaste brands, toasters, and nearly all kinds of products imaginable. Seems like testimonials about self-driving cars ought to work similarly.

Some pundits point out that the self-driving cars industry has been somewhat slow or behind the wheel, if you can so allow, in terms of marketing their efforts. Some suggest this is due to the technological bent of the automakers and self-driving tech firms involved. For them, the focus is primarily on making a better mousetrap, in this case devising a self-driving car, and little energy goes toward the aims of marketing or promoting their wares.

Others emphasize that the industry went over its toes and marketed itself too early and with so much bravado that it backfired. All those tall tales about self-driving cars suddenly inhabiting all of our highways and roadways overnight have not come to pass. The public came to realize that the prophecies were premature. As such, there is a certain sensitivity nowadays about those that inflate expectations, though there are some that seem to still be able to get away with this via their ardent fanbase support and maverick style charm.

The use of testimonials by riders is a seemingly ideal way to gently nudge back into public view.

Having riders offer their opinions is pretty nifty. Testimonials tend to be assumed as coming from the hearts of those that proffer the testimonials. It takes the attention away from the maker of the product and turns the eyes toward someone like us. You say to yourself, that could be me, touting how great that toothpaste is, or how toasty that toaster is, or how wonderful a ride it was in that self-driving car.

This also allows the maker of the product to stand tall. They are merely legitimately putting forward a customer that wants to express their views. What could be wrong with that? Indeed, it seems to not only offer an unbiased and forthright assessment, but it also seems chancy for the product maker since the customer telling their story might go afield of what the company might prefer to be said.

There is another facet about testimonials related to self-driving cars though that differs substantively from testimonials about products such as shampoos and skin creams.

Life or death.

That's right, the act of riding in a car is altogether a life-or-death matter.

You might not think of being inside a car as a life-or-death kind of activity, but it assuredly is. Each time that you get behind the wheel of a car, you are putting yourself at risk of getting into a car crash. Similarly, each time that you get into a car as a rider, whether in a ridesharing vehicle or a taxi, or a friend's car, you are also absorbing the risk of getting into a car crash.

We are so used to using cars that the daily risk involved is either immensely discounted or outright ignored.

In the United States alone, there are annually about 40,000 car crash-related fatalities and about 2.5 million injuries. Few that drive a car are aware of those statistics. Few that go for a ride in a car are aware of those statistics. Even if you know about those figures, you probably would proceed to drive and ride in cars anyway, because you need to get from point A to point B and the assumption is that nothing is going to happen to you during that driving journey (or, that the odds are extremely remote and therefore worth the marginal risks entailed).

But would you feel the same way about getting into a self-driving car?

People are unlikely to assume that their personal risk is minuscule when taking a ride in a car that is not being driven by a human. Actually, people are likely unsure of what the risk is. They know that human drivers have lots of driving foibles and issues. There are drunk drivers. There are distracted drivers.

Which is the better bet, namely to have a human at the wheel or have an AI driving system doing the driving?

There is an obvious risk-reducing factor that the AI won't be drunk driving and will presumably not be a distracted driver. On the other hand, the AI is an unseen and unknown element. You can size-up a human driver and make your own decision about whether they seem worthy as a driver.

There aren't any apparent means to do the same for an AI driving system.

Thus, the vital nature of testimonials.

Perhaps those that are riding in self-driving cars can inform us about the safety and validity of those AI driving systems. These fellow humans, albeit seemingly daring riders, took a chance and opted to go for a ride. Are they akin to astronauts that are willing to break the sound barrier and act as first-movers that heroically can attest to what they felt and saw? That's one view of how powerful such testimonials can be in shaping public opinion about self-driving cars.

Not everyone is convinced that these testimonials are fair game, so to speak.

There is controversy afoot about testimonials associated with riding in self-driving cars.

Here then is an important question to ponder: *What ought we sensibly derive from the ongoing and expanding use of personal testimonials about riding in self-driving cars during these public roadway tryouts?*

Before we unpack that matter, let's make sure we are all in concordance about what is meant by referring to those vehicles that are considered true self-driving cars.

Self-Driving Cars And Rider Testimonials

For Level 4 and Level 5 true self-driving vehicles, there won't be a human driver involved in the driving task.

All occupants will be passengers.

The AI is doing the driving.

A rider gets into a self-driving car and goes for a ride. Eventually, this will be a daily occurrence and nothing to write home about per se. The notion of going somewhere via a self-driving car will be as natural and mundane as going somewhere by the hands of a human driver being at the driving controls.

Right now, going for a ride in a true self-driving car is extremely rare.

Since most people aren't likely to be a rider in a self-driving car for some years to come, they are intensely curious about what it must be like. Voila, thus the keen interest in reading, hearing, or otherwise finding out about personal testimonials by those that have gone for a ride in a self-driving car.

This doesn't seem to evoke any controversy whatsoever.

Turns out, there are quite a number of qualms being expressed. One of which is that these riders don't know what the heck they are seeing and experiencing. To some degree, they are neophytes and are ill-equipped to be offering any insights about self-driving cars, goes the criticism about this latest spate of testimonials.

Consider an analogous situation to a magic act and magicians.

You take someone that is not versed in how a rabbit is pulled out of a hat, or how an ace card is startlingly yanked out of a deck of cards, and you ask them about the show they just experienced.

Wonderful, they might exclaim.

Amazing and breathtaking, they might say gushingly.

But if you had a fellow magician watch that same act, they might tell you that the effort you just saw was quite simplistic and had tons of glitches, none of which the non-magician noticed or realized was taking place. Someone that has no training in such matters and otherwise is a complete neophyte is unable to readily discern that which is well orchestrated from that which is perhaps an abysmal mess (the performance nonetheless was sufficiently able to pull the wool over the eyes of said uninitiated).

Harry Houdini was reportedly known for saying, what the eyes see and the ears hear, the mind believes. In short, when a rider of a self-driving car provides a testimonial, this raises the unstated question of whether they are capable of rendering a sound judgment or not.

The maker of a self-driving car would likely insist that a neophyte is the ideal source of a testimonial.

Regular people are going to be going in self-driving cars, therefore regular people ought to be the ones that tell us what the ride is like. You don't need to be an expert automotive engineer to go for a ride in an Uber or Lyft ridesharing car that is being driven by a human driver, and thus the same should be the case for self-driving cars.

In fact, if the only way to ride in a self-driving car required that the passenger had to be versed in automotive technology or AI, this would surely undercut the value of having self-driving cars, since very few would be suitably versed to ride in them. There is a clearcut need to demonstrate that there is no requirement of having any background about self-driving cars in order to ride in and leverage the utility of using a self-driving car.

Those facets are certainly notable, yet this does not respond to the concern that such riders are unable to "fairly and adequately" assess what they have experienced. Yes, they can report what they believe they saw, but akin to a magic act, the whole experience could be smoke and mirrors, yet they were oblivious to the trickery involved.

How could a self-driving car be somehow tricky as a driving journey experience?

Suppose a self-driving car drove you from your home to the mall.

It is a sunny day. There is very little traffic on the roadways as it is midday, before any commuter traffic. The self-driving car takes you primarily onto side streets and only rarely gets onto any major thoroughfare. During the journey, few if any bike riders are encountered. No pedestrians try to dart into the street. No loose dogs running out of someone's front yard. Etc.

The rider provides a testimonial about how incredible the ride was. Smooth ride, no sudden stops at all. The ride was so seamless that the rider nearly fell asleep. Gosh, it would be great if human drivers could drive as well as this self-driving car.

Notice that from the testimony itself, we have no idea of the context of the driving journey.

Turns out, there wasn't any arduous traffic to contend with, there weren't any jaywalking pedestrians, and so on. It wasn't raining, the day was sunny and the roads were readily drivable. On and on, one can go. All of those are crucial aspects that can take place during any driving effort. We do not know from the testimonial that *none* of those aspects occurred. It was an easy-peasy driving effort and not at all of the quality and complexity that even an everyday drive might consist of.

So, a bona fide qualm about neophyte first-time riders is that they are likely to provide a glowing testimony that appears to suggest that the self-driving car can do the same depth and breadth of driving that a human driver can do, and yet that is not at all showcased by the ride experience per se. The testimony is essentially hollow, but it nonetheless seems legitimate since it comes from an everyday person that is innocently and sincerely expressing an everyday opinion.

Presumably, an expert that knew about self-driving cars would indeed observe that the driving journey did not particularly stretch the boundaries of a driving effort. This would be akin to the versed magician, knowing when the "act" was able to deftly do something and when it was not doing so. A neophyte has no such awareness and therefore cannot fully express what took place.

A counterargument about using an expert is that they would be unlike an average rider and therefore not be able to report the experience as though they were an everyday person. The public perception would be that only an expert would be willing to ride in a self-driving car, and somehow, therefore, being a passenger requires specialized skills and expertise.

Another claim is that an expert would likely focus on trivia or insider details of little concern for the ordinary rider. All that matters to a passenger is whether the ride proceeds safely and whether they get to their destination. No need to know about how the sensors were working or the maneuvering of the vehicle by the AI driving system.

Conclusion

There are numerous other considerations to keep in mind about the controversies on this topic.

For example, there is a selectively "bias" associated with the rider testimonials.

Here's what that entails.

Suppose there are ten people that each went for a ride, doing so on separate journeys. Let's pretend that nine of them thought the ride was terrible, for whatever reason. One rider thought the ride was astonishing. The self-driving car maker posts the remarks of the one rider that relished the journey but does not publicize the remarks of the other riders.

All that you see is the commentary by the one rider. That particular rider was presumably selected due to their praise for the self-driving car experience. We have no semblance of how many other riders there were and nor whether those other riders did not like the experience. Nonetheless, we are likely to assume that the one rider is representative of the entirety of the riders.

Of course, the self-driving car company can point out that they did not claim that the testimonial by the one rider was necessarily representative of the overarching sentiment. That was a *rash* conclusion made by those that see the testimonial.

Furthermore, if pressed, the self-driving car maker might contend that the dissatisfied riders were confused or otherwise off-the-mark. Imagine that an upset rider was out-of-sorts that there wasn't a cup holder for their soda during the self-driving car journey. If that was the sum total of their beef, it certainly seems sensible to not let such a myopic viewpoint overstate the nature of the self-driving car experience.

Round and round the testimonial merry-go-round we go.

In general, testimonials for any kind of product will have the same types of limitations and problems, and everyone ought to judge all testimonials with a jaundiced eye. You can't toss onto the backs of self-driving carmakers culpability about testimonials as though they are the only ones to have ever taken that route. Thus, self-driving cars are not somehow unique when it comes to the strengths and the drawbacks of testimonials. Someone that provides a testimonial about a shampoo might have no idea about the chemistry involved and cannot properly judge whether their hair might fall out in a month's time.

The difference though with self-driving cars is the life-or-death element, and so there is a case to be made that perhaps the use of testimonials should be undertaken more somberly than with the latest kitchen cutlery or trendiest vacuum cleaner.

Testimonials are valuable, but as always, make sure to be on the watch for illusions and sleight of hand, and let Houdini's advice guide you in ascertaining the veracity of what you read or here.

CHAPTER 23
VERBAL COMMANDS AND SELF-DRIVING CARS

Stubborn as a mule.

Sometimes it seems as though a car is about as stubborn as a mule or perhaps being downright bull-headed.

Here's an example of something I witnessed first-hand the other day.

A tow truck was getting ready to take a car for a tow.

This was a flatbed style tow truck, consisting of a flat and rear raised area that serves to hold and essentially piggyback a car for being transported. In that sense, the tow truck isn't particularly towing the car and instead of giving it a ride.

The tail end of the flatbed portion tilts at a somewhat acute angle to allow for driving a car up onto the riding platform. This forms a ramp for the car to traverse upward onto the empty and awaiting flatbed area.

If needed, a car could be towed from ground level and pulled agonizingly up the ramp by a special winching apparatus. Presumably, this feature is reserved for cases of a car that is unable to be driven, such as after a car crash or when the engine has conked out and won't start. In this instance, the car appeared to be quite drivable, and thus things were readied for the car to make its way up the ramp, ultimately aiming to become nestled and secured onto the flatbed.

The person that owned the car got into the driver's seat and aligned the vehicle with the skids of the tilting rampway. You could see that the driver was a bit nervous about this kind of driving predicament.

I say predicament because whoever is driving the car will need to make sure the tires of the car are able to perfectly make their way into the ramp skids. Next, you need to give the car enough gas to get it to readily accelerate up the steep ramp. Of course, you also need to make sure that you come to a proper stop once you've made your way up the ramp and ended up on the flatbed portion.

There is a danger that you might overshoot the acceleration needed, possibly zooming up the ramp and onto the flatbed, and subsequently find yourself zipping forward out-of-control and ramming into the back of the tow truck itself. This car did not *yet* seem to have any outward appearance of damages. It would certainly be a shame to crush the front of the car or otherwise dent this pristine-looking vehicle, simply by the act of trying to get it onto the tow truck flatbed.

The tow truck driver made no effort to assuage the car driver's qualms.

I'm sure that if the tow truck driver had offered to do the driving, the driver would likely have acquiesced, gleefully so. Meanwhile, the driver looked to be the type of person that would not ever ask to have the tow truck driver do the driving. This would be a driver's loss of face, as it were, and an admission of weakness or helplessness that this particular car driver seemed unwilling to concede.

There you have it, a moment whereby a reluctant car driver wants to undertake a driving activity that is rarely performed in any semblance of ordinary daily driving, and a tow truck driver that probably has done this driving act a thousand times but is deferring to the ordinary driver in this case.

What might happen?

I felt as though I might be witnessing a car accident in the making. It seemed like going to a bullfight and awaiting the moment that the bullfighter might get gored. You assume that the matador is probably unlikely to get into any problematic circumstance, though there is a tense air of possibility and thus the whole thing is certainly worth watching.

The driver began to inch up the ramp.

When referring to inches, I mean inches. Time was nearly standing still, that's how slowly the car was making its way up the ramp. The car was straining to do so. Gravity was working its magic and the weight of the vehicle was helping out. You could tell that the driver was not willing to apply a lead foot to the gas pedal and instead was hoping that the car could crawl rather than dart aboard the flatbed.

The expression on the face of the tow truck driver was priceless.

He was somewhat bemused at the difficultly of the car driver. Imagine that you are an artist, and you see someone flail around with a paintbrush and not know how to properly cast paint onto a canvas. The tow truck driver was undoubtedly imbued with car-up-the-ramp artistry after years of toil and was now witnessing the rather lame and ineffectual efforts of a layman at his same craft.

That being said, bemusement does not necessarily translate into cash in one's pocket. It is doubtful that the tow truck driver was getting paid by the hour. He wanted to finish this job, expediently, and take the car to wherever it had to go. The longer this snail-paced inching took, it meant the tow truck driver was losing out on future opportunities awaiting his valued towing services.

The tow truck driver yelled to the car driver and inquired as to whether he needed any help. That seemed to spur the car driver to take heightened risks, and sure enough, the car finally bolted up the rest of the ramp and landed squarely onto the flatbed.

No harm, no foul.

It is a sure bet that the car driver went home that night and bragged about his driving prowess. You can also bet that the tow truck driver got home and carped about a car driver that took eons to get a car onto his flatbed. Two different views involving two people living in different worlds, as it were.

Anyway, you could assert that the car was stubborn and didn't want to go up that ramp.

I doubt any of us would seriously though contend that the car "knew" it was going up a ramp. All that happened was that physics was working against the car as it tried to climb the ramp. That's about it.

You might say the stubbornness was rooted in the car driver. He was unable to smoothly drive the car up the ramp. He wasn't stubborn in the sense of not wanting to drive the car, it was more like stubbornness about insisting on driving in a situation that he wasn't versed in driving (and, for which he had an immediate substitute on-hand that did know how to do so). Maybe the car driver was worried that the tow truck driver would be overly callous and not gingerly drive his prized baby (car) onto the flatbed. Or perhaps the car driver wanted the thrill of trying a new and tricky maneuver. People have innumerable reasons for what they do.

Shifting gears, and since we are discussing the topic of cars, the future of cars entails self-driving cars. This stubbornness element in the flatbed truck tale brings up an interesting facet about self-driving cars and one that few are giving much attention toward.

First, be aware that true self-driving cars are driven by an AI-based driving system and not by a human driver. Thus, in the case of this flatbed truck scenario, if the car had been a self-driving car, the AI driving system would have been trying to get the car up that ramp and onto the flatbed.

Secondly, there are going to be instances wherein a human wants a self-driving car to go someplace, but the AI driving system will "refuse" to do so.

I want to clarify that the AI is not somehow sentient since the type of AI being devised today is not in any manner whatsoever approaching sentience. Perhaps far away in the future, we will achieve that kind of AI, but that's not in the cards right now.

This latter point is important because the AI driving system opting to "refuse" to drive someplace is not due to the AI being a sentient being, and instead is merely a programmatic indication that the AI has detected a situation that it is not programmed to drive in. Please dispense with any anthropomorphizing of the AI and realize that this is merely automation that is providing an automation-based invoked response.

Today's then intriguing question consists of this: *How can you convince a self-driving car to go where you want it to go when it won't go there?*

We'll use the loading of the car onto the flatbed as a handy exemplar.

Time to unpack this matter and see.

Self-Driving Cars And Going Beyond

For Level 4 and Level 5 true self-driving vehicles, there won't be a human driver involved in the driving task.

All occupants will be passengers.

The AI is doing the driving.

Envision a self-driving car that is supposed to get itself onto the flatbed of a tow truck.

We'll assume that the self-driving car is fully operational. This is worthwhile mentioning because any problems associated with the autonomous driving capabilities could readily undermine the capability of the AI driving system to perform this particular driving task.

For example, if the sensors needed for driving weren't working properly, the car isn't likely going to be able to drive itself up that ramp and onto the flatbed. The sensor suite, consisting usually of video cameras, radar, LIDAR, ultrasonic units, and the like, is used to detect the driving environment. Without those devices functioning properly, the AI driving system is essentially blind to the world around the vehicle. By-and-large, the AI driving system is programmed to not proceed with driving if the sensors aren't able to work right.

If this was a scenario whereby the self-driving car was generally inoperable, presumably the tow truck would use the winch to drag the self-driving car up onto the flatbed. This is the same activity that would take place if a conventional car was otherwise inoperable.

One small twist is that it could be that the normal car aspects of the self-driving car are within operable capacity, and only the AI and related self-driving aspects are out-of-whack. In other words, the car might be a fully drivable car, by a human being, assuming that there are still human-drivable driving controls available in the self-driving car.

The future design of self-driving cars is that they will likely eliminate the incorporation of human driving controls. Your first thought might that doing so is counterintuitive. It seems like keeping the driving controls intact would be handy in any circumstance involving the AI driving system being unable to adequately drive the car. A human could takeover.

Well, the counterargument is that a key premise for the advent of self-driving cars is that they will reduce dramatically the annual number of car crashes and fatalities thereof. In the United States alone, there are about 40,000 annual car crash-related fatalities and approximately 2.5 million injuries. Much of that is due to drunk drivers, distracted driving, and other foibles of human drivers. By excising the human driver from behind the wheel, the hope is that the AI driving systems won't incur those kinds of car statistics (AI driving systems won't drive drunk, they won't be distracted, etc.).

Thus, if you retain the human driving controls, you are keeping the door open to human driving, and ergo not going to gain the full semblance of benefits by having AI driving systems. The nightmare is that a human will decide to turn-off the AI driving system, perhaps doing so after coming out of a nighttime bar and having had too much to drink, and opt to drive the vehicle. Rather than allow that temptation, some assert that the best bet is to remove the human-accessible driving controls entirely.

We don't yet know how this will playout. Some insist that no one will ever take away their driving privileges, at least not until you pry their cold dead hands from the steering wheel.

Returning to the flatbed tow truck scenario, assume that the AI driving system of the self-driving car is working fine and that the car aspects of the self-driving car are working fine too. Okay, you might be tempted to assume that the AI driving system will just zip up that ramp and park that self-driving car on the flatbed, doing so like a jet plane that lands on an aircraft carrier deck.

Indeed, perhaps the AI driving system would undertake this flatbed tow truck driving challenge a lot better than the car driver did. We wouldn't expect the AI to be quite so timid as the human driver. By taking the nervousness out of the driving equation, we seem to have a robot-like system that will drive without emotion and therefore drives more straightforwardly.

Going even further, it causes one to wonder whether the AI driving system might do better at this task than the tow truck driver. Since we are comparing the AI driving system to human drivers, we ought to not just look at the car driver that was a neophyte at driving up onto the flatbed. Indubitably, it makes sense to compare to the expert driver, the tow truck driver, having done this same action zillions of times.

In theory, if the AI driving system has been programmed for this kind of driving task, one supposes that it will potentially do a better job than the car driver did. And, there is a chance too that might do the same in terms of equally or besting the tow truck driver (perhaps).

The problem is that the AI driving system probably has not been programmed for this specific kind of driving task.

Keep in mind that the automakers and self-driving tech firms are focusing their energies on getting AI driving systems to drive a car safely from point A to point B, such as going from someone's home to the mall. This involves driving on normal streets and highways. It involves coping with bike riders and pedestrians. And so on.

That alone is a moonshot-like load of car driving difficulties.

Programming an AI driving system to climb up a ramp onto a flatbed is not very high on the list of top priority development efforts. At best, it is on the edge or corner cases list, meaning that it is something identified as eventually worth pursuing, but considered a low priority right now.

Aha, you are thinking, maybe the AI doesn't need specific programming for going up a ramp and parking on the flatbed. Seems like that type of driving is generalizable and can be devised by anyone or anything that knows how to drive.

In other words, pretend we went and found a teenage novice driver. They barely know how to drive a car. We present them with the situation of the flatbed tow truck. Could this newbie driver figure out what to do? The reasonable answer is that yes, they could. The teenager might not like doing so, or might have difficulty with the task, but overall, we can likely agree that they could get the job done.

Unfortunately, there are very few AI driving systems that have that kind of generalizable capability. In fact, we would want to think twice about that kind of capacity. There is a chance that the AI driving system might attempt to drive in inherently dangerous settings. Realize that the AI has absolutely no sense of common sense or common-sense reasoning.

No matter what you might say about a teenager, they do have some modicum of common sense. Sure, go ahead and scoff at this point, but when comparing a thinking human being, albeit an immature one, they still have a common-sense facility that no one has been yet able to get an AI system to imbue. Admittedly, the teenager might "reason" themselves into a really bad situation, and for that, we would all be saddened, though nonetheless they at least had some capacity to reason about what they are doing.

Here's then where this all lands in terms of the flatbed truck scenario.

Unless an AI driving system has been programmed or ostensibly trained to cope with the tow truck matter, the odds are that the AI driving system would be ill-prepared to drive up that ramp.

In addition, the sensors would likely be detecting the tow truck and the flatbed, and not be able to discern what it all portended. In short, the tow truck and its elements would be a blob that is blocking the path forward.

The AI driving system would likely balk at being commanded to drive ahead. There are too many obstacles and seemingly unknown objects that are in the path forward. In a similar manner to how the AI driving system might be programmed to avoid ramming a parked car that is ahead of the self-driving car, by refusing to move forward into the rear-end of a parked car, this same reaction is bound to be the response by the AI driving system to the flatbed truck.

You could say that the AI driving system would "refuse" to try and drive up the ramp. Again, recall that the refusal is not by a conscious effort. This is a refusal in the same manner that you might have a garage door with a built-in obstruction detector that won't finish closing the garage door because an object is in the way.

How can you convince the AI driving system to get up that darned ramp?

Setting aside the earlier point that you could winch the self-driving car up the ramp, which doesn't count per se since the self-driving car is merely a hefty paperweight in that instance (that's not the spirit of the problem being tackled herein), we can consider some other options.

You could try to trick the AI driving system.

Perhaps mask the appearance of the tow truck and its ramp, making it look more like a normal road is ahead of the self-driving car.

This is pretty much a really bad idea.

Some are worried that it might be overly easy to fool a self-driving car into driving in settings that it should not be doing so. Various adversarial attacks have been experimented with. In any case, the idea of doing this even with good intentions (versus evildoer intentions) is also rife with problems and dangers. You might regrettably fool the AI into getting the self-driving car into a quite dicey predicament for everyone involved.

Another approach would be to contact the fleet operator of the self-driving car.

Here's what that means.

Unlike conventional cars, it is anticipated that all self-driving cars will be part of some fleet, of one kind or another. The fleet operator will be able to use OTA (Over-The-Air) electronic communications to download software updates into the on-board AI driving system. Also, the OTA can be used to collect or upload data from the self-driving car, such as the driving scene data that was derived by the sensor suite.

It could be that the AI driving system has a special software-enabled mode or added software component that has been devised to cope with this kind of tow truck flatbed driving scenario. Maybe it hasn't been loaded into the self-driving car as yet, or maybe it is on-board and dormant until activated by an authorized remote indication.

In that case, in theory, the component could be downloaded and then invoked, or if already on-board then simply activated. This is a bit of a stretch in that doing so on-the-fly is rather sketchy, but this does count as a possibility.

Another thought you might have would be to ask a remote operator to take over the driving controls and manually drive the self-driving car up that vaunted ramp.

Well, now you've opened an entire can of worms.

Some self-driving cars are going to be outfitted with remote accessible driving controls, and some will not be so adorned. Those that are opposed to remote accessible driving controls point out that such a capacity could be used by bad actors and in insidious ways. I won't say much more about that here. Even if such remote driving were done by an authorized person, they are reliant upon the electronic communication connection between the vehicle and the agent that is doing the driving.

You might be somewhat okay with the electronic communication delays or disruption that could occur, depending upon the driving setting involved. For example, when a remotely driven rover on another planet is remotely controlled, you have to expect that the communications are time-delayed and fractured. Of course, here on earth, the danger is that the vehicle is potentially surrounded by humans that are going to get hit, and a disruption in the communications linkage could lead to dire consequences.

In short, there is a great deal of controversy about having remote driver accessibility to self-driving cars and you cannot pin your hopes on that kind of feature existing to solve the flatbed truck conundrum that we are discussing.

There is a notable variant of that kind of approach.

The variation is that a remote agent can provide advice to the AI driving system. This is an important distinction, namely between remote driving and the alternative of providing remote guidance or advice. In the use case of remote guidance, the AI driving system is still considered in-charge of the driving task.

The remote human makes recommendations to the AI driving system. The AI driving system must use its own capabilities to then ascertain whether to proceed.

This has various limitations and tradeoffs, somewhat trying to get the best of both worlds, and might be viable to cope with the flatbed tow truck situation.

Conclusion

A self-driving car is not a mule.

That being said, you could assert that at times an AI driving system will be stubborn in terms of "refusing" to drive where you want it to go. The beauty of human driving is that a human can drive however they want, meaning they can drive in places that you wouldn't think a car could go. The downside and ugliness of human driving involve driving places you ought to not go.

Perhaps someday AI systems will be astute and cunning, able to navigate all kinds of driving situations that it has not heretofore seen. Until then, it won't make sense to get mad at the mule, and definitely don't kick one, since it will only hurt your own foot and won't especially bother the AI.

CHAPTER 24
COMPUTER CHIP SHORTAGES AND SELF-DRIVING CARS

Computer chips don't grow on trees.

Imagine if they did.

In that dream world, you could be walking in a forest and find all the micro-chips that you need for your smartphone, laptop, video gaming devices, and the like.

Heck, no need to roam a forest, since the trees lining your local neighborhood would undoubtedly have those prized electronics hanging freely and ready to be plucked whenever so desired. One supposes though that the dangling computer chips might only appear on a seasonal basis, so you'd want to plan for the proper harvesting time and be ready before the chips begin precipitously falling to the ground on their own (ouch, yet another micro-chip bit the dust by a sizable fall from the top of that towering redwood tree!).

Switching back to reality, chipmakers are the ones that make our revered semiconductors, doing so in production facilities and so-called fabs.

Turns out that it is pretty costly to make those sought-after chips. In addition, there is a substantive lead time required from the initial concept of what a chip will be and subsequently manufacturing that chip, ultimately becoming available for everyday use. No magic wands will make this any easier and nor any faster. That being said, there are increasingly sophisticated ways to speed-up the time from design to produced chips, and ways too to bring down the costs, but all-in-all this is going to continue to be a relatively cost-high and long-delayoriented process.

You've undoubtedly seen the blaring headlines recently that decry the existing chip shortages. This is especially bumming out the automotive sector.

Here's why.

Modern-day cars need gobs of computer chips.

Those ubiquitous electronics are found within nearly all aspects of a contemporary automobile. The braking system, yes, likely has some micro-chips. The transmission, sure, indubitably has micro-chips involved. We can go on like this all day long. Beyond the driving-oriented elements, there are chips needed for those fancy in-car infotainment systems that blare out those wonderful tunes and display captivating cat videos while you are on a driving journey. Etc.

If cars were the only source of demand for chips, perhaps there might be large stockpiles waiting at the doors of the automakers. Of course, the automakers need to compete with the hunger and thirst for computer chips as exhibited by all other electronic-using contraptions. Smartphone makers want chips. Refrigerator makers want chips (we certainly do need "smart" refrigerators). Anybody that makes something that can be enhanced or stand tall by adding a computer chip is either already on that bandwagon or eagerly soon going to join the parade.

In short, automakers need to stand in line with all those other fevered buyers of chips.

This brings up the equally important factor that ordering computer chips is a dicey game.

Suppose an automaker wants computer chips for their cars and realizes that the timing involves a years-ahead prediction of how many chips will be needed, based on the volume of cars anticipated to be made and sold. So, a guess is made at the need for some high number of chips to be delivered. These will ultimately be included in the cars during their assembly and manufacturing of the cars.

Meanwhile, imagine additionally that the upcoming future market for car purchases is starting to dry up and the initial rosy predictions were off-base. Darn, all those computer chips are not going to be needed. But that won't matter to the chipmakers that are churning out the chips since they will insist that the automaker ordered them and will need to receive them, regardless of what the automaker opts to do with the vaunted pieces of electronic wizardry.

You might be thinking that it would be wiser for the automaker to have originally lowballed the number of needed chips. Thus, if the prediction for future sales began to diminish, they would not be high-and-dry with those unused computer chips. The tough problem of course is that if demand is high, and you don't have the chips, this means that those cars aren't going to be made that could have been selling like hotcakes.

Though this admittedly is a somewhat simplistic portrayal of the global situation, you likely get the gist that there is a fine line to walk in terms of how many chips an automaker should be ordering. If you aim too low, this could mean that you won't be able to have enough chips to meet demand and will lose out on selling cars that people would have readily bought. If you aim too high, you could end-up with pallets upon costly pallets of unused computer chips that you've paid good money for and are now overpriced doorstops.

For the overall nature of today's supply chain for computer chips, predictably is king.

Returning to the woes facing automakers right now, they had to make predictions last year about their future car sales and accordingly adjusted when the pandemic came along. Some assert that their pullback in chip orders has now left them somewhat flatfooted. When the demand for chips is coming from all angles, the automakers cannot just hop to the front of the line for those savory micro-chips.

The catchphrase being used is *car-chip pain.*

Others are describing the whole matter as a self-inflicted wound.

Those are fighting words for some, and they would argue that the problem has to do with insufficient available capacity to produce chips. Were there more capacity, it wouldn't matter that the lead time forecasts were misaligned. Assuredly, if you want to get into an unpleasant fistfight with someone in the automotive industry, merely bring up the semiconductor "shortage" issue and be ready for a quite bruising discourse on the heated topic.

Anyone that is not currently in the market seeking to buy a car is probably amused by the whole conundrum and could care less that the automotive sector is feeling the squeeze of insufficiently available micro-chips. People that own stocks of automakers are likely watching the unfolding situation with rapt attention. Obviously, the automakers are anxiously trying to figure out what to do and probably are having daily nightmares, staying awake at night over the situation, and ever hopeful of dealing adequately with the dilemma.

Shifting gears, keep in mind that the future of cars will consist of true self-driving cars (I'll explain the word "true" in a moment).

I bring this up because the same type of conundrum or challenge will undoubtedly occur whence self-driving cars become available. You see, self-driving cars are going to need even more of those micro-chips than a normal conventional car requires.

Think of self-driving cars as a micro-chips bonanza on steroids.

Assuming that the same or similar issues about the supply chain and the back-and-forth of chip availability will prevail in the future, this means that the same disruption or perturbations could impact the making of self-driving cars. A maker of self-driving cars will need to render a prediction of how many self-driving cars they plan on making in some timeframe ahead, and chip makers will produce the requested chips accordingly. But, suppose the self-driving car predicted volume is too low or too high? Once again, akin to today's woes, it could be that the number of self-driving cars able to be produced would be undercut by not enough chips, or the makers of the self-driving cars could get stuck with too many chips.

Some pundits claim that this will not happen because the number of predicted self-driving cars will be readily predictable, meaning that the automakers and the chipmakers will be seamlessly aligned and dancing with great aplomb. There won't be any chip shortages for self-driving cars, and there won't be any untoward overages of micro-chips for self-driving cars, so they assert.

This is the proverbial Goldilocks envisioned future for self-driving cars and micro-chips. The porridge won't be too hot and it won't be too cold. Instead, it will be just the right temperature.

Sorry, that seems like a wee bit of a fairytale.

This brings up today's intriguing question to ponder: *Will AI-based true self-driving cars get caught by these miseries of prediction-affliction and at times suffer the angst of car-chip pain, or will they skate along freely and be in micro-chip heaven?*

Let's unpack the matter and see.

Self-Driving Cars And Those Micro-Chips

For Level 4 and Level 5 true self-driving vehicles, there won't be a human driver involved in the driving task.

All occupants will be passengers.

The AI is doing the driving.

AI is most definitely not a free lunch.

To have a suitable AI driving system, you need lots of computer chips. For example, there are specialized computer chips for the Machine Learning and Deep Learning aspects of AI capabilities. Also, computer chips are running the AI algorithms for keeping track of the driving scene and planning the actions needed for undertaking the driving task. There are computer chips needed for the sensors that are used by a self-driving car. You've got the video cameras, radar, LIDAR, ultrasonic devices, and the rest of the extensive sensor suite, all of them utilizing various computer chips.

Chips, chips, and more chips.

And that's just the micro-chips that are devoted to the AI driving system. A self-driving car is still a car and thus this requires all those other computer chips that go into the same uses that occur in a conventional car. For whatever amount of chips embedded into a conventional car, including a car with ADAS, make sure to increase that number by the additional chips constituting the AI driving system facilities for a self-driving car.

I don't think anyone can argue that AI-based true self-driving cars aren't going to be chip gobbling beasts.

One aspect that silo-focused pundits oftentimes don't do is think about the world beyond the realm of self-driving cars. In short, self-driving cars won't be the only seeker of micro-chips. You can certainly expect that the incorporation of chips and AI-based capabilities will inhabit all manner of other types of electronic systems.

The point is that once again, there is going to be fierce competition over the availability of computer chips, by just about everyone that walks and breathes. Self-driving cars will be amid the computer chip insatiable demand.

The question is whether self-driving cars will be able to get their portion of the chip pie.

This is where some paths begin to diverge.

Some believe that the adoption of self-driving cars will be a smooth curve that gradually builds and can be perfectly predicted.

In this scenario, there are initially those timid and tiny tryouts of true self-driving cars. Out of those tryouts becomes confidence that self-driving cars can be expanded in terms of their adoption. There will be a somewhat slow up-curve as efforts ramp-up, and then it will climb like wildfire.

The reason for the leap in the curve will be that people will crave the advantages of self-driving cars. No longer will you need to find a human driver to give you a lift. Self-driving cars have a driver already included, namely an AI-based system that doesn't tire, doesn't need food breaks and will work tirelessly and 24x7 without any qualms or complaints. The public will tend to eschew human-driven cars in favor of using self-driving cars.

Furthermore, it is anticipated that self-driving cars are not going to drink and drive, nor drive while distracted. There are currently about 40,000 annual fatalities in the United States alone due to car crashes and around 2.5 million injuries as a result. Those horrific stats are principally attributed to the foibles of human driving. The hope and assumption are that the number of car crashes is going to drop enormously by the use of self-driving cars and a concomitant reduction in the use of human-driven cars.

Overall, the emphasis related to computer chips is that the rollout of self-driving cars will be as easy to forecast as it is to fall off a log.

By having a quite predictable semblance of how many self-driving cars will be produced, year after year, in the many years ahead, it will be relatively straightforward to line-up the needed chip supply. Chipmakers will know far in-advance what capacity to put in place and can nearly fall asleep at the wheel as they let their plants crank out those wonderments of technology.

You can even put aside the difficulties associated with competition for computer chips, since the makers of self-driving cars will be able to "guarantee" what their demand consists of, and the chipmakers will have a nice steady sales flow to the self-driving car businesses, meanwhile contending with the fluidity and staggered fluctuations with the rest of the chips-desiring marketplace.

Those self-driving cars are the ideal cash cow for chipmakers.

No more car-chip bellyaches or pains, and you can relax on the sunny beaches of Hawaii as you delight in the car-chip nirvana involving self-driving cars.

Hold on for a moment, that above picturesque imagery seems rather quaint, akin to an enchanting storybook. Since I earlier invoked the fable of Goldilocks, perhaps now might be a handy moment to recall the famed story of the emperor that had no clothes. I mention this because the aforementioned idealized vision for the adoption of self-driving cars seems just a tad over-the-top.

Let's revisit how the future rollout of self-driving cars is more likely to occur, including all the unfettered grime and sordid gristle.

First, realize that the existing tryouts of Level 4 self-driving cars involve an Operational Design Domain (ODD). The ODD refers to the aspect that the self-driving car will only function within a stated operational domain, such as perhaps within a boxed geographical area and only when particular weather conditions exist (sunny versus rainy, snow versus no snow, etc.), and so on. The ODD varies by the brand of a self-driving car and can vary too by the model of a self-driving car within a given brand.

The point is that even if a particular self-driving car brand can showcase sufficiently that it seems safe to be used, this is going to primarily be bounded by whatever ODD the self-driving car is operating under. This does not immediately imply that the self-driving car can be used anywhere else that you want to adopt that same brand, and in fact, the notion is that it won't be readily applied to other areas that are beyond the tested ODD.

This becomes a kind of bottleneck in expanding the self-driving car brand adoption. Only until the ODD is widened and tested sufficiently would the self-driving car be viable for adoption in other areas that require a more suitable ODD.

That is one gotcha as it relates to forecasting the volume of self-driving cars.

Another catch will be the safety topic.

Right now, almost everyone in the self-driving car industry is holding their breath. The reason for this being on edge is that we all know that if even one instance occurs of a self-driving car that somehow gets involved in a car crash and someone is killed (recall the Phoenix prior instance, as covered extensively), the full weight of regulators and public opinion about self-driving cars could turn on a dime, overnight.

The counterargument about being overly reactive to one such instance is that the use of self-driving cars is projected to ultimately save lives, in terms of reducing demonstratively the 40,000 car crash-related deaths occurring annually in the U.S. In short, suppose that the number of car crash-related fatalities dropped in half (just for sake of discussion), we should all be heralding the vast number of lives saved. In that sense, if one person let's say is harmed, and certainly, all lives are precious and vital, the matter ought to be viewed in the context of the overall number of lives being saved, one might assert.

Reality suggests that even one such instance will be a staggering blow to all self-driving car initiatives. There will be an immense inspection of the self-driving cars arena in a manner that heretofore has not taken place. Currently, things are relatively quiet since there haven't been any recent clear-cut self-driving car blowback incidents.

The outcry and clamor will be deafening if triggered into action. And, mark my words, that time will come.

From the computer chips perspective, this suggests that the predictability of self-driving car adoption is once again hampered. You can make all the predictions you want, but if the big freeze suddenly happens due to regulatory oversight or public outrage, those forecasts go out the window.

We also don't know how things are going to go in terms of whether people will avidly want to ride in self-driving cars. The argument made about the ease of going for a ride and not having to find a human driver is one side of the coin. Other sides of the coin include that perhaps some people won't trust the AI driving system, some people won't like interacting with an AI system and will prefer to have a human driver, and so on.

There is a sinking feeling among some that this building of a better mousetrap might not be grandly and immediately accepted by the world at large. We all tend to assume that by-gosh if self-driving cars were to exist, they would be irresistible and they would be needed by all. This is not the kind of assumption that you can necessarily take to the bank.

Conclusion

Do not misinterpret the somewhat doomsday appearing remarks as though self-driving cars aren't going to make the cut. I am a firm and fervent believer in the future of self-driving cars. The real point to the portrayal of the self-driving car adoption lifecycle is that it is not going to be as rosy as some might imagine or that they are pitching with glee. The real-world of rolling out self-driving cars are going to be a battle. There will be moments of great success, and other instances of setbacks and difficulties.

Trying to make a nice-looking curve out of the starts and stops of self-driving car adoption does not comport with what will really happen. It is going to be jagged, ups and downs, and not something that you can layout as though the numbers of self-driving cars and the needed numbers of computer chips are superbly going to be aligned.

As the tale of Little Red Riding Hood informs us, a seemingly peaceful and uneventful trip ahead is not always in the cards. There are wolves assuredly in the way of self-driving car widespread adoption, and will inexorably upend any expectation of a delightful and smooth romp in these woodlands.

Might as well face it, there will be computer chip shortages that get entangled in the arrival of self-driving cars. The happy side of that face is that self-driving cars will persevere and there will ultimately be a massive boon, in both self-driving cars and the shortages of computer chips for them

CHAPTER 25
CHASING DOGS AND SELF-DRIVING CARS

Dogs love to chase after all kinds of things such as weathered tennis balls or worn-out frisbees.

Unfortunately, dogs also delight in chasing after passing cars, which is a really bad idea.

If you've ever witnessed first-hand as a brazen dog wildly ran to catch a car coming swiftly down your neighborhood street, it is a quite scary affair and will undoubtedly make your heartbeat uncontrollably. One possibility is that the driver decides to swerve or hit the brakes, any of which might end up with the dog getting hit by the car. More likely, and usually with a more adverse outcome, some other upcoming car will not see the dog that is running in the street and will accidentally ram smackdab into or entirely run over the canine.

We know that these pell-mell pursuits of a moving car are fraught with grave danger.

Dogs might not realize the peril and instead perceive the car as a shiny object that is well-worth chasing. In some ways, it seems like a fun game for the dog to be playing, at least that's what the dog is possibly thinking. Those brash dogs that undertake this form of a daredevil sporting endeavor are usually trying to catch up with the moving vehicle, and at least are not running face-forward into the path of the car per se.

If the car keeps going on its existing traversal, ostensibly away from the pursuing pooch, the odds are that the dog won't reach the vehicle and will by happenstance escape the particular danger of getting entangled with the car. Still, there is the frightening aspect that the animal is likely now stranded in the middle of the street and other cars could fail to spy the beloved hound.

Some believe that dogs chase after cars as part of a herding instinct. Maybe in the minds-eye of a dog, the car is akin to a ferocious wolf and the dog is saving all the rest of us from the wickedness of a vicious wolf-pack style attack. Another theory is that the dog is merely utilizing its innate ability to stalk after prey. This seems somewhat questionable since the dog is typically making all sorts of howling noises and not slinking quietly up upon the passing car, but it nonetheless could be a strategy used for capturing quarry that potentially works in the wild and therefore might work on everyday streets.

It is hard to know what the dog is thinking.

Perhaps there is fear involved. The dog might be intrinsically fearful of this large-sized unknown object that is steadily moving along. A reaction to the fear could be to lash out at the massive thing and try to stop it or maybe damage it. Some say this shows how gutsy dogs can sometimes be. This same possibility relates to the dog as a heroic figure, trying to save the pedestrians and other humans walking around from the mysterious contraption that seemingly endangers everyone in the vicinity.

Trying to make somewhat lighter remarks, some jokingly suggest the dog wants to catch and keep the car as a prized possession. Imagine how impressed the other dogs in the community would be if the capturing dog was able to showcase that they had wrangled a car to the ground and dragged it back to their private doghouse. One supposes that the proud winning dog might even dig a large hole and try to bury the car, as though the vehicle was the largest bone that the dog had ever managed to collect.

You might go so far as to suggest that the dog wants to drive the car.

Some say the real reason a dog chases after a car is because it can.

Let's dig into that remark a bit more so.

Assuming that a human owner is responsible for the dog, that person is allowing the pooch to do something it shouldn't be doing. In essence, it is the fault of the human and not particularly the fault of the dog. People ought to take care of their dogs and either keep their pets from being freely able to chase after a car or as a minimum train their dogs to decidedly not partake in such a hazardous practice, goes this logic.

Sure, it can be challenging to teach a dog to not chase after cars. The arduous task can involve hours upon hours of careful and conscientious effort with your treasured pet. There isn't much argument about the difficulties involved. That being said, the time is well spent and necessary for the well-being of all parties.

The other obvious point to be made is that if a dog is routinely kept on a leash, for which most locales have pointed leash laws, there is not much chance that a dog can indeed chase after a car. Unless the human relinquishes the leash or allows their dog out of a fenced area, presumably the opportunity to actively give chase after a car is nearly nonexistent.

Of course, slipups can occur. The most faithful of owners could inadvertently let the leash escape from their grasp while walking their dog, especially if the enthused animal suddenly and surprisingly darts away without any warning. Or perhaps a fenced area has a gate that wasn't properly locked, and the dog shoved at the potential opening while fiercely intent on watching that car travel down the street. For those myriads of reasons, training a dog to not chase a car has added merits.

Why all this talk about dogs chasing cars?

Consider that the future of cars consists of self-driving cars. In the case of true self-driving cars, there won't be a human driver at the wheel. An AI driving system will be in charge of the driving controls and determining how the car will be driven.

Tying together these two topics, it will be important for AI driving systems and thus self-driving cars to be able to contend with dogs that opt to chase cars. Yes, it would seem just as likely that a dog might chase a self-driving car as they would a human-driven car.

Today's intriguing question is this: *How will an AI-based true self-driving car contend with dogs that chase cars and can we rest easy knowing that those self-driving cars will do the right thing?*

Let's unpack the matter and see.

Self-Driving Cars And Those Dogs That Chase Cars

For Level 4 and Level 5 true self-driving vehicles, there won't be a human driver involved in the driving task.

All occupants will be passengers.

The AI is doing the driving.

One aspect to immediately discuss entails the fact that today's AI is not sentient. In other words, the AI is altogether a collective of computer-based programming and algorithms, and most assuredly not able to reason in the same manner that humans can. For example, current AI lacks any semblance of common sense and nor has any kind of common-sense reasoning.

This is important to keep in mind when considering the matter of a dog that chases after a self-driving car.

A human driver would realize the significance of a chasing dog. The driver would comprehend that a dog is, well, a dog. It can scamper and run. It can do things that aren't wise to do. It can veer this way and that way, nearly erratically. The dog might pursue the chasing car and abruptly decide it has had enough and come to a halt. Or the dog might run up onto lawns and across homes to try and reach the car, thus not taking a straight path toward reaching the in-motion vehicle.

None of that is "understood" within an AI driving system, and even if the AI driving system is programmed to cope with the act of dogs that chase cars, keep in mind that the programming is only programming and does not have the robustness of human thinking intertwined.

Consider this weighty facet in a somewhat different light.

Suppose you had a teenage novice driver that was just initially in the throes of learning to drive. The neophyte is barely able to use the pedals and the steering wheel, in the sense that they are unsure of how to perform the driving task.

If that teenager was driving in a local neighborhood and all of a sudden a dog started to give chase, there is no question that the young adult would indubitably comprehend the significance of what a dog is, how a dog acts, and the qualms associated with having a dog chasing their car. Unless the teenager has been living in a cave their whole life, they would inarguably know what dogs are and what they can do.

I'm not suggesting that the novice driver would know what to do in such a driving circumstance and simply emphasizing that the human driver would realize the nature of dogs. This goes into the earlier exhortation about a semblance of common sense. Despite those that might chortle about ascribing common sense to teenagers, you must admit that a teenager is quite likely to have rather extensive knowledge and awareness about dogs.

An AI driving system of today is unlikely to have anything at all that provides background about dogs. There is no overarching reason to go to the trouble to infuse this kind of information into an AI driving system at this time (exceptions do apply). The developers have enough on their hands in terms of getting a self-driving car to be able to safely go from point A to point B, and thus the so-called edge case or corner case involving a chasing dog is very low on the priority list.

In essence, the AI driving system might do something like this.

First, realize that the sensors of the self-driving car usually include video cameras, radar, LIDAR, ultrasonic units, and the like. These are akin to being the eyes and ears of the AI driving system. Via those sensors, the AI driving system interprets the data being collected and attempts to discern the driving scene. Aspects include notable particulars such as where is the roadway, are there are other cars nearby, are there pedestrians nearby, and so on.

Trying to detect a dog is not particularly easy.

Dogs tend to be relatively low to the ground. Their movement can be quite quick. With pedestrians, you can oftentimes examine a visual image to figure out which way a pedestrian is possibly going to turn, or whether they have got their arms out and maybe are going to run into the street. Trying to do a similar analysis about dogs is relatively hard to do.

So, you've got a dog, as an object, which is low to the ground, moving fast, and difficult to predict in terms of what the object might do.

On top of those complexities, let's assume the dog is coming up toward the self-driving car, doing so from behind the vehicle. By-and-large, the focus of the sensors and the AI driving system has to do with what's ahead of the car, not especially what is behind the car (obviously, another car that is coming up fast from behind and that might ram the self-driving car is a vital consideration, though realize that another vehicle is a relatively larger object, more commonly expected, and generally easier to detect and predict).

All in all, the bad news for the dogs that chase cars are that few if any self-driving cars of today are prepared to cope with the specifics of a dog that is chasing the car. There are (at this time) not many AI driving systems that have a pre-programmed response to deal with a chasing dog. And, as mentioned, even trying to detect the dog is problematic, to begin with.

In the discussion earlier it was pointed out that the car being chased is perhaps less likely to end-up striking a dog and it might be more likely that other nearby cars might do so, assuming that there is other traffic. In that use case, the odds are a little better about the AI-based self-driving cars because they are perhaps diligently scanning the area and trying to continually ferret out what is going on in the driving scene.

Human drivers oftentimes will drive while distracted, ironically watching cat videos just when a dog happens to be in the middle of the street. The hope is that AI driving systems will be as safe or possibly safer than human drivers, partially due to the lack of distractions and also since the AI won't be drinking and driving.

In short, one can be somewhat hopeful that if a self-driving car comes upon a situation wherein a dog is chasing after a car that is ahead of the self-driving car, there is some semblance of a chance that the AI driving system might detect the dog. Though the AI might not be able to classify what the object is, nonetheless, there is an object that has been detected and is presumably in the roadway, thus, it becomes an object to be given due consideration.

Most AI driving systems would interpret the object as something to be tracked and monitored, waiting to ascertain what the detected object is going to do. From the AI programming viewpoint, the object might just as well be a tumbleweed that has come onto the street and is weaving to and fro. Of course, a car can ram into a tumbleweed if needed, but ramming into a dog or other living creature is a different matter.

We can add a variety of twists to this dilemma.

A human driver is driving along, and a dog starts to chase after the moving car. A self-driving car is behind the car that is being chased by the dog. One concern involves the dog. Another concern involves the potential actions of the human driver.

Envision that the human driver in this scenario decides to "freak out" and slams on their brakes. Maybe the person believes that the best course of action is to come to a sudden halt. The dog will then be able to catch-up with the car. The human driver doesn't have to worry about running over the dog since the car is now at a standstill.

Seems like impeccable logic.

Don't though forget that there is another car immersed in this driving scenario, namely the self-driving car that is behind the human-driven car. It is conceivable that the abrupt act of the human driver might lead to the self-driving car rear-ending the human-driven car. This could certainly happen too if the car that was behind the stopped car was being driven by a person, and thus you cannot somehow ascribe that this would only happen to an AI-based self-driving car.

The crux of this twist is that the AI driving system has to be programmed to anticipate the reactions of other objects in the driving scene, including what the human-driven cars are going to do or react in response to the bolting dog.

Another object that might get involved in this expanding scenario could be a pedestrian or perhaps a slew of pedestrians, all of whom suddenly decide they will come into the street to try and save the dog. You can easily imagine this kind of reaction. People that see a dog in danger are likely to take dangerous actions themselves, doing so in hopes of saving the dog and without necessarily giving due thought to their own safety, and nor the safety of the passengers in the cars entangled in the entire affair.

The point is that a dog chasing a car can be an entangling web of activities that rapidly unfold or evolve while the driving action is underway. If you only construe the matter as one dog and one car, you have demonstrably understated the nature of the problem and the life-or-death consequences that can arise.

Conclusion

Some believe that dogs won't chase after a self-driving car.

Here's why they say this.

Dogs are aware today that a human is at the wheel, presumably being able to see the person, and therefore they are chasing not merely a car, they are also chasing the person. Since an AI-based true self-driving car does not have a human driver at the wheel, dogs will no longer feel any need or incentive to chase after cars.

Sorry, but as they say, that logic won't hunt.

First, it seems questionable to assume that dogs can connect the notion that a car is being driven by a human with the aspect that this big shiny object is coming down the street. In many cases, the human driver is not readily seen anyway. All in all, the odds are higher than the dog is chasing the car, and not somehow trying to chase the human driver (to clarify, sure, there are rarer instances of the dog spying their owner driving a car and wanting to follow their owner, that kind of situation).

Secondly, there are going to be passengers inside self-driving cars. Not all of the time, since it is abundantly possible for self-driving cars to be roaming around without passengers, or possibly doing a delivery chore and there is no need for any riders inside. In any case, for likely much of the time, there are going to be people riding inside self-driving cars.

Can the dog distinguish between humans that are driving a car versus humans merely residing in a car?

Look, I am the first to say that dogs are darned smart, and we ought to give them immense credit, but it seems rather farfetched to claim that dogs principally choose to chase cars due to there being a human driver at the wheel, and furthermore that these savvy pooches would ergo also mentally calculate that human riders inside a self-driving car are not serving as human drivers.

Since my dog does the balancing of my checkbook each month for me, I'll bring this up during the time that we have together for doing my accounting and see what the dog says. Probably will cost me some of his favored dog biscuits, but it will be worth it to find out exactly why dogs do indeed chase cars.

I'll let you know.

CHAPTER 26
ROLLING HOUSE AND SELF-DRIVING CARS

Sometimes, you can be quite surprised by what you might see on the sunny streets of San Francisco.

For example, this proverbial City by the Bay is a Silicon Valley favorite right now, allowing an abundance of self-driving cars to crisscross the steep hills and teeming streets, doing so in a visionary flurry of experimental tryouts for emergent driverless cars.

If that isn't enough of an unusual scenery for you, there is something else that San Francisco also is known for, namely houses that from time-to-time are rolling throughout the avenues and keep afar from the fabled cable cars. Though some have jokingly said that these slinking along homes have a mind of their home, the reality is that there is a long history of putting treasured houses up on giant dollies and moving them to other parts of town.

To be clear, there are humans at the wheel of those moving homes (not ghosts and nor any venerated AI-based driving systems).

In this latest case, a picturesque Victorian home that is popularly known as the Englander House was moved to make way for a proposed apartment complex. One supposes the easiest path would have been to simply demolish the now outdated and somewhat dilapidated house, crushing it to the bone and carting away the remains. Instead, the more than five-thousand square-foot structure was carefully and gently rolled to a new spot, which though admittedly only six blocks away, nonetheless constituted a heck of a distance to cart an entire two-story home (you might think of this as the celebrated notion of having seen *it* on Mulberry Street, though in this case, the street names differed).

By lifting the home onto rollable wheels, the affair became one of trying to navigate the winding and hilly streets of famed San Francisco, known as being one of the hilliest cities in the world. Fortunately, no need, in this case, to try and shove the house across the Golden Gate Bridge. The local streets that would witness the inching along house were prepared beforehand to make way. This included cutting back overstretched tree limbs, removing parking meters, temporarily taking down road signs that were potential obstructions, and the like.

You might be wondering whether the posted speed limit sign was perhaps also removed, and in which case, could the house opt to sprint its way to the new location. Sorry to disappoint, the speed limit still applied, though it wasn't a consideration since the rolling process had a top speed of about 1 mile per hour anyway. No sense in laying out rubber on the roadway from doing any kind of tire screeching starts or donuts, and just make sure that the house safely reached its ultimate destination.

Here's a question for you.

Suppose you were driving your car in San Francisco on that particular day, and also assume that you did not know beforehand that a house was being moved. In that scenario, you would have been quietly driving along, minding your own business, and upon turning a corner on some ordinary street there would suddenly be looming ahead of you a house.

Mind you, not a house that was on the sides of the street and sitting still, nailed to the perch, but instead a home smack dab in the middle of the street. Perhaps you would end-up going head-to-head with this menacing figure. In a street duel involving going face to face with a house versus a car, consider the likely winner of this driving battle. The house weighs a lot more and has quite a hefty size advantage, while your car is nimble and can make circles around the snail-paced home.

I'd bet that most drivers would have let the house win.

The odds are that you would have been caught off-guard at seeing a house coming down the street toward you. Since this was happening in slow motion, you would have plenty of time to take in the sight and mentally calculate what was taking place. Other than a mild surprise and perhaps giving you a bit of a chuckle, it seems likely that you would have taken the matter in stride.

That being said, it is not every day that you manage to observe a house in the middle of the roadway and that is moving along too. Someone visiting San Francisco as a tourist might immediately assume it was a touristy act being undertaken by the authorities that run Frisco, possibly attempting to gain renewed attention to the Golden Gate City. I suspect that it would be easy to shrug off the experience and maybe make a posting on social media in a nonchalant manner, doing a trendy insta-bragging or a so-called humble-brag about what you just saw.

The odds are that you would have made a U-turn and made your way beyond the reach of the iceberg-slow moving house. Of course, the reality is that you probably would not have gotten especially close to the being-moved home anyway. There were plenty of barricades and road closures, along with bright and flashing warning signs and police enforcing the right-of-way for this Victorian-style masterpiece.

All told, a human driver would have presumably remained calm and at most been curious about how a house managed to get onto the street. Despite never having seen such a roadway condition before (how many of us have ever experienced a rolling home coming down the street?), a person witnessing such a spectacle can readily make a mental sense of what they are seeing.

It is a house. It is on the street. It is slowly moving. It poses no immediate danger. I can drive away without difficulty. That's the extent of the driving mental contortions, and the remaining cognitive action can entail the why and how of the story behind a house confronting you while on a normal driving journey.

Shifting gears, the future of cars consists of self-driving cars. The AI-based *true* self-driving cars are driven entirely by an AI driving system. There isn't a human at the wheel, and in fact, the expectation is that most self-driving cars will not provide any provision of human-accessible driving controls. The AI will be the sole driver and no human will directly be involved.

This gives rise to today's intriguing question: *What would a self-driving car do when suddenly facing a house that was moving down the middle of the street?*

Let's unpack the matter and see.

Self-Driving Cars And Those Rolling Houses

For Level 4 and Level 5 true self-driving vehicles, there won't be a human driver involved in the driving task.

All occupants will be passengers.

The AI is doing the driving.

One aspect to immediately discuss entails the fact that today's AI is not sentient. In other words, the AI is altogether a collective of computer-based programming and algorithms, and most assuredly not able to reason in the same manner that humans can. For example, current AI lacks any semblance of common sense and nor has any kind of common-sense reasoning.

This is important to keep in mind when considering the matter of a house coming down the middle of a street on a driving trek.

Humans comprehend that the object ahead of them is a house. Houses are usually not in the middle of the street. Houses rarely move, other than perhaps shifting here and there due to earth movement or seismic activity. Overall, a human would readily grasp that this is an unusual situation and would realize that this Victorian house is in the wrong place and doing something it should not be doing, namely cruising along on a presumably active street meant for cars, bikes, motorcycles, vans, and the like.

The house is altogether out of place. A human would reason that there must be some logical explanation for this oddball circumstance. How could a house get into the street? It is not as though a house is like a pet dog that got off its leash and sneaked out to play in the middle of the roadway. A house is not a dog. Houses do not customarily of their own volition opt to stray.

A quick visual scan of the driving scene would undoubtedly showcase the special roadway and moving crews that were shlepping along with the house. The street would be barren of all of the usual trappings that you'd expect to see on a typical everyday roadway. Thus, even if you somehow did not notice the blizzard of warning signs and somehow avoided getting stopped by those esteemed guardians securing the route, you nonetheless would reason about what you are seeing and be able to turn the extraordinary setting into something sensible and understandable.

What would an AI driving system do?

As mentioned, today's AI is not sentient. It cannot "reason" in the manner that humans can. Let's trace the technological aspects of what might occur.

The odds are that the sensors would detect that things were amiss. Self-driving cars are loaded with various sensors such as video cameras, radar, LIDAR, ultrasonic devices, and the like. You can certainly assume that all of those sensors are pretty much going to detect a house that is sitting in the middle of the street.

Realize though that the various sensors each have their own range of detection. This means that some of the sensors would sooner detect the object than others. Within the AI driving system, there is a function or component that undertakes Multi-Sensor Data Fusion (MSDF). This capability is programmed to compare and contrast the results of the sensor data collections and try to resolve any differences and also amplify any similarities. The visual imaging interpretations would be indicating that a large object is blocking the roadway. The radar and LIDAR would likewise be reporting that a large object is straight ahead. Etc.

The AI driving system maintains a virtual world model, essentially an internal frame of reference about what the outside world of the surrounding driving scene seems to consist of. Based on the sensor data and the algorithmic interpretation of the sensor indications, the AI driving system likely would make a mark in the virtual world model that something rather monstrous in size is blocking the roadway ahead.

Notice that I have carefully worded that description to refer to the thing as an object and not refer to it as a house.

We don't know that the AI driving system would necessarily classify the massive object as a house per se. For some AI driving systems, a house is considered an object that sits outside of the roadway. It could be the case that the AI driving system would be trying to compare the house to objects that are usually found within the path of the street, such as other cars, trucks, moving vans, pedestrians, and the like.

The AI doesn't "know" that a house is a house, at least not in the manner that you and I understand the meaning of the word. Any programming related to the object that is being called a "house" would likely have simple attributes associated with it. There is no semblance of realization that a house can have a family that grew-up within the home and lived a wonderful life there, enjoying the company of others and the raising of children, and so on.

Consider for a moment all of the memories and thoughts you might embody about the nature of houses and homes. Essentially, none of that robust wealth of knowledge and understanding is within the reach of today's AI systems.

Okay, we hopefully all agree that the AI driving system is unaware of what a house per se is (and, please avoid anthropomorphizing AI). At this juncture of the step-by-step exploration, the AI driving system has detected a large-sized object, taking up the majority of the ahead driving scene. This is beyond the size of a tumbleweed. It is beyond the size of a piece of furniture that might have dropped off the back of a truck.

All told, the odds are that the AI driving system would feed this indication about a colossal blockage up ahead into the portion of the driving system that plans what to do next. The routing algorithm would potentially have various digital maps and would refer to the maps. If the street ahead is unavailable for traversal, the AI driving system would be seeking to identify an alternative path.

We can assume that the self-driving car would seemingly aim to make a U-turn, and head some other way, utilizing other streets to avoid getting blocked by the object on this particular street.

In that case, consider this matter from the perspective of a car. A human driver would likely have made a U-turn and found some other path to proceed. An AI driving system would also have likely made a U-turn and opted to take a different route to proceed on its driving journey. If you were standing on the street and watching a car that came up to the situation, you would see the car make a U-turn and try to navigate away from the house coming down the roadway.

Could you immediately discern whether the car was being driven by a human versus being driven by an AI driving system?

Not really.

Sure, if you could see into the car, you would obviously have seen a human sitting in the driver's seat in the case of the human-driven car, and you would presumably have observed that there wasn't anyone sitting in the driver's seat of the self-driving car. In that manner, you could readily tell the difference.

But suppose you couldn't see into the car or the car was far enough away that you couldn't discern the nature of what might or might be inside the car. From the external behavior of the car, you would not seemingly be able to discern whether it was being human-driven or being driven by an AI driving system.

Is that good or bad?

Well, you have now reached a vociferous question that many are scratching their heads about.

On the one hand, yes, the AI driving system seemed to do the same thing that a human driver would have done. That seems reassuring.

Per my aforementioned depiction about the AI driving system, you undoubtedly realize that the AI didn't know anything at all about a house or a home, at least in comparison to a human. In this specific setting, it would seem that not "knowing" about houses or homes did not make a notable or discernible difference. The resulting driving actions were the same.

Not all driving actions are of the same ilk.

There are driving actions that entail human thinking that AI driving systems are not yet able to attain, and for which it is unclear if such AI will ever be possible. As such, the AI driving systems are going to be quite rudimentary and lacking in the depth of comprehension that humans have and that humans seemingly leverage when driving a car.

Some worry that as a society we are going to piecemeal allow ourselves into having self-driving cars on our roadways that seem or appear to be driving as though a human was at the wheel, and yet the AI driving system is not even in the same ballpark as human cognition.

The other side of that coin is that humans have all kinds of human foibles that come to play when they are driving. There are about 40,000 car crash-related fatalities each year in the United States alone and approximately 2.5 million related injuries.

Much of those statistics are due to drunk driving and distracted driving. The AI driving systems won't be driving while drunk and will not be watching cat videos when driving the vehicle.

Are we willing to trade off the advantages of AI driving systems over the foibles of human drivers, though also realizing that the AI is not sentient?

We will need to accept the notion that the AI will be of a merely mechanical and programmatic capability, and overcome a false sense that the AI is of caliber with human thinking and intrinsic human capabilities.

Conclusion

You might have been surprised to discover that the mere presence of a slowly rolling house in the middle of a street could spur this kind of illustrious discussion.

Turns out fortuitously that the quirkiness and mystery of a house existing where it is not expected serves as a marvelous foil upon which to reveal the oft unspoken aspects about AI and the capabilities of today's AI driving systems.

The day-to-day acts of self-driving cars starting to roam our streets can inadvertently lull us into assuming that AI driving systems are the same as human drivers, embodying the same cognitive capacities, and meanwhile excising the adverse role of human emotions and human faults that occur while driving a car.

There is no free lunch.

The AI driving systems are limited in what they can do. A tough tradeoff is going to occur as society has to decide between the advantages of self-driving cars versus the advantages of human drivers. If driving a car is relatively routinized, and some sufficient range of driving scenarios are programmed to be handled, this might be enough to weigh the scales toward those AI driving systems and avert the downsides of human-driven cars.

Time will tell.

Meanwhile, I am determined to put some sturdy wheels onto my house and take it for a spin, including refining my homegrown AI driving system to be able to drive a house rather than a car. One thing seems pretty sure, my AI driving house can stomp on any of those pesky AI self-driving cars, in a heartbeat.

CHAPTER 27
MULTI-CLOUD AND AUTONOMOUS VEHICLES

What happens when you put multiple clouds together?

If your first thought drifts toward wonderous clouds in the sky, perhaps your answer might be that you end-up with clouds that could be described as cirrus, alto, stratus, or perhaps cumulonimbus in nature. For those that relish watching the formation of clouds, lazily observing as the fluffy crystals gently float along, you can witness quite a dance taking place. There are fractious portions that seem to go in their own desired direction. You might watch in rapt amazement as they gingerly float off toward the horizon.

Meanwhile, there is also something soothing and heartwarming when a multitude of seemingly disparate clouds opt to join together, creating a breathtaking amalgamation. Did the winds by happenstance alone bring them together? Or maybe the hand of fate was involved and somehow shepherded or guided those clouds into becoming a mutually beneficial cooperative.

I don't want to interrupt your idyllic daydreaming, but the kind of clouds that I was referring to is the type that embodies state-of-the-art computing resources and has become an essential element for any modern-day company.

A recent news announcement that garnered some outsized headlines provides ample indication of how multi-cloud amalgamations are soon going to emerge as a vital cornerstone of commerce and proffer savvy opportunities across all industries and sectors of business.

A cavalcade of hospitals announced that they are banding together to create a supercharged data collection of health data. Top named hospital systems such as Tenet Healthcare, Trinity Health, Aurora Health, Providence, and others are forming a virtual multi-cloud collective, doing so as part of the startup launch of Truveta Inc. (a newly formed company that will aggregate, analyze, and sell anonymized health-related golden nuggets, as it were).

Besides bringing together data on a massive scale that no singular hospital system solely would have available, this soon-to-emerge cooperative aims to go beyond just being a mighty storehouse of health-related info. The belief is that via the use of AI systems, the abundance of data will be turned into actionable results. Stated overarching aspirations include that cures for diseases will be discovered sooner, personalized medicine will finally become a reality, and vast improvements in health equity will occur.

A tagline that astutely goes with this multi-cloud formulation is the notion of saving lives with data.

Of course, they will have to stridently showcase that the data so collected is well-protected and fulfills their assertion that all will be anonymized. Estimates are that they will initially be able to bring together nearly 13% of the clinical care data across the entire United States. Pulling together this immensity of data is a huge lift onto itself, let alone also ensuring that there are appropriate privacy controls, security locks, and everything else needed to make sure this valuable data asset is used for good and not for bad.

In any case, thinking big is important and can provide benefits of scale that otherwise would never by perchance alone be encountered. You can chalk up this business-oriented cloud formation to the hands of humanity and not merely attributable to the whims and whisps of the winds.

What other industries or business sectors are ripe for a multi-cloud bonanza?

Yes, you might have guessed that I am thinking about the realm of autonomous vehicles.

Those readers that follow my coverage know that autonomous vehicles are predicted to demonstrably change our world.

This is not just going to merely alter how we get from point A to point B. All manner of vehicles, including cars, trucks, busses, trains, drones, planes, ships, submersibles, and the like will inevitably and inexorably become autonomous. There will be a wholescale and mammoth disruption in most of what we do, which if aimed right will provide widespread benefits. Take a moment to reflect on how society could be reshaped via having vehicles that no longer require humans at the wheel, and you will undoubtedly come to realize that this emergence will transform our existence.

If the enormity of widespread adoption of autonomous vehicles seems like a rather large bite to chew on, let's take a focused look at the advent of *true* self-driving cars and see how a multi-cloud amalgamation will arise and be a tremendous treasure trove for all. We can then consider how this same visionary perspective can be further expanded to encompass the full range of autonomous vehicles.

Let's first take a moment to clarify what I mean by my reference to *true* self-driving cars.

Self-Driving Cars And Multi-Clouds

For Level 4 and Level 5 true self-driving vehicles, there won't be a human driver involved in the driving task.

All occupants will be passengers.

The AI is doing the driving.

One crucial factor to keep in mind is that the automakers are each devising their own brand and models of self-driving cars (typically in conjunction with a firm devoted to crafting self-driving capabilities, or having bought such a firm, or having assembled an in-house crew for said purposes).

To clarify, my point is that not all self-driving cars will be the same.

Thus, automaker X might have their particular brand and models of self-driving cars. Meanwhile, automaker Y will have its own brand and models. The same for automaker Z, and so on. Of course, some automakers are joining together in onesie-twosie type arrangements, but the point overall is that we won't have a monolith of all self-driving cars being exactly the same.

I mention this salient aspect because some outside of the self-driving industry has a misimpression that somehow all self-driving cars are going to be identical, consisting of the same AI driving systems, the same sensor suites, etc. Nope, that won't be the case. There will be a variety of both hardware and software involved in crafting self-driving cars.

Another important element of self-driving cars involves the data aspects.

A self-driving car includes a suite of sensors encompassing video cameras, radar, LIDAR, thermal imaging, ultrasonic devices, etc. These are the proverbial eyes and ears of the self-driving car. The AI driving system receives the data flowing from the sensors and has to try and interpret the data to determine the driving scene and how to best utilize the driving controls of the car.

The data collected from the sensors are initially kept on-board the processing systems within the self-driving car. There is a great deal of ongoing debate and discussion regarding how much of the data is or ought to be stored on-board the vehicle versus instantly purged.

Via the use of OTA (Over-The-Air) electronic communications, the self-driving car can upload data into the cloud of the automaker or fleet operator. Similarly, software patches for the AI driving system can be remotely downloaded via the OTA from the cloud and placed into use inside the vehicle.

There is an additional twist to the data facets.

Imagine that a self-driving car is driving down an ordinary neighborhood street. The sensors are collecting a boatload of data about whatever they happen to encounter. You might assume that the only data being sought involves figuring out where the road is and how to navigate safely on the given street.

The thing is, the sensors are collecting whatever they can get.

Consider the video cameras. The video cameras are not only obtaining visual images of the roadway, but they are also capturing whatever is happening on the sidewalks, and whatever is occurring in the front yards of the houses on the block, and so on. All told, the data from the sensors can engulf a vast array of whatever perchance is occurring around the self-driving car as it makes its way throughout a neighborhood, or a community, or a town and a city. I've referred to this as the roving eye.

Okay, this all sets the stage for getting to the gist of this discussion.

Let's assume that each of the automakers decides to upload the data that was being collected by their fleet of self-driving cars (it could be the entirety of the data or a subset). On each day, a particular automaker or fleet operator is going to collect a massive volume of data about the locales and activities taking place in a given area. Realize that their self-driving cars are continually crisscrossing the geographical realm in which the vehicles are being operated.

Automaker X brings the data from their self-driving cars into their cloud, which we'll call cloud X. It is vital data that they can use to try and improve their self-driving capabilities (and, as you'll see in a moment, has a lot of other uses too). Meanwhile, automaker Y is bringing the data from their self-driving cars into their cloud, which we'll call cloud Y.

On and on this goes.

Suppose automaker X has their self-driving cars roaming on the west side of town. Automaker Y has their self-driving cars roaming on the east side of town. Logically, this implies that automaker X has a lot of useful data about the nature of the west side of town, while automaker Y has a lot of useful data about the east side of town. It also implies that automaker X has very little if any data about the east side of town (since their self-driving cars aren't roaming there), and similarly that automaker Y has little if any data about the west side.

Normally, you might expect that these are fierce competitors, and they would each keep their own collected data as stored in their respective clouds from the eyes of their respective self-driving car rival across town. That does make sense and you can certainly expect everyone to hold their aces close to their chest, at first.

Hark back momentarily to the news story about the hospitals that have decided to band together. We would not normally expect hospitals to do so, especially if they are essentially competing in the same marketplaces. Like any business, they prize the data that they have collected about their "customers" and are apt to keep it private and apart from others (of course, they also need to abide by stringent regulatory requirements too).

It took a while for the lightbulb to brighten and the right convergence of societal and technological factors to make the timing for a multi-cloud incarnation feasible, viable, and presumably rewarding.

My prediction is that gradually and inexorably the automakers and fleet operators will begin to realize that the self-driving car collected data in their respective clouds can be synergistically amalgamated to proffer added benefits that each alone could not otherwise attain.

It won't happen overnight. Realistically, you've got to expect that they all first need to get their ducks in order. There is enough newness about self-driving cars and the self-driving collected data in the cloud that trying to go beyond their singular efforts is something nearly unimaginable at this time.

You have to crawl before you can walk, and walk before you can trot, etc.

When the timing is right, what sensibly and profitably can be accomplished via a multi-cloud amalgamation of self-driving collected data?

Let's take a quick look at a readily apparent seven ways to leverage such data (there are many more ways, I assure you).

- **Roadway Infrastructure**

Many deplore the lousy status of our existing roadways, replete with potholes, insufficient markers, and a slew of problems that endanger drivers and pedestrians alike. Self-driving cars are going to be collecting tons of data about our roadways. This can be used by governmental bodies to determine where to best spend precious infrastructure dollars. It can also be used to predict where human-driven car crashes are likely to occur and shore-up high-priority spots. Using the example of cloud data being collected by automaker X and automaker Y, amalgamating their collected cloud data would empower an assessment of the entirety of the local town, both west, and east, which otherwise by one cloud collection we would only gauge one-half of the local roadway infrastructure.

- **Up-to-date Maps**

For many of today's digitally available maps, they are based on a periodic scan of a given locale, such as once per month or maybe once per year. This means that the map that you are using is potentially out-of-date. Self-driving cars are going to be daily able to update maps (furthermore, able to do so in near real-time). The data they collect into the cloud can be used to indicate when say a bridge is out of commission for a few days due to heavy rainfall. Envision that via the multi-cloud amalgamation, a comprehensive semblance of mapping would take place over an entire community or city or state, daily and be immediately available.

- **Real Estate**

If you've been looking to buy a home lately, you might have noticed that most real estate agents these days are uploading pictures of the homes they have for sale. These pictures are oftentimes poorly taken or worse are somewhat misleading in the nifty way that the property is portrayed. In any case, the self-driving data is going to have gobs of real estate video and imagery, collected daily. In addition, consider that commercial real estate is also another aspect of what the video is going to include. Owners of commercial property can get a daily tally of how their property looks, such as whether it got tagged with graffiti or was properly cleaned yesterday. Just imagine how the multi-cloud amalgamation could be monetized for the real estate industry all told, and you are already salivating at the possibilities.

- **Crime-Fighting**

I've previously pointed out that the data from self-driving cars can be potentially used for crime-fighting. Currently, when a crime occurs, there is a wild rush to discover whether any stationary video cameras managed to catch the crime or the criminals, and likewise, the public at large is asked to provide any smartphone video that might be relevant. The multi-cloud amalgamation collected from the roaming self-driving cars could be utilized to figure out the whodunit and be a handy means of reducing crime in a given area (of course, this raises various notable privacy issues, as do each of these potential uses of the data).

- **Pedestrian Safety**

Most towns have pedestrian crosswalks that are quite dangerous, yet few realize the dangers involved and sadly only take corrective action after an injury or fatality occurs. Self-driving cars routinely scan for pedestrians to try and determine whether someone is going to suddenly dart into the street or otherwise put themselves into harm's way by stepping off the curb at the wrong moment. From this data, analyses can reveal where the public is most tempted to jaywalk or where human drivers tend to be least attentive to the rights of pedestrians.

- **Human-Driven Cars**

Realize that there are still going to be human drivers during the emergence of self-driving cars. In essence, you'll have some smattering of self-driving cars on the roadways and mixing with some smattering of human-driven cars on the highways and byways too. Perhaps, far in the future, we will have only self-driving cars, but no one can say whether or when that will occur. Meanwhile, self-driving cars are intently observing the actions of human-driven cars (actually, all cars, though especially human-driven cars). This data can indicate places that seem to inspire human drivers to drive recklessly, and there might be ways to lessen the number of annual car crashes (and fatalities) accordingly.

- **Anonymized Passenger Behavior**

What will people opt to do while riding in self-driving cars? Those that had begrudgingly driven in heavy traffic to work each day will now be able to sit back and relax while the AI driving system contends with the road rage entailments. I've pointed out in my columns that an estimated 70 billion hours annually of human driving time will eventually be given back to humanity and can be used for other purposes. Most self-driving cars are going to have inward-facing cameras, doing so to allow for doing interactive Zoom-like discussions while riding in a self-driving car, perhaps doing work meetings while on-the-road or helping your kids with their homework while commuting home at night. The general activities of passengers could be anonymized and used to indicate what people do during their self-driving car journeys, which certainly would be of interest to advertisers (big bucks there!).

Conclusion

The aforementioned uses of the multi-cloud amalgamated self-driving collected data are but the tip of the iceberg, as they say. Uses range the full gamut from fundamental research to everyday practical application.

In some ways, the data would be beneficial for society overall.

That's a big-picture perspective and admirable. There is also a tremendous amount of monetization that can be gleaned from the multi-cloud endeavor.

For the hospitals that are embarking down this same path, they are emphasizing that data can save lives. The same type of mantra can readily be applied to the self-driving see-all data. Pedestrian lives can be potentially saved or at least injuries averted. Car crash fatalities can be reduced. Admittedly, the hospitals have a greater claim to the lives saved moniker, but the point being that the self-driving collected data has a lot of potential in amazing ways that might not at first blush be evident.

Finally, now that we've covered the advent of self-driving cars as an instance of autonomous vehicles, widen the scope to include other types of autonomous vehicles.

There are going to be disparate clouds devoted to for example one commercially utilized autonomous drone versus other such autonomous drones. You can tie their data together and get synergies. There will be disparate clouds across the myriad of types of autonomous vehicles. Imagine the synergies from piecing together cloud-based data from self-driving cars with self-driving trucks and toss into the mix the data from those ubiquitous autonomous drones that we keep hearing about (they will eventually get here).

A treasure trove of data awaits.

Come on, autonomous vehicles, get your act together, and move forward to enable the multi-cloud amalgamations to arise.

Think about all of this as you gaze idly up at the cumulus clouds in the sky, and imagine how those computing clouds down here on the earth will soon be forming into cooperatives that provide some pretty equally breathtaking results.

CHAPTER 28
STEEP HILLS
AND
SELF-DRIVING CARS

Have you ever been driving and found yourself at the edge of a really steep incline?

I'm talking about a monster of a slope.

A gradient of tremendous and heart-pounding fear-inducing scope. The downward tilt is seemingly equal to being on a roller coaster at the moment that you are looking below you and praying that things hold together, and you'll live through the experience.

Of course, when on an active roadway in the real-world, the qualms about being on a steep incline are more pressing than a joyous ride on a roller coaster, especially since you are at the wheel of the car and ultimately responsible for any life-or-death consequences that might arise. You are the captain of the ship. The car is at the crest of a tsunami-sized wave and you don't know for sure that the craft won't be crumpled as it descends the mighty swell.

When caught in such a dire predicament, you likely are pressing your face forward toward the front windshield of your car, hoping to somehow peek over the hood and manage to see what is on the other side of this monstrous hill you are on. The thing is, you probably cannot see the road at all due to your car being pitched somewhat upward at the crest, and all that exists beyond your vision is the vast skyline.

This means that you cannot directly see the road.

For all you know, your car is going to gingerly pass over this toppling crest and then shockingly end-up falling into an endless abyss. You don't believe in your heart of hearts that such an outcome is possible. There is supposed to be a roadway ahead, and you are assuming that there must be since otherwise, you would have to abandon all hope.

So, you tease forward by giving your car just a slight inch of pressure on the accelerator pedal. The vehicle crawls over the crest like those old war serials that showcased military tanks trying to get over rows of blocking hedges. For a few heart-stopping moments, your car is seemingly in nowhere land as it comes off the upward slope and pitches downward.

Then, with a gasp of relief, you realize that there is indeed a road and your tires are thankfully still engaged with the surface of the street. You can see the roadway once again!

The problem now becomes one of quickly scanning the driving scene ahead of you. Are there any parked cars that are threatening to be in the way as you come down this steep incline? Are pedestrians anywhere in the street or nearby to the roadway? Is there any traffic coming up the incline that might be dangerously close to your car as you make your way downward?

All of those factors would normally be scanned for and be detected long in-advance when driving on a relatively flat and altogether horizontal roadway. This vertical drop makes for some dicey driving. You don't know exactly what you will confront after successfully navigating the crest. You have just a few split seconds to rapidly examine the road conditions ahead and make any nearly instantaneous adjustments to your steering, your braking, and your acceleration, hoping to contend with whatever exists on the other side of this cliffhanging experience.

Maybe you don't live in an area that has roads of this nature. If so, perhaps be thankful you don't need to contend with them, else your heart might give out. Or, you might readily get into a car wreck, which can happen easily in these crazy gradient circumstances.

Generally, many localities put up warning signs for any streets that might involve a 7% or greater grade (the higher the number, the greater the degree of tilt). In technical terms, the grade of a road is its vertical location with respect to the ground surface, measured typically via the tangent of the angle of that surface to the horizontal. In layman's language, if your breath is taken away by the slope or pitch, the road is probably a darned steep one.

Various roadway infrastructure reporting suggests that the following list constitutes the Top 10 steepest inclines in the United States for drivable roadways that are publicly available for driving on (though, there is plenty of argument and debate over such lists):

1. 45% gradient in Hawaii (Waipio Rd. in Honokaa)
2. 37% gradient in Pennsylvania (Canton Ave. in Pittsburgh)
3. 33% gradient in California (Eldred St. in Los Angeles)
4. 33% gradient in California (28th St. in Los Angeles)
5. 32% gradient in California (Baxter St. in Los Angeles)
6. 32% gradient in California (Fargo St. in Los Angeles)
7. 32% gradient in California (Maria Ave. in Spring Valley)
8. 32% gradient in Pennsylvania (Dornbush St. in Pittsburgh)
9. 32% gradient in California (22nd St. in San Francisco)
10. 32% gradient in California (Filbert St. in San Francisco)

Those are assuredly whoppers, regardless of whether they belong on a Top 10 list or not.

Truth be told, any such steep street is a danger to society, sorry to say.

Despite the thrill or excitement involved in traversing such a road, you have to take into account the fact that these steep streets are patently hazardous for all concerned parties. The driver is blindly proceeding ahead. There might be everyday pedestrians in the street and they'll get run down. There might be a car coming up the hill and you'll ram head-to-head into the vehicle. You might sideswipe parked cars that have been (riskily) parked on the sloping street and thus lose total control of your vehicle. And so on.

Technically, these are referred to as terrain slope-induced driving problems.

As a human driver, some take all this in stride. People that drive down these roads on a daily basis might vehemently swear that they've never encountered any difficulties. To them, the massive descent is no different than driving on the flats of a pancaked desert.

Good for them, but this doesn't provide proof of safety. They have managed to somehow exploit their lucky rabbits' foot and never had any issues arise on the slope. One might argue they are living on borrowed time.

There is also the matter of drivers that encounter the steep slope for the first time. Those first-timers are not only faced with the challenges of driving the steepness in a safe manner, but they might also react adversely to the situation and become panicked in their drivable ways. In essence, the human reaction to the predicament could produce an untoward outcome, regardless of whether by default alone a calamity might have laid in wait.

For those of you that are movie buffs, you undoubtedly have watched the famous car chase scene by Steve McQueen in the action-thriller movie *Bullitt.* He drives a Ford Mustang GT Fastback through the hilly streets of San Francisco while chasing after the villains in a Dodge Charger. If you want to virtually get a palpable sense of what it is like to drive down steep slopes, make sure to watch the video posting of this iconic car chase. Be prepared for a bit of vertigo and being on the edge of your seat.

Why all this discussion about driving down steeply sloped streets?

Consider that the future of cars entails the advent of self-driving cars. AI-based true self-driving cars will drive autonomously, meaning that the AI is doing all of the driving. There is no human involvement and the AI is utterly in-charge of the driving controls.

Here is today's intriguing question: *When a true self-driving car comes upon the precipice of a really steep street, how good will it do at coping with such a driving dilemma?*

Let's unpack the matter and see.

Self-Driving Cars And Daredevil Gradients

For Level 4 and Level 5 true self-driving vehicles, there won't be a human driver involved in the driving task.

All occupants will be passengers.

The AI is doing the driving.

One aspect to immediately discuss entails the fact that today's AI is not sentient. In other words, the AI is altogether a collective of computer-based programming and algorithms, and most assuredly not able to reason in the same manner that humans can. For example, current AI lacks any semblance of common sense and nor has any kind of common-sense reasoning.

This is important to keep in mind when considering how a self-driving car will deal with a steep slope and a potentially daredevil descent. There isn't any semblance of human judgment, human intuition, or similar human-specific qualities. Of course, the other side of that coin can be argued as doing away with the emotional reactions that can arise when confronting a dicey driving situation such as a steep decline.

In any case, let's start at the beginning.

A self-driving car contains a slew of sensors to aid in detecting the outside world. The typical sensor suite includes video cameras, radar, LIDAR, ultrasonic units, and the like. These electronic devices are intended to be the veritable eyes and ears of the self-driving car. Mounted on various positions of the self-driving car, these sensors are continually collecting data about whatever is detectable in the surrounding driving scene.

The AI driving system then mathematically examines the sensory data and tries to figure out what the driving scene consists of. Crucial fundamentals such as where the drivable roadway surface exists have to be calculated and ferreted out. Humans take for granted that they can see the road and divine that the road is drivable. All of that has to be painstakingly computed by the AI driving system.

One aspect that outsiders of the self-driving industry do not take into account is the inherent limitations of those sensors. Different types of sensors are detecting the surroundings in differing ways. Some types of sensors do better in certain kinds of conditions, such as whether it is sunny versus cloudy, dry versus raining, etc. Also, various sensors have key differences in terms of how far away they can detect objects. And so on.

Another key consideration is where the sensors are mounted.

Generally, the higher up the sensor is placed, the more likely the sensor will be unobstructed and be able to glean a wider expanse. If you have a sensor on the lower bumper of the car, the odds are that it can only do detection closer to the ground. Meanwhile, a sensor sitting atop the roof of the car is bound to have a more pronounced detection capacity (these are generalizations and dependent upon the nature of the sensors being used).

Okay, this sets the stage for the saga of arriving at a street that has a steep decline.

The self-driving car is cruising along and comes to the precipice of the sloped street. In many ways, the AI driving system is going to be confounded akin to how a human is confounded (do not though anthropomorphize the AI, as stated, it is not sentient). The odds are that the sensors will not readily be able to detect the road that lies ahead.

Assuming that the sensors are statically fixed in place on the vehicle, they will be aiming at a somewhat upward angle when the self-driving car reaches the crest. This limits their facility of detecting what is over-the-hill and down along the downward sloping street. In short, a significant aspect of the terrain slope-induced driving problem for self-driving cars is that the forward visibility is severely limited in settings such as a high gradient steeply sloped downward pitched street.

Humans take for granted that the road will continue. They make this assumption because they believe that other humans would have made sure the road continues (well, this applies in cities and is not necessarily the case for off-road driving). Furthermore, one would assume that unless a sign or warning signal is posted to alert you about some disaster waiting ahead, you are relatively safe to proceed.

In that same manner of logic, a self-driving car generally is programmed to make the same set of assumptions.

Note that this implies the self-driving car ought to be first detecting whether there are any posted warnings. Thus, a vital aspect of the AI driving system involves scanning the area while at the top of the crest, attempting to discover any signage or indication that perhaps the road ahead is not traversable.

You might be thinking that this is somewhat unnecessary since the self-driving car would certainly be armed with digitized maps and have GPS. In that case, there is no need to presumably be looking around for signage. Instead, merely consult the map. If the map indicates the road continues ahead, you are good to proceed. Case closed.

Well, maybe, maybe not.

First, you are making quite a big bet with the lives of all parties involved, as based solely on a map. The reality at the driving scene can oftentimes differ from a prior digitized map. Perhaps the map was updated a month ago. Meanwhile, there was roadwork done and just beyond the crest, there is a mighty pothole, waiting to ensnare cars that come down that street.

The use of a map is undoubtedly vital and an important element, but a map alone is not how anyone or anything should be driving a car. It is a reasonable expectation that the AI driving system ought to be using all of its sensors to try and figure out what the real-time situation consists of, in addition to using any available digitized maps.

Besides scanning for warning signs, another factor would be the status of other cars.

For example, suppose a car that was being human-driven was ahead of the self-driving car, reaching the summit first. Imagine that the human-driven car reaches the crest, comes to a halt, and then makes a U-turn. If you were driving in the car that was behind that turning around the car, what would you think? Most cautious drivers would think that maybe this other driver has determined that something ahead is amiss. Of course, that driver might simply be "a chicken" in that they don't want to tempt fate by going down the gradient, or it could be that they saw something that alerted them to avoid a potential catastrophe.

One would also expect that the AI driving system will drive slowly, cautiously, and not try to breeze over the crest. Human drivers love to drive fast and especially on a hill that has steep slopes. Perhaps these daredevils get a rush or envision themselves acting like Steve McQueen. In any case, it is reasonable to expect that the AI driving system should not proceed brazenly and instead be soberly measured in how it approaches the setting.

That being said, there is a consequent danger that nearby human-driven cars will react adversely if they get stuck behind a self-driving car that seems to be inching along in such circumstances. This might prompt human drivers into veering around the snail-paced self-driving car. The end result could be quite dangerous for all concerned. Your first impulse is to assert that this is a problem associated with the human drivers and not the "fault" of the AI driving system. That seems like a satisfying reply, but it lacks real-world value and we need to ensure that self-driving cars can mix ably with human-driven traffic too.

After the crest, the AI driving system will need to quickly scan the road ahead, having (safely, one hopes) gone over the crest and now aiming downward on the steep slope. The sensors will once again have a viable chance of being able to discern what the roadway status is. This includes examining the sensory data to figure out where the roadway is, where pedestrians are, where parked cars are, and the rest.

If a self-driving car has previously driven that route, there can be a kind of templated expectation of what the upcoming driving scene is going to be like. This reduces the computational workload in the manner that the AI driving system only needs to update an expected scene, rather than render one from scratch.

An advantage of self-driving cars is that if even one self-driving car of a given fleet has ridden down a particular street, this, in theory, can be applied to the other self-driving cars in the fleet (using OTA, Over-The-Air electronic updating capabilities).

Conclusion

To help the AI driving system, other anticipated innovations are coming down the pike (whoa, that was a bit of a pun).

There are efforts underway to provide a paired drone with self-driving cars.

Essentially, a self-driving car would have a drone that sits atop the vehicle or maybe in a compartment on the trunk and can be launched into the air when so needed. The drone could fly ahead and look down upon the steep road, providing sensory data electronically to the vehicle and thus allow the self-driving car to readily be aware of what lies ahead.

Another upcoming innovation is the use of V2V (vehicle-to-vehicle) electronic communication.

This allows a self-driving car to broadcast an electronic message to other nearby self-driving cars. For example, if debris is sitting in the middle of a road, a self-driving car that detects the debris might emit a warning electronically to other self-driving cars that are within the same vicinity. Similarly, a self-driving car that goes down the steep slope can be transmitting V2V and inform other self-driving cars nearing the top crest about what to expect on the road below.

As much as possible, the hope is that the makers of self-driving cars will be on their toes and finding ways to reduce the risks of driving down those wildly steep avenues. Rather than passengers having to hold their breaths and make a leap of blind faith that the AI driving system has been well-devised, we are all likely only going to accept self-driving cars on our public roadways if they can manage to deal with all types of driving quandaries.

Think about this the next time you are in a human-driven car, and you are watching the face of the driver as they either tense-up when approaching a steep slope, or they get that devil-may-care look and decide to floor it for a car-rocking bone-jarring high-risk reckless drive on a slope meant for seasoned skiers in the snow-capped Alps.

CHAPTER 29
BOOTSTRAPPING AND SELF-DRIVING CARS

Sure, there is an ebb-and-flow at times, including that self-driving cars have witnessed a recent slowing of new AV firms, but you've got to think more widely and include the full gamut of autonomous vehicle types such as self-driving trucks, self-driving delivery carts, self-driving motorcycles, self-driving drones, self-driving submersibles, self-driving surface ships, self-driving planes, and any other manner of transportation that is amenable to autonomous capabilities.

The big picture is looking mighty fine.

Let's go over some of the crucial success factors that underpin an AV startup that wants to make its mark. Those AV startups aim to get a viable product avidly underway and showcase that they are more than just some flash-in-the-pan semblance of vacuous ideas and words on a page.

The odds are that a savvy approach to an AV startup is going to outlast the AV startups that are based solely on whim and guts. I mention the guts aspect because there is truth to the notion that embarking upon a startup, and especially in the tough and unforgiving world of AVs, takes a sturdy and hefty amount of guts.

That being said, guts alone are insufficient, sorry to say.

Sadly, way too many AV startups never see the light of day. I see them all the time, before their collapse or fade-out, and can readily discern which will make it and which will be no more than a dream that was never realized.

To help any AV startups that are open to helpful advice, I'll include herein some handy insights that I've gleaned via my time as a top exec at a major Venture Capital (VC) firm, along with ongoing efforts as an incubator mentor to AV startups and a frequent pitch judge at local and global Shark Tank-style competitions.

One overarching theme that will become apparent is that the use of cloud computing is an important bootstrapping mechanism and ought to be on the top of your list for matters to be undertaken from the get-go of your startup.

Strap yourself into your seat and get ready for a startup boosting ride.

We'll begin by clarifying what the AV market space consists of.

Classifying By AV Scope

When thinking about AVs, I've found it useful to classify startups into one of two buckets, the AV-totality bucket, and the AV-element bucket.

The AV-totality category entails startups that attempt to do the whole ball of wax, the A to Z, the end-to-end facets of creating an autonomous vehicle. This encompasses the essence of the hardware involved, along with the entirety of the software stack. These are the so-called big-chew visionaries that say they want to reimagine what the underlying vehicular facility is, trying to begin with a fresh look at how that form of transport ought to be devised.

Those of these veritable all-you-can-eat buffet AV startups are glaringly ambitious, outlandish in their aspirations, and are tackling oftentimes more than they can adequately get their hands around. I'm not saying they shouldn't embark upon those outsized goals, only that it will be a lot harder to pursue than they might otherwise assume or outright claim. Good luck to them and one has to earnestly root for an underdog that fights way above its weight class.

More realistic are the AV startups that go the AV-elements route.

They carve out a segment or portion of the autonomous vehicle market and aim to become the go-to choice in that niche. This might be in the sensors arena, offering a new kind of sensor, or a sensor that is less costly than the prevailing products, or a sensor that is several times as efficient or effective, and so on. It might be that the niche is chosen has to do with software, such as providing a newly crafted AI capability, perhaps leveraging Machine Learning and Deep Learning innovatively and as applied to autonomous vehicles. Etc.

I realize that the AV-element strategy might seem timid or narrow to some that insist on the grandiose AV plays, but any startup that is truly just a startup and not already backed by heavy hitters will have a much greater chance of survival and existence by taking the elements-oriented avenue. You can be an AV-element provider and still knock things out of the ballpark.

When pitching an AV startup, make sure to clarify whether you are the AV-totality or the AV-element gambit. Believe it or not, many startups make a pitch that is so jampacked that it is not readily feasible to figure out what their aim is. A startup might emphasize the AV-totality and turnout to be the AV-element type, and meanwhile, a startup that appears to be an AV-element goer is actually an outstretched attempt to be an AV-totality.

Handy tip: When you confound or confuse potential investors and mentors, you are doing quite a disservice to your own ambitions and are usurping the limited time-attention those funding and advice-giving sources have (it will backfire on you, tarnishing your reputational goodwill).

Of course, if a startup is embarking upon a step-at-a-time approach toward an AV-totality, doing so by gradually pursuing a series of AV-elements that will plug-and-play together, this is certainly worth mentioning and can provide some satisfaction for those investors that are seeking a grand scheme.

You also don't have to pretend to have a veiled desire to be an AV-totality and can at least explain how your AV-element fits into the

AV-totality efforts taking place elsewhere.

Let's dovetail the cloud computing aspects.

You will want to indicate how the AV-totality or the AV-element will be designed, developed, tested, and fielded. Those activities are going to require the collecting of, access to, and use of data. Those activities are also certainly going to require the running of or crafting of software.

Where will those computing resources come from?

The days of buying a server and keeping it in your backyard garage as you gather together your fellow intrepid founders and crank out your MVP (Minimally Viable Product) are no longer in vogue. Indeed, such a proclamation of how you are intending to proceed is pretty much like waving a large-sized red flag.

An investor wants to know that the funds going into the startup are going to have legs, meaning that if the whole thing falls apart, there will be something salvageable. For whatever you've pieced together so far, there ought to be a secure and safe place for it to be found. That's where cloud computing comes to the fore.

By placing your data into the cloud, it means that even if that endearing garage has a tree that falls onto it, the data and software will still be available, residing securely in the cloud. It also means that you and your fellow startup creators can access the data and software from wherever they might be, at any time, and not be constrained by having to be in the particular township that your garage resides in.

In the past, some startups did not begin their founding trek by using the cloud because it was perceived as overly costly or overly arduous to get underway. They believed that the faster and easier path was to establish their own servers and try and find any software that they could get their hands on, either legally or at times under-the-table. Scrambling and street hustle was the right buzz for any tech startup such as those in the AV realm.

That's not the way things are done nowadays.

Investors will sleep better at night (that's important if you want to attract them and keep them engaged), by knowing that the intellectual property assets of the startup are safely in the cloud and are legitimately licensed and properly-being utilized. Nobody but nobody wants to get into some protracted legal battles over licensed software, and you can be sure that whatever vendor's tools you choose to use will come after those that aren't in compliance (it is their bread-and-butter to do so).

Those are primarily protective measures and highlight how the cloud helps in that perspective. There are also the go-forward aspects that the cloud also provides enabling capacity for. We can touch upon those go-forward synergies in a moment.

It will be useful to first clarify the nature of AV functionality that is likely integral to your AV startup.

AV Functionality

An important means to establish what your AV pursuit consists of can be illuminated via the use of a typical AV-functionality indication.

In brief, nearly all AVs are going to have these five key functional aspects:

- Sensing of the world around the AV
- Interpretation of the detected surroundings
- Virtual world modeling
- Planning for vehicular movement
- Carrying out AV motion

If you are an AV-element startup, make sure to clearly identify which of the AV functionality domains you are inhabiting. It is okay to be in just one. It is also okay to be in more than one. Furthermore, you might be devising your AV-element to initially be in just one but are doing so with the larger eye of incrementally expanding the AV-element into the other domains.

For an AV-totality, presumably, the startup is going to attain all of those AV functionalities. It could be that the startup is going to handcraft them all from scratch, which is the proverbial reaching for the star's ambition. More likely, the startup is going to leverage other companies or other resources that entail some of those domains. In that case, make sure to explain how those will end-up dovetailing into your efforts and what if any chokepoints this might imbue.

Let's now consider how the cloud is essential for the go-forward activities when pursuing the chosen AV functionality.

You and your buddies want to make a new kind of sensor and seek to showcase what it can do for AVs (this will be an example that can be equally applicable to the other AV functionality stages).

The sensor will be used to collect data. The data will have to be examined to ascertain that the sensor is aptly detecting the outside world. If the sensor is glitching, this needs to be figured out and corrected. Furthermore, the data is only useful if it can be turned into something useable by the rest of the AV stack.

Okay, so you need to decide where to put the data, housing it someplace that it can be kept secured, where it can be accessed globally by your scrappy startup team and will accommodate a likely large growth in the volume of data that will be stored (increasing in some proportional way to the growth of your startup).

The cloud provides a means to store the data, doing so in a flexible manner of both how to store the data (structures and formats), and at a cost that is commensurate with the amount of volume at-hand. You can start with smaller data volumes, paying less, and then rachet to larger volumes when the timing is right, and the cost gradually ratcheting in concordance.

You'll likely need software for examining the data being generated via your new sensor.

Most full-bodied cloud services have available a slew of data-related online tools. This includes the predominant AI packages for

Machine Learning and Deep Learning. Rather than wasting time trying to figure out where to find the right AI packages, such precious and valuable time is usually better spent by adeptly using tools that are known to work, already at your fingertips, and then getting those packages underway expeditiously for your AV efforts.

All told, the notion is that the cloud provides a ready-made platform to readily proceed with your AV startup.

Going other routes will typically entail lots of added overhead, for which the savvy investor is going to want to know why your energies and attention are being diverted to such activities when the cloud is today such an instant-on, available, and cost-reasonable option.

Conclusion

There is a sage line that some like to use, admittedly perhaps a bit over-the-top, but nonetheless catchy, consisting of the assertion that you can start with the cloud, grow with the cloud, and eventually exit with the cloud for an AV startup.

The assertion seems readily apparent about the starting and growing stages of an AV startup, but might cause you to scratch your head about the allusion to the exit stage.

Here's what that refers to.

Assume that eventually, you will have some form of exit from your startup. This might involve an IPO or maybe using a SPAC to go public (Special Purpose Acquisition Companies are the darling of the market right now). Or you might agree to be acquired by another company that is directly in AV and wants to swallow-up and embody your AV capabilities. Perhaps you'll merge with another peer AV firm rather than being acquired outright. And so on.

Those myriads of exits are typically contingent upon the startup being considered viable for an exit. If the startup has a demonstrative weakness or difficulty, the odds are this will be discovered during the due diligence process leading to the exit. The exit itself could be soured and fall apart. Another possibility is that the exit continues unabated, but the value of the startup is demonstrably downgraded. Consider where the cloud comes into this picture.

Using the example of a startup with a new sensor, they are courted by a larger company that makes a full suite of sensors. The interest in the startup involves being able to quickly include the new sensor into the existing suite of this larger company.

This acquiring company is already using the cloud for its AV efforts. If the AV startup is also using the cloud, the odds are that the integration of this new sensor into the suite of the acquiring company will be relatively streamlined. This makes the startup especially attractive. Time is money, as they say. Other similar AV startups that were not using the cloud would be considered riskier choices, and costlier to bring into the fold.

The same kind of business logic applies to the IPO or SPAC routes too. A startup in the AV arena that has all their ducks lined-up, using the cloud, and able to readily assure that the data is there, the software is there, and the whole shebang is available without any missing components is going to get a green light to proceed. Auditors that have to dig into arcane corners and off-the-beaten-path computing resources will put up huge warnings that the entire core of the startup is potentially scattered, unreproducible, and not able to hang together.

The overall mantra for an AV startup ought to be that establishing the proper infrastructure is crucial. This includes the initial phases of a startup, such as at the pre-seed and seed stages. Trying to after-the-fact get the right infrastructure is doable, though there is an added cost and delay that can frustrate and disrupt the growth path of the AV startup.

As Mark Twain was known for having stated, do the right thing since it will gratify some people and astonish the rest. Be assured that investors in the AV realm are eager to be astonished and are continually on the search for that next gobsmacking AV startup coming down the pike.

CHAPTER 30
TEENAGE DRIVERS AND SELF-DRIVING CARS

Adult drivers oftentimes detest teenage drivers.

This is not ostensibly a generational differences issue.

The cold hard facts are that teenage drivers are newbie drivers, and there is little question that neophyte drivers tend to make more driving mistakes than seasoned drivers. You can passionately argue whether these driving foibles are due to inexperience at the wheel, or whether they are due to the intrinsic immaturity associated with being a teenage adolescent.

Perhaps a combination of factors comes to play.

One supposes that the good news is that there aren't as many teenage drivers as you might otherwise assume. Of the approximately 225 million driver's licenses in the U.S., about 10 million are associated with teenagers. That means that less than about 5% of all drivers are teenage drivers.

Do not rest easy.

According to additional U.S. stats, the fatal crash rate per mile driven for teens is about three times as high as the rate for all other drivers that are over the age of 19.

Yikes!

Adding to these alarming statistics is that the fatal crash rate for those that are 16 and 17 years of age is about twice the rate of drivers that are ages 18 and 19. This suggests that the younger the driver within the drivable teenage years, the greater the relative chance of getting into a fatal car crash.

Parents that have second thoughts about their teenage offspring getting a driver's license have an exceedingly reasonable basis for having trepidations about the matter. Parental love knows no bounds, including ensuring that their budding teenager lives to the ripe age of say twenty.

The teen is likely insisting that they are ready and eager to drive.

For teenagers, the act of driving is ostensibly a rite of passage, giving them entry into what will eventually become adulthood. There is also the sense of independence that comes from driving a car, a kind of freedom that is both imagined and altogether real. Even the seemingly banal act of being able to drive to the grocery store, on your own, can seem like a Herculean accomplishment of independence for a teen, a sensation that is unfathomable to adults that have forgotten how enthralling the driving privilege can be.

I'd be willing to bet my bottom dollar that your teen is going to say that all their peers are driving and how dare you as a parent deny them the same equity as those other teens.

This is the classic ploy to shame the parents into letting the teen be an equal among their friends and acquaintances. It certainly has a convincing ring. Apparently, the parents of those other teens made a reasoned and sound decision to let their offspring drive, thus the FOMO (fear of missing out) catches the mindset of the parent teetering on letting their teenager learn to drive.

Try it out, the logic goes, and if the teen overplays their hand while at the wheel, you can always ground them and deny them the revered parental-granted driving rights.

Here's a stat that your teen won't like, thus if they are reading this discussion, it is a likely guess they will try to edit out this sentence and keep you from ever seeing it: *Only about one-third or statistically 34.8% of teens in the 16-to-19 age bracket have a driver's license.*

In other words, nearly *two-thirds* of them do not have a driver's license.

That kind of deflates the crafty argument that since everyone else has a driver's license, they ought to have one too.

But, since I want those teens to keep on reading, here's a counterargument. The one-third is across all teenagers in the age 16 to 19 age bracket encompassing the entire U.S.A. In your particular town or city, it could be that the percentage is a lot higher. Furthermore, in your particular clique of friends and acquaintances, it could be nearly one hundred percent (other than your kid, of course).

Hey, teens, make sure to mention that factoid to your parents, maybe it will help bolster your case.

One crucial point to make here is that not all teens are the same.

There is a substantial difference in driving behavior among teens.

Some teens think they own the roadways. Those teens tend to drive with reckless abandon. Some teens drive while distracted, and illegally drive while intoxicated. All manner of bad driving is bound to be found amongst teens, just as similarly you can find bad driving among those drivers over the age of 19.

On the opposite extreme of the lousy teenage drivers, some teens drive quite carefully and thoughtfully. They are extremely dutiful while at the wheel. They make complete stops at stop signs. They stay back from the crosswalk when they bring their car to a halt on active streets. Traffic laws are nearly always strictly obeyed. These teens relish the driving act and will do whatever they can to keep it intact.

Each parent has to make a singular decision about driving based on the maturity of their teen.

It can be gut-wrenching, that's for sure. Also, there are often compelling reasons to take a chance. Perhaps the only seemingly viable way for your teen to get to school or get to a job is via the use of a car and doing their own driving. Everybody has their own cost-benefit analysis to be made about whether teen driving is worth the risks involved.

Another twist, though, involves that even if a teen seems relatively mature and ready to drive, they are nonetheless still a newbie driver.

This means that they have not yet experienced the range and depth of tricky driving scenarios that more seasoned drivers have encountered. As such, the teen will have to "learn" in real-time and make split-second decisions, which could be taxing for anyone that has never logged lots of miles of driving effort, no matter what the age. In short, a teen that is a responsible person and diligent at the wheel still has the unfortunate and inarguable disadvantage of not being an experienced driver.

Sorry to say it that way, but it is true.

Swinging back over to the side favoring the teen, they can undoubtedly point at adult drivers that are seasoned and yet drive quite dangerously. That is abundantly true too. Experience alone does not mean that someone is going to drive properly. In fact, some studies suggest that the experienced driver tends to take more outsized risks while driving, under the somewhat egotistical belief that they can handle anything that the road tosses in their direction.

Experienced drivers get into car crashes, let there be no doubt about that fact.

Returning to the earlier point about adult drivers not welcoming teenage drivers (while amid everyday traffic), part of the problem entails that the teenage drivers are perceived as problematic in one of two major ways.

Teen drivers either are overly cautious, crawling along at a snail's pace and gum up the traffic or those darned no-good teens of a brazen nature are overly careless and cut off other drivers and run red lights.

Is this really a fair assessment of teenage drivers?

Some would argue that it is an unfair characterization and disproportionality that overstates that there are indeed sometimes timid teenage drivers and sometimes daredevil teenage drivers. Whether it is reasonable to cast all teens into those two buckets of driving behaviors does seem a bit outlandish and a mightier-than-though phenomenon that teens would certainly suspect that adults might entertain.

Anyway, I'm not going to try and solve world hunger and nor the question of teenage driving in this particular discussion. Those are large-scale topics and deserving of their respective devoted attention.

Shifting gears, keep in mind that the future of cars consists of self-driving cars.

For AI-based true self-driving cars, there won't be any humans at the wheel. Many are eagerly awaiting that day, partially to ease the burden on having to drive a car, and furthermore to potentially extend driving to those that today are disadvantaged when it comes to the accessibility to driving (see my column coverage about those topics for further info).

There is also a belief that the number of annual car crashes will drop precipitously, saving lives and reducing the annual heart-wrenching injuries that arise. All in all, the hope is that the advent of self-driving cars will produce a mobility-for-all outcome and be a lifesaver in a multitude of figurative and literal ways.

Some seem to think that there will be an overnight switchover to self-driving cars, as though one day we are driving human-driven cars, and suddenly the next day we all wake-up and there are only self-driving cars on our highways, streets, and byways. Right now, there are about 250 million conventional cars in the United States alone, and those are not going to disappear and be magically replaced with self-driving cars with the push of a button or any hocus-pocus.

This is an important point, and here's why.

Human-driven cars and self-driving cars are going to be mixing together in traffic for many years to come, probably many decades. We don't even know whether there will come a day when there won't be conventional cars on the roadways. Some vehemently argue that you only will take away their driving privileges when you pry their cold dead hands from the steering wheel.

Okay, so you hopefully get the idea that there will be human-driven cars and self-driving cars that are side-by-side while on our neighborhood streets, while on our city streets, while on our freeways, and so on. Human drivers of all ilk will be driving within traffic that also contains self-driving cars.

That means that teenagers will be driving nearby to self-driving cars too.

I'm not implying that only teenage drivers will be driving amongst self-driving cars. That doesn't make any sense. What I am saying is that since teenage drivers are, well, car drivers, they will accordingly be on the roads and driving, doing so when self-driving cars are driving too.

Teenage drivers will need to contend with other teenage drivers, adult drivers, and now they will have the added combatant of self-driving cars. Turning that on its head, since this is a two-way street, as it were, self-driving cars also have to contend with adult drivers and with (of course!) teenage drivers.

Here is today's mighty question: *What happens when teenage drivers are amidst self-driving cars, considering the point of view of the teens and the point of view of those self-driving cars?*

Great question and one worthy of some noodling over. Before we jump into the fray, let's first clarify what I mean when referring to true self-driving cars.

Self-Driving Cars And Teenage Drivers Nearby

For Level 4 and Level 5 true self-driving vehicles, there won't be a human driver involved in the driving task.

All occupants will be passengers.

The AI is doing the driving.

One aspect to immediately discuss entails the fact that today's AI is not sentient.

In other words, the AI is altogether a collective of computer-based programming and algorithms, and most assuredly not able to reason in the same manner that humans can. I mention this aspect because many headlines boldly proclaim or imply that AI has turned the corner and become equal to human intelligence. As if that wasn't bad enough, the outsized headlines seek to amp further the matter by contending that AI is reaching superhuman capabilities (for why the use of "superhuman" as a moniker is especially misleading and inappropriate).

Why this emphasis about the AI not being sentient?

Because the AI driving system has to be explicitly established programmatically to cope with human drivers, including the ranklings of teenage drivers.

And, as mentioned earlier, this is a two-way street metaphorically in that teenage drivers need to successfully cope with self-driving cars while both are driving around on our public roadways.

This brings up a somewhat lofty topic known as the theory of mind.

When you are driving a car, you are guessing about what other drivers are going to do. You have an overall semblance of what other drivers do. If you see a car ahead of you that appears to be approaching a piece of debris on the roadway, you are likely to envision that once the other driver sees the debris, the driver will take some form of evasive action.

Because you placed yourself into the shoes of the other driver, you realize that this other car might suddenly come to a stop or veer to the side, all in an attempt by the driver to avoid striking the debris. In a sense, you have a theory about the mind of that other driver.

You don't personally know that driver (let's assume they are a complete stranger). Nonetheless, you size-up the other driver and do so based on clues about how they are driving. Did this driver recently pump their brakes when other traffic got nearby? If so, it is perhaps a telltale clue that this particular driver is quite cautious, bordering on being overly wary.

By watching the cars around you, you try and divine what might be in the minds of those various drivers. This, in turn, allows you to make reasoned guesses about what those drivers will do. The aim of predicting their actions is especially crucial when trying to avoid getting into car crashes. We all know that a driver weaving back-and-forth is probably drunk, and therefore we can assess their state of mind, doing so without actually speaking with the person or smelling their breath directly.

Now that we've covered that background, consider what your theory of mind consists of for teenage drivers. As an adult driver, you likely have a templated perspective about teenage drivers, and the moment you get a glance and see that a car has a teenager at the wheel, your template gets loaded into the forefront of your driving tactics.

Similarly, if you see a car making certain kinds of motions and moves, you might suspect that the driver is a teenage driver. This becomes your default assumption at that moment, until or if something else occurs that causes you to either cement that assumption or to reject it.

What theory of mind do you have about self-driving cars and the capabilities of the AI driving system?

The answer that most people would give is that they have absolutely no clue as to what might be going on "in the mind" of the AI driving system (I loath to use the word "mindset" or anything similar when referring to AI, since anthropomorphizing AI is a bad idea).

Generally, most people tend to assume that an AI driving system is probably a lot like a teenage driver in many ways, such as having a timidity of driving and driving slowly (recall, that was one of the two major ways that people tend to categorize teenage drivers). People also assume that a self-driving car will be a polite driver, civil in sharing the roadway, along with always properly coming to a full stop at red lights and otherwise abiding by the stated traffic laws.

Consider this:

- What theory of mind do teenagers have about self-driving cars?
- What kind of programming do self-driving cars have with regard to the efforts of teenage drivers?

By-and-large, it would seem that the teenagers that I regularly interact with are about in the same headspace as the general public about self-driving cars. These teen drivers make the same assumptions that I've earlier mentioned.

Having seen these teens driving on the roadways where self-driving cars are traversing about (as part of the tryouts underway on our public roadways), it is apparent that the teens generally give a wide berth to the self-driving cars. When you aren't sure what a car driver might or might not do, it seems readily sensible to try and keep sufficient separation to allow for anything at all that might transpire.

There is an old line that familiarity sometimes breeds contempt.

This is a seemingly applicable saying about drivers that get used to being around self-driving cars (see my coverage of human car drivers that are bullying self-driving cars). People that drive frequently in traffic with self-driving cars are bound to over time find themselves getting used to the driving behaviors of the AI driving systems. Since it is indeed the case that most of the AI driving systems are cautious and attempt to unerringly be law-abiding, this tends to provoke human drivers into reacting by trying to go around self-driving cars or otherwise fool self-driving cars (such as grabbing the right-of-way at a four-way stop sign).

Yes, even teens get this way too.

What is especially interesting though is that these teens say that they often get bullied by cars containing adult drivers while in traffic, or so they believe to be the case.

The teens that are the good drivers are seemingly being treated as though they are bad drivers. Perhaps this is because the proverbial bad apple in the barrel spoils the entire barrel. Maybe there are adult drivers that had foul-tasting encounters with bad teenage drivers and became conditioned to assume that all teenage drivers must be bad. Whether that is a valid concern is not significant to the adult, since the adult likely figures it is "safest" to merely assume that all teens are bad drivers and therefore be prepared for the worst-case at any time.

Unfortunately, this tends to spur the teens toward somewhat adverse and perhaps unexpected consequential actions. The teens begin to seemingly resent the bulk of adult drivers, believing that the adult drivers are taking advantage of them. This, in turn, makes the teen drivers decide to either become exaggeratingly slow and ponderous, trying to keep their distance from the offending adult drivers, or the teens decide that if you can't beat them that you, therefore, might as well join them, meaning that the teens become aggressive drivers in a fit of survival on the roadways.

Into this melee comes the self-driving cars.

The less cynical teen drivers seem to suggest that they favor the driving tactics of self-driving cars. They find that self-driving cars are consistent and relatively predictable. Meanwhile, adults are, yes, you know it, wild and unpredictable (wait for a second, isn't that what adults say about the teens?).

In terms of self-driving cars being programmed to cope with teenage drivers, you would be hard-pressed to have anyone indicate that they are purposely programming a specialty of the AI driving system to contend with teenage drivers. What you would hear instead is that the AI driving system is being prepared to cope with drivers that are timid or that are overbearing, and the age of the driver is immaterial to those driving antics.

Conclusion

For a worried parent, the aspect that your teenage driver is driving amidst self-driving cars should not alter your perception of the risks associated with driving. There is and will continue to be a plethora of adult drivers on the roads for a long time to come, and only very few self-driving cars. Thus, the preponderance of your teenager's driving time will be among those fearsome and pesky adult human drivers.

If there were a lot of self-driving cars and only a few adult drivers, this would certainly help presumably reduce the risks for your teenage driver. Of course, a self-driving car and an AI driving system can only achieve so much. If a teenage driver were to ram into the rear-end of a self-driving car, there really isn't much the self-driving car could have done to avoid the crash, assuming that the teen was at fault.

As a final thought for now, and one that will maybe give you some peace of mind, someday in the future there will be a sufficient prevalence of self-driving cars such that your teen won't necessarily need to be a driver. They will instead use self-driving cars to get around. Some believe this will be a godsend, while others are worried about what will happen once teens in the driving age can go in a car and do so without any adult supervision (well, but hey, that would be the case anyway if they had a license to drive!).

Some say that teens are already starting to back away from wanting to drive. Driving is certainly a hassle. Taking a self-driving car would be a lot easier. No worries about the driving. You can play online video games during a driving journey. And so on.

I'm sure though that as a doting parent, you would insist (or urge) your teen to be working on their homework while riding in a self-driving from school or extracurricular activities. Yes, those teens already feeling saddled by their parents watching over their every action will soon discover that the time spent in a self-driving car won't go unsupervised since the parent will likely instruct the AI system to make sure the teen is dutifully studying their algebra and classics of literature while getting a lift to wherever they might be heading.

Hey, AI, please give those teens a break.

APPENDIX

APPENDIX A
TEACHING WITH THIS MATERIAL

The material in this book can be readily used either as a supplemental to other content for a class, or it can also be used as a core set of textbook material for a specialized class. Classes where this material is most likely used include any classes at the college or university level that want to augment the class by offering thought provoking and educational essays about AI and self-driving cars.

In particular, here are some aspects for class use:

- Computer Science. Studying AI, autonomous vehicles, etc.
- Business. Exploring technology and it adoption for business.
- Sociology. Sociological views on the adoption and advancement of technology.

Specialized classes at the undergraduate and graduate level can also make use of this material.

For each chapter, consider whether you think the chapter provides material relevant to your course topic. There is plenty of opportunity to get the students thinking about the topic and force them to decide whether they agree or disagree with the points offered and positions taken. I would also encourage you to have the students do additional research beyond the chapter material presented (I provide next some suggested assignments they can do).

RESEARCH ASSIGNMENTS ON THESE TOPICS

Your students can find background material on these topics, doing so in various business and technical publications. I list below the top ranked AI related journals. For business publications, I would suggest the usual culprits such as the Harvard Business Review, Forbes, Fortune, WSJ, and the like.

Here are some suggestions of homework or projects that you could assign to students:

a) Assignment for foundational AI research topic: Research and prepare a paper and a presentation on a specific aspect of Deep AI, Machine Learning, ANN, etc. The paper should cite at least 3 reputable sources. Compare and contrast to what has been stated in this book.

b) Assignment for the Self-Driving Car topic: Research and prepare a paper and Self-Driving Cars. Cite at least 3 reputable sources and analyze the characterizations. Compare and contrast to what has been stated in this book.

c) Assignment for a Business topic: Research and prepare a paper and a presentation on businesses and advanced technology. What is hot, and what is not? Cite at least 3 reputable sources. Compare and contrast to the depictions in this book.

d) Assignment to do a Startup: Have the students prepare a paper about how they might startup a business in this realm. They must submit a sound Business Plan for the startup. They could also be asked to present their Business Plan and so should also have a presentation deck to coincide with it.

You can certainly adjust the aforementioned assignments to fit to your particular needs and the class structure. You'll notice that I ask for 3 reputable cited sources for the paper writing based assignments. I usually steer students toward "reputable" publications, since otherwise they will cite some oddball source that has no credentials other than that they happened to write something and post it onto the Internet. You can define "reputable" in whatever way you prefer, for example some faculty think Wikipedia is not reputable while others believe it is reputable and allow students to cite it.

The reason that I usually ask for at least 3 citations is that if the student only does one or two citations they usually settle on whatever they happened to find the fastest. By requiring three citations, it usually seems to force them to look around, explore, and end-up probably finding five or more, and then whittling it down to 3 that they will actually use.

I have not specified the length of their papers, and leave that to you to tell the students what you prefer. For each of those assignments, you could end-up with a short one to two pager, or you could do a dissertation length paper. Base the length on whatever best fits for your class, and the credit amount of the assignment within the context of the other grading metrics you'll be using for the class.

I mention in the assignments that they are to do a paper and prepare a presentation. I usually try to get students to present their work. This is a good practice for what they will do in the business world. Most of the time, they will be required to prepare an analysis and present it. If you don't have the class time or inclination to have the students present, then you can of course cut out the aspect of them putting together a presentation.

If you want to point students toward highly ranked journals in AI, here's a list of the top journals as reported by *various citation counts sources* (this list changes year to year):

- Communications of the ACM
- Artificial Intelligence
- Cognitive Science
- IEEE Transactions on Pattern Analysis and Machine Intelligence
- Foundations and Trends in Machine Learning
- Journal of Memory and Language
- Cognitive Psychology
- Neural Networks
- IEEE Transactions on Neural Networks and Learning Systems
- IEEE Intelligent Systems
- Knowledge-based Systems

GUIDE TO USING THE CHAPTERS

For each of the chapters, I provide next some various ways to use the chapter material. You can assign the tasks as individual homework assignments, or the tasks can be used with team projects for the class. You can easily layout a series of assignments, such as indicating that the students are to do item "a" below for say Chapter 1, then "b" for the next chapter of the book, and so on.

a) What is the main point of the chapter and describe in your own words the significance of the topic,

b) Identify at least two aspects in the chapter that you agree with, and support your concurrence by providing at least one other outside researched item as support; make sure to explain your basis for disagreeing with the aspects,

c) Identify at least two aspects in the chapter that you disagree with, and support your disagreement by providing at least one other outside researched item as support; make sure to explain your basis for disagreeing with the aspects,

d) Find an aspect that was not covered in the chapter, doing so by conducting outside research, and then explain how that aspect ties into the chapter and what significance it brings to the topic,

e) Interview a specialist in industry about the topic of the chapter, collect from them their thoughts and opinions, and readdress the chapter by citing your source and how they compared and contrasted to the material,

f) Interview a relevant academic professor or researcher in a college or university about the topic of the chapter, collect from them their thoughts and opinions, and readdress the chapter by citing your source and how they compared and contrasted to the material,

g) Try to update a chapter by finding out the latest on the topic, and ascertain whether the issue or topic has now been solved or whether it is still being addressed, explain what you come up with.

The above are all ways in which you can get the students of your class involved in considering the material of a given chapter. You could mix things up by having one of those above assignments per each week, covering the chapters over the course of the semester or quarter.

As a reminder, here are the chapters of the book and you can select whichever chapters you find most valued for your particular class:

Chapter Title
1 Eliot Framework for AI Self-Driving Cars
2 Move Over and Self-Driving Cars
3 Crossing Chicken and Self-Driving Cars
4 Code Breaches and Self-Driving Cars
5 Car Paint Colors and Self-Driving Cars
6 Bait Cars and Self-Driving Cars
7 Jinxes and Self-Driving Cars
8 Bouldering and Self-Driving Cars
9 Drivers Speeding and Self-Driving Cars
10 Snitch On Drivers and Self-Driving Cars
11 Reprogramming Pedestrians and Self-Driving Cars
12 Points Of Failure and Self-Driving Cars
13 Minecraft and Self-Driving Cars
14 Add-on Options and Self-Driving Cars
15 Car Pile-Ups and Self-Driving Cars
16 Crossing Guards and Self-Driving Cars
17 Driving Robots and Self-Driving Cars
18 Rain Driving and Self-Driving Cars
19 Stop Signs and Self-Driving Cars
20 Cloud and Autonomous Vehicles
21 Opposition to Self-Driving Cars
22 Neophyte Testimonials and Self-Driving Cars
23 Verbal Commands and Self-Driving Cars
24 Computer Chip Shortages and Self-Driving Cars
25 Chasing Dogs and Self-Driving Cars
26 Rolling House and Self-Driving Cars
27 Multi-Clouds and Autonomous Vehicles
28 Steep Hills and Self-Driving Cars
29 Bootstrapping and Self-Driving Cars
30 Teenage Drivers and Self-Driving Cars

Companion Book By This Author

Advances in AI and Autonomous Vehicles: Cybernetic Self-Driving Cars

Practical Advances in Artificial Intelligence (AI) and Machine Learning

by

Dr. Lance B. Eliot, MBA, PhD

Chapter Title

1 Genetic Algorithms for Self-Driving Cars
2 Blockchain for Self-Driving Cars
3 Machine Learning and Data for Self-Driving Cars
4 Edge Problems at Core of True Self-Driving Cars
5 Solving the Roundabout Traversal Problem for SD Cars
6 Parallel Parking Mindless Task for SD Cars: Step It Up
7 Caveats of Open Source for Self-Driving Cars
8 Catastrophic Cyber Hacking of Self-Driving Cars
9 Conspicuity for Self-Driving Cars
10 Accident Scene Traversal for Self-Driving Cars
11 Emergency Vehicle Awareness for Self-Driving Cars
12 Are Left Turns Right for Self-Driving Cars
13 Going Blind: When Sensors Fail on Self-Driving Cars
14 Roadway Debris Cognition for Self-Driving Cars
15 Avoiding Pedestrian Roadkill by Self-Driving Cars
16 When Accidents Happen to Self-Driving Cars
17 Illegal Driving for Self-Driving Cars
18 Making AI Sense of Road Signs
19 Parking Your Car the AI Way
20 Not Fast Enough: Human Factors in Self-Driving Cars
21 State of Government Reporting on Self-Driving Cars
22 The Head Nod Problem for Self-Driving Cars
23 CES Reveals Self-Driving Car Differences

This title is available via Amazon and other book sellers

Companion Book By This Author

Self-Driving Cars:
"The Mother of All AI Projects"

by Dr. Lance B. Eliot, MBA, PhD

Chapter Title

1 Grand Convergence Explains Rise of Self-Driving Cars
2 Here is Why We Need to Call Them Self-Driving Cars
3 Richter Scale for Levels of Self-Driving Cars
4 LIDAR as Secret Sauce for Self-Driving Cars
5 Pied Piper Approach to SD Car-Following
6 Sizzle Reel Trickery for AI Self-Driving Car Hype
7 Roller Coaster Public Perception of Self-Driving Cars
8 Brainless Self-Driving Shuttles Not Same as SD Cars
9 First Salvo Class Action Lawsuits for Defective SD Cars
10 AI Fake News About Self-Driving Cars
11 Rancorous Ranking of Self-Driving Cars
12 Product Liability for Self-Driving Cars
13 Humans Colliding with Self-Driving Cars
14 Elderly Boon or Bust for Self-Driving Cars
15 Simulations for Self-Driving Cars: Machine Learning
16 DUI Drunk Driving by Self-Driving Cars
17 Ten Human-Driving Foibles: Deep Learning
18 Art of Defensive Driving is Key to Self-Driving Cars
19 Cyclops Approach to AI Self-Driving Cars is Myopic
20 Steering Wheel Gets Self-Driving Car Attention
21 Remote Piloting is a Self-Driving Car Crutch
22 Self-Driving Cars: Zero Fatalities, Zero Chance
23 Goldrush: Self-Driving Car Lawsuit Bonanza Ahead
24 Road Trip Trickery for Self-Driving Trucks and Cars
25 Ethically Ambiguous Self-Driving Car

This title is available via Amazon and other book seller

Companion Book By This Author

Innovation and Thought Leadership on Self-Driving Driverless Cars

by Dr. Lance B. Eliot, MBA, PhD

Chapter Title

1 Sensor Fusion for Self-Driving Cars
2 Street Scene Free Space Detection Self-Driving Cars
3 Self-Awareness for Self-Driving Cars
4 Cartographic Trade-offs for Self-Driving Cars
5 Toll Road Traversal for Self-Driving Cars
6 Predictive Scenario Modeling for Self-Driving Cars
7 Selfishness for Self-Driving Cars
8 Leap Frog Driving for Self-Driving Cars
9 Proprioceptive IMU's for Self-Driving Cars
10 Robojacking of Self-Driving Cars
11 Self-Driving Car Moonshot and Mother of AI Projects
12 Marketing of Self-Driving Cars
13 Are Airplane Autopilots Same as Self-Driving Cars
14 Savvy Self-Driving Car Regulators: Marc Berman
15 Event Data Recorders (EDR) for Self-Driving Cars
16 Looking Behind You for Self-Driving Cars
17 In-Car Voice Commands NLP for Self-Driving Cars
18 When Self-Driving Cars Get Pulled Over by a Cop
19 Brainjacking Neuroprosthetus Self-Driving Cars

This title is available via Amazon and other book sellers

Companion Book By This Author

New Advances in AI Autonomous Driverless Cars Self-Driving Cars

by Dr. Lance B. Eliot, MBA, PhD

Chapter Title

1 Eliot Framework for AI Self-Driving Cars
2 Self-Driving Cars Learning from Self-Driving Cars
3 Imitation as Deep Learning for Self-Driving Cars
4 Assessing Federal Regulations for Self-Driving Cars
5 Bandwagon Effect for Self-Driving Cars
6 AI Backdoor Security Holes for Self-Driving Cars
7 Debiasing of AI for Self-Driving Cars
8 Algorithmic Transparency for Self-Driving Cars
9 Motorcycle Disentanglement for Self-Driving Cars
10 Graceful Degradation Handling of Self-Driving Cars
11 AI for Home Garage Parking of Self-Driving Cars
12 Motivational AI Irrationality for Self-Driving Cars
13 Curiosity as Cognition for Self-Driving Cars
14 Automotive Recalls of Self-Driving Cars
15 Internationalizing AI for Self-Driving Cars
16 Sleeping as AI Mechanism for Self-Driving Cars
17 Car Insurance Scams and Self-Driving Cars
18 U-Turn Traversal AI for Self-Driving Cars
19 Software Neglect for Self-Driving Cars

This title is available via Amazon and other book sellers

Companion Book By This Author

Introduction to Driverless Self-Driving Cars

by Dr. Lance B. Eliot, MBA, PhD

Chapter Title

1 Self-Driving Car Moonshot: Mother of All AI Projects
2 Grand Convergence Leads to Self-Driving Cars
3 Why They Should Be Called Self-Driving Cars
4 Richter Scale for Self-Driving Car Levels
5 LIDAR for Self-Driving Cars
6 Overall Framework for Self-Driving Cars
7 Sensor Fusion is Key for Self-Driving Cars
8 Humans Not Fast Enough for Self-Driving Cars
9 Solving Edge Problems of Self-Driving Cars
10 Graceful Degradation for Faltering Self-Driving Cars
11 Genetic Algorithms for Self-Driving Cars
12 Blockchain for Self-Driving Cars
13 Machine Learning and Data for Self-Driving Cars
14 Cyber-Hacking of Self-Driving Cars
15 Sensor Failures in Self-Driving Cars
16 When Accidents Happen to Self-Driving Cars
17 Backdoor Security Holes in Self-Driving Cars
18 Future Brainjacking for Self-Driving Cars
19 Internationalizing Self-Driving Cars
20 Are Airline Autopilots Same as Self-Driving Cars
21 Marketing of Self-Driving Cars
22 Fake News about Self-Driving Cars
23 Product Liability for Self-Driving Cars
24 Zero Fatalities Zero Chance for Self-Driving Cars
25 Road Trip Trickery for Self-Driving Cars
26 Ethical Issues of Self-Driving Cars
27 Ranking of Self-Driving Cars
28 Induced Demand Driven by Self-Driving Cars

This title is available via Amazon and other book sellers

Companion Book By This Author

Autonomous Vehicle Driverless Self-Driving Cars and Artificial Intelligence

by Dr. Lance B. Eliot, MBA, PhD

Chapter Title

1 Eliot Framework for AI Self-Driving Cars
2 Rocket Man Drivers and AI Self-Driving Cars
3 Occam's Razor Crucial for AI Self-Driving Cars
4 Simultaneous Local/Map (SLAM) for Self-Driving Cars
5 Swarm Intelligence for AI Self-Driving Cars
6 Biomimicry and Robomimicry for Self-Driving Cars
7 Deep Compression/Pruning for AI Self-Driving Cars
8 Extra-Scenery Perception for AI Self-Driving Cars
9 Invasive Curve and AI Self-Driving Cars
10 Normalization of Deviance and AI Self-Driving Cars
11 Groupthink Dilemma for AI Self-Driving Cars
12 Induced Demand Driven by AI Self-Driving Cars
13 Compressive Sensing for AI Self-Driving Cars
14 Neural Layer Explanations for AI Self-Driving Cars
15 Self-Adapting Resiliency for AI Self-Driving Cars
16 Prisoner's Dilemma and AI Self-Driving Cars
17 Turing Test and AI Self-Driving Cars
18 Support Vector Machines for AI Self-Driving Cars
19 "Expert Systems and AI Self-Driving Cars" by Michael Eliot

This title is available via Amazon and other book sellers

Companion Book By This Author

Transformative Artificial Intelligence Driverless Self-Driving Cars

by Dr. Lance B. Eliot, MBA, PhD

Chapter Title

1 Eliot Framework for AI Self-Driving Cars

2 Kinetosis Anti-Motion Sickness for Self-Driving Cars

3 Rain Driving for Self-Driving Cars

4 Edge Computing for Self-Driving Cars

5 Motorcycles as AI Self-Driving Vehicles

6 CAPTCHA Cyber-Hacking and Self-Driving Cars

7 Probabilistic Reasoning for Self-Driving Cars

8 Proving Grounds for Self-Driving Cars

9 Frankenstein and AI Self-Driving Cars

10 Omnipresence for Self-Driving Cars

11 Looking Behind You for Self-Driving Cars

12 Over-The-Air (OTA) Updating for Self-Driving Cars

13 Snow Driving for Self-Driving Cars

14 Human-Aided Training for Self-Driving Cars

15 Privacy for Self-Driving Cars

16 Transduction Vulnerabilities for Self-Driving Cars

17 Conversations Computing and Self-Driving Cars

18 Flying Debris and Self-Driving Cars

19 Citizen AI for Self-Driving Cars

This title is available via Amazon and other book sellers

Companion Book By This Author

Disruptive Artificial Intelligence and Driverless Self-Driving Cars

by Dr. Lance B. Eliot, MBA, PhD

Chapter Title

1 Eliot Framework for AI Self-Driving Cars

2 Maneuverability and Self-Driving Cars

3 Common Sense Reasoning and Self-Driving Cars

4 Cognition Timing and Self-Driving Cars

5 Speed Limits and Self-Driving Vehicles

6 Human Back-up Drivers and Self-Driving Cars

7 Forensic Analysis Uber and Self-Driving Cars

8 Power Consumption and Self-Driving Cars

9 Road Rage and Self-Driving Cars

10 Conspiracy Theories and Self-Driving Cars

11 Fear Landscape and Self-Driving Cars

12 Pre-Mortem and Self-Driving Cars

13 Kits and Self-Driving Cars

This title is available via Amazon and other book sellers

Companion Book By This Author

State-of-the-Art
AI Driverless Self-Driving Cars

by Dr. Lance B. Eliot, MBA, PhD

Chapter Title

1 Eliot Framework for AI Self-Driving Cars

2 Versioning and Self-Driving Cars

3 Towing and Self-Driving Cars

4 Driving Styles and Self-Driving Cars

5 Bicyclists and Self-Driving Vehicles

6 Back-up Cams and Self-Driving Cars

7 Traffic Mix and Self-Driving Cars

8 Hot-Car Deaths and Self-Driving Cars

9 Machine Learning Performance and Self-Driving Cars

10 Sensory Illusions and Self-Driving Cars

11 Federated Machine Learning and Self-Driving Cars

12 Irreproducibility and Self-Driving Cars

13 In-Car Deliveries and Self-Driving Cars

This title is available via Amazon and other book sellers

Companion Book By This Author

Top Trends in AI Self-Driving Cars

by Dr. Lance B. Eliot, MBA, PhD

Chapter Title

1 Eliot Framework for AI Self-Driving Cars

2 Responsibility and Self-Driving Cars

3 Changing Lanes and Self-Driving Cars

4 Procrastination and Self-Driving Cars

5 NTSB Report and Tesla Car Crash

6 Start Over AI and Self-Driving Cars

7 Freezing Robot Problem and Self-Driving Cars

8 Canarying and Self-Driving Cars

9 Nighttime Driving and Self-Driving Cars

10 Zombie-Cars Taxes and Self-Driving Cars

11 Traffic Lights and Self-Driving Cars

12 Reverse Engineering and Self-Driving Cars

13 Singularity AI and Self-Driving Cars

This title is available via Amazon and other book sellers

Companion Book By This Author

AI Innovations
and Self-Driving Cars

by Dr. Lance B. Eliot, MBA, PhD

Chapter Title

1 Eliot Framework for AI Self-Driving Cars

2 API's and Self-Driving Cars

3 Egocentric Designs and Self-Driving Cars

4 Family Road Trip and Self-Driving Cars

5 AI Developer Burnout and Tesla Car Crash

6 Stealing Secrets About Self-Driving Cars

7 Affordability and Self-Driving Cars

8 Crossing the Rubicon and Self-Driving Cars

9 Addicted to Self-Driving Cars

10 Ultrasonic Harm and Self-Driving Cars

11 Accidents Contagion and Self-Driving Cars

12 Non-Stop 24x7 and Self-Driving Cars

13 Human Life Spans and Self-Driving Cars

This title is available via Amazon and other book sellers

Companion Book By This Author

Crucial Advances for AI Self-Driving Cars

by Dr. Lance B. Eliot, MBA, PhD

Chapter Title

1 Eliot Framework for AI Self-Driving Cars

2 Ensemble Learning and AI Self-Driving Cars

3 Ghost in AI Self-Driving Cars

4 Public Shaming of AI Self-Driving

5 Internet of Things (IoT) and AI Self-Driving Cars

6 Personal Rapid Transit (RPT) and Self-Driving Cars

7 Eventual Consistency and AI Self-Driving Cars

8 Mass Transit Future and AI Self-Driving Cars

9 Coopetition and AI Self-Driving Cars

10 Electric Vehicles (EVs) and AI Self-Driving Cars

11 Dangers of In-Motion AI Self-Driving Cars

12 Sports Cars and AI Self-Driving Cars

13 Game Theory and AI Self-Driving Cars

This title is available via Amazon and other book sellers

Companion Book By This Author

Sociotechnical Insights and AI Driverless Cars

by Dr. Lance B. Eliot, MBA, PhD

Chapter Title

1 Eliot Framework for AI Self-Driving Cars

2 Start-ups and AI Self-Driving Cars

3 Code Obfuscation and AI Self-Driving Cars

4 Hyperlanes and AI Self-Driving Cars

5 Passenger Panic Inside an AI Self-Driving Car

6 Tech Stockholm Syndrome and Self-Driving Cars

7 Paralysis and AI Self-Driving Cars

8 Ugly Zones and AI Self-Driving Cars

9 Ridesharing and AI Self-Driving Cars

10 Multi-Party Privacy and AI Self-Driving Cars

11 Chaff Bugs and AI Self-Driving Cars

12 Social Reciprocity and AI Self-Driving Cars

13 Pet Mode and AI Self-Driving Cars

This title is available via Amazon and other book sellers

Companion Book By This Author

Pioneering Advances for AI Driverless Cars

by Dr. Lance B. Eliot, MBA, PhD

Chapter Title

1 Eliot Framework for AI Self-Driving Cars

2 Boxes on Wheels and AI Self-Driving Cars

3 Clogs and AI Self-Driving Cars

4 Kids Communicating with AI Self-Driving Cars

5 Incident Awareness and AI Self-Driving Car

6 Emotion Recognition and Self-Driving Cars

7 Rear-End Collisions and AI Self-Driving Cars

8 Autonomous Nervous System and AI Self-Driving Cars

9 Height Warnings and AI Self-Driving Cars

10 Future Jobs and AI Self-Driving Cars

11 Car Wash and AI Self-Driving Cars

12 5G and AI Self-Driving Cars

13 Gen Z and AI Self-Driving Cars

This title is available via Amazon and other book sellers

Companion Book By This Author

Leading Edge Trends for AI Driverless Cars

by Dr. Lance B. Eliot, MBA, PhD

Chapter Title

1 Eliot Framework for AI Self-Driving Cars

2 Pranking and AI Self-Driving Cars

3 Drive-Thrus and AI Self-Driving Cars

4 Overworking on AI Self-Driving Cars

5 Sleeping Barber Problem and AI Self-Driving Cars

6 System Load Balancing and AI Self-Driving Cars

7 Virtual Spike Strips and AI Self-Driving Cars

8 Razzle Dazzle Camouflage and AI Self-Driving Cars

9 Rewilding of AI Self-Driving Cars

10 Brute Force Algorithms and AI Self-Driving Cars

11 Idle Moments and AI Self-Driving Cars

12 Hurricanes and AI Self-Driving Cars

13 Object Visual Transplants and AI Self-Driving Cars

Companion Book By This Author

The Cutting Edge of AI Autonomous Cars

by Dr. Lance B. Eliot, MBA, PhD

Chapter Title

1 Eliot Framework for AI Self-Driving Cars

2 Driving Controls and AI Self-Driving Cars

3 Bug Bounty and AI Self-Driving Cars

4 Lane Splitting and AI Self-Driving Cars

5 Drunk Drivers versus AI Self-Driving Cars

6 Internal Naysayers and AI Self-Driving Cars

7 Debugging and AI Self-Driving Cars

8 Ethics Review Boards and AI Self-Driving Cars

9 Road Diets and AI Self-Driving Cars

10 Wrong Way Driving and AI Self-Driving Cars

11 World Safety Summit and AI Self-Driving Cars

This title is available via Amazon and other book sellers

Companion Book By This Author

The Next Wave of AI Self-Driving Cars

by Dr. Lance B. Eliot, MBA, PhD

Chapter Title

1 Eliot Framework for AI Self-Driving Cars

2 Productivity and AI Self-Driving Cars

3 Blind Pedestrians and AI Self-Driving Cars

4 Fail-Safe AI and AI Self-Driving Cars

5 Anomaly Detection and AI Self-Driving Cars

6 Running Out of Gas and AI Self-Driving Cars

7 Deep Personalization and AI Self-Driving Cars

8 Reframing the Levels of AI Self-Driving Cars

9 Cryptojacking and AI Self-Driving Cars

This title is available via Amazon and other book sellers

Companion Book By This Author

Revolutionary Innovations of AI Self-Driving Cars

by Dr. Lance B. Eliot, MBA, PhD

Chapter Title

1 Eliot Framework for AI Self-Driving Cars

2 Exascale Supercomputer and AI Self-Driving Cars

3 Superhuman AI and AI Self-Driving Cars

4 Olfactory e-Nose Sensors and AI Self-Driving Cars

5 Perpetual Computing and AI Self-Driving Cars

6 Byzantine Generals Problem and AI Self-Driving Cars

7 Driver Traffic Guardians and AI Self-Driving Cars

8 Anti-Gridlock Laws and AI Self-Driving Cars

9 Arguing Machines and AI Self-Driving Cars

This title is available via Amazon and other book sellers

Companion Book By This Author

AI Self-Driving Cars
Breakthroughs

by Dr. Lance B. Eliot, MBA, PhD

Chapter Title

1 Eliot Framework for AI Self-Driving Cars

2 Off-Roading and AI Self-Driving Cars

3 Paralleling Vehicles and AI Self-Driving Cars

4 Dementia Drivers and AI Self-Driving Cars

5 Augmented Realty (AR) and AI Self-Driving Cars

6 Sleeping Inside an AI Self-Driving Car

7 Prevalence Detection and AI Self-Driving Cars

8 Super-Intelligent AI and AI Self-Driving Cars

9 Car Caravans and AI Self-Driving Cars

This title is available via Amazon and other book sellers

Companion Book By This Author

Trailblazing Trends for
AI Self-Driving Cars

by Dr. Lance B. Eliot, MBA, PhD

Chapter Title

1 Eliot Framework for AI Self-Driving Cars

2 Strategic AI Metaphors and AI Self-Driving Cars

3 Emergency-Only AI and AI Self-Driving Cars

4 Animal Drawn Vehicles and AI Self-Driving Cars

5 Chess Play and AI Self-Driving Cars

6 Cobots Exoskeletons and AI Self-Driving Car

7 Economic Commodity and AI Self-Driving Cars

8 Road Racing and AI Self-Driving Cars

This title is available via Amazon and other book sellers

Companion Book By This Author

Ingenious Strides for
AI Driverless Cars

by Dr. Lance B. Eliot, MBA, PhD

Chapter Title

1 Eliot Framework for AI Self-Driving Cars

2 Plasticity and AI Self-Driving Cars

3 NIMBY vs. YIMBY and AI Self-Driving Cars

4 Top Trends for 2019 and AI Self-Driving Cars

5 Rural Areas and AI Self-Driving Cars

6 Self-Imposed Constraints and AI Self-Driving Car

7 Alien Limb Syndrome and AI Self-Driving Cars

8 Jaywalking and AI Self-Driving Cars

This title is available via Amazon and other book sellers

Companion Book By This Author

AI Self-Driving Cars Inventiveness

by Dr. Lance B. Eliot, MBA, PhD

Chapter Title

1 Eliot Framework for AI Self-Driving Cars

2 Crumbling Infrastructure and AI Self-Driving Cars

3 e-Billboarding and AI Self-Driving Cars

4 Kinship and AI Self-Driving Cars

5 Machine-Child Learning and AI Self-Driving Cars

6 Baby-on-Board and AI Self-Driving Car

7 Cop Car Chases and AI Self-Driving Cars

8 One-Shot Learning and AI Self-Driving Cars

This title is available via Amazon and other book sellers

Companion Book By This Author

Visionary Secrets of
AI Driverless Cars

by Dr. Lance B. Eliot, MBA, PhD

Chapter Title

1 Eliot Framework for AI Self-Driving Cars

2 Seat Belts and AI Self-Driving Cars

3 Tiny EV's and AI Self-Driving Cars

4 Empathetic Computing and AI Self-Driving Cars

5 Ethics Global Variations and AI Self-Driving Cars

6 Computational Periscopy and AI Self-Driving Car

7 Superior Cognition and AI Self-Driving Cars

8 Amalgamating ODD's and AI Self-Driving Cars

This title is available via Amazon and other book sellers

Companion Book By This Author

Spearheading AI Self-Driving Cars

by Dr. Lance B. Eliot, MBA, PhD

Chapter Title

1 Eliot Framework for AI Self-Driving Cars

2 Artificial Pain and AI Self-Driving Cars

3 Stop-and-Frisks and AI Self-Driving Cars

4 Cars Careening and AI Self-Driving Cars

5 Sounding Out Car Noises and AI Self-Driving Cars

6 No Speed Limit Autobahn and AI Self-Driving Car

7 Noble Cause Corruption and AI Self-Driving Cars

8 AI Rockstars and AI Self-Driving Cars

This title is available via Amazon and other book sellers

Companion Book By This Author

Spurring AI Self-Driving Cars

by Dr. Lance B. Eliot, MBA, PhD

Chapter Title

1 Eliot Framework for AI Self-Driving Cars

2 Triune Brain Theory and AI Self-Driving Cars

3 Car Parts Thefts and AI Self-Driving Cars

4 Goto Fail Bug and AI Self-Driving Cars

5 Scrabble Understanding and AI Self-Driving Cars

6 Cognition Disorders and AI Self-Driving Car

7 Noise Pollution Abatement AI Self-Driving Cars

This title is available via Amazon and other book sellers

Companion Book By This Author

Avant-Garde
AI Driverless Cars

by Dr. Lance B. Eliot, MBA, PhD

Chapter Title

1 Eliot Framework for AI Self-Driving Cars

2 Linear Non-Threshold and AI Self-Driving Cars

3 Prediction Equation and AI Self-Driving Cars

4 Modular Autonomous Systems and AI Self-Driving Cars

5 Driver's Licensing and AI Self-Driving Cars

6 Offshoots and Spinoffs and AI Self-Driving Car

7 Depersonalization and AI Self-Driving Cars

Companion Book By This Author

AI Self-Driving Cars Evolvement

by Dr. Lance B. Eliot, MBA, PhD

Chapter Title

1 Eliot Framework for AI Self-Driving Cars

2 Chief Safety Officers and AI Self-Driving Cars

3 Bounded Volumes and AI Self-Driving Cars

4 Micro-Movements Behaviors and AI Self-Driving Cars

5 Boeing 737 Aspects and AI Self-Driving Cars

6 Car Controls Commands and AI Self-Driving Car

7 Multi-Sensor Data Fusion and AI Self-Driving Cars

Companion Book By This Author

AI Driverless Cars Chrysalis

by Dr. Lance B. Eliot, MBA, PhD

Chapter Title

1 Eliot Framework for AI Self-Driving Cars
2 Object Poses and AI Self-Driving Cars
3 Human In-The-Loop and AI Self-Driving Cars
4 Genius Shortage and AI Self-Driving Cars
5 Salvage Yards and AI Self-Driving Cars
6 Precision Scheduling and AI Self-Driving Car
7 Human Driving Extinction and AI Self-Driving Cars

This title is available via Amazon and other book sellers

Companion Book By This Author

Boosting
AI Autonomous Cars

by Dr. Lance B. Eliot, MBA, PhD

Chapter Title

1 Eliot Framework for AI Self-Driving Cars

2 Zero Knowledge Proofs and AI Self-Driving Cars

3 Active Shooter Response and AI Self-Driving Cars

4 Free Will and AI Self-Driving Cars

5 No Picture Yet of AI Self-Driving Cars

6 Boeing 737 Lessons and AI Self-Driving Cars

7 Preview Tesla FSD and AI Self-Driving Cars

8 LIDAR Industry and AI Self-Driving Cars

9 Uber IPO and AI Self-Driving Cars

10 Suing Automakers of AI Self-Driving Cars

11 Tesla Overarching FSD and AI Self-Driving Cars

12 Auto Repair Market and AI Self-Driving Cars

This title is available via Amazon and other book sellers

<u>Companion Book By This Author</u>

AI Self-Driving Cars
Trendsetting

by Dr. Lance B. Eliot, MBA, PhD

<u>Chapter Title</u>

1 Eliot Framework for AI Self-Driving Cars
2 OTA Myths and AI Self-Driving Cars
3 Surveys and AI Self-Driving Cars
4 Tech Spies and AI Self-Driving Cars
5 Anxieties and AI Self-Driving Cars
6 Achilles Heel and AI Self-Driving Cars
7 Kids Alone and AI Self-Driving Cars
8 Infrastructure and AI Self-Driving Cars
9 Distracted Driving and AI Self-Driving Cars
10 Human Drivers and AI Self-Driving Cars
11 Anti-LIDAR Stance and AI Self-Driving Cars
12 Autopilot Team and AI Self-Driving Cars
13 Rigged Videos and AI Self-Driving Cars
14 Stalled Cars and AI Self-Driving Cars
15 Princeton Summit and AI Self-Driving Cars
16 Brittleness and AI Self-Driving Cars
17 Mergers and AI Self-Driving Cars

This title is available via Amazon and other book sellers

Companion Book By This Author

AI Autonomous Cars
Forefront

by Dr. Lance B. Eliot, MBA, PhD

Chapter Title

1 Eliot Framework for AI Self-Driving Cars
2 Essential Stats and AI Self-Driving Cars
3 Stats Fallacies and AI Self-Driving Cars
4 Driver Bullies and AI Self-Driving Cars
5 Sunday Drives and AI Self-Driving Cars
6 Face Recog Bans and AI Self-Driving Cars
7 States On-The-Hook and AI Self-Driving Cars
8 Sensors Profiting and AI Self-Driving Cars
9 Unruly Riders and AI Self-Driving Cars
10 Father's Day and AI Self-Driving Cars
11 Summons Feature and AI Self-Driving Cars
12 Libra Cryptocurrency and AI Self-Driving Cars
13 Systems Naming and AI Self-Driving Cars
14 Mid-Traffic Rendezvous and AI Self-Driving Cars
15 Pairing Drones and AI Self-Driving Cars
16 Lost Wallet Study and AI Self-Driving Cars

This title is available via Amazon and other book sellers

Companion Book By This Author

AI Autonomous Cars
Emergence

by Dr. Lance B. Eliot, MBA, PhD

Chapter Title

1 Eliot Framework for AI Self-Driving Cars
2 Dropping Off Riders and AI Self-Driving Cars
3 Add-On Kits Drive.AI and AI Self-Driving Cars
4 Boeing 737 Emergency Flaw and AI Self-Driving Cars
5 Spinout Tesla Autopilot and AI Self-Driving Cars
6 Earthquakes and AI Self-Driving Cars
7 Ford Mobility Lab and AI Self-Driving Cars
8 Apollo 11 Error Code and AI Self-Driving Cars
9 Nuro Self-Driving Vehicle and AI Self-Driving Cars
10 Safety First (SaFAD) Aptiv and AI Self-Driving Cars
11 Brainjacking Neuralink and AI Self-Driving Cars
12 Storming Area 51 and AI Self-Driving Cars
13 Riding Inside An AI Self-Driving Car
14 ACES Acronym and AI Self-Driving Cars
15 Kids Bike Riding and AI Self-Driving Cars
16 LIDAR Not Doomed and AI Self-Driving Cars

This title is available via Amazon and other book sellers

Companion Book By This Author

AI Autonomous Cars Progress

by Dr. Lance B. Eliot, MBA, PhD

Chapter Title

1 Eliot Framework for AI Self-Driving Cars
2 Risk-O-Meters and AI Self-Driving Cars
3 Eroding Car Devotion and AI Self-Driving Cars
4 Drunk Driving Rises With Smart Cars
5 Driver's Difficulties and Smart Cars
6 Millennials Aren't As Car Crazed As Baby Boomers
7 Risks Of AI Self-Driving Cars
8 Major Phase Shift and AI Self-Driving Cars
9 Level 3 Tech Misgivings For Smart Cars
10 Presidential Debate Lessons and AI Self-Driving Cars
11 Cloud Breeches and AI Self-Driving Cars
12 The Moral Imperative and AI Self-Driving Cars
13 Freed Up Driver Time And AI Self-Driving Car
14 Deadliest Highways and AI Self-Driving Cars
15 Your Lyin' Eyes and AI Self-Driving Cars
16 Elon Musk Physics Mindset and AI Self-Driving Cars

This title is available via Amazon and other book sellers

Companion Book By This Author

AI Self-Driving Cars
Prognosis

by Dr. Lance B. Eliot, MBA, PhD

Chapter Title

1 Eliot Framework for AI Self-Driving Cars
2 Roadkill and AI Self-Driving Cars
3 Safe Driver Cities and AI Self-Driving Cars
4 Tailgate Parties and AI Self-Driving Cars
5 Tesla's AI Chips and AI Self-Driving Cars
6 Elites-Only and AI Self-Driving Cars
7 Four Year Lifecycle and AI Self-Driving Cars
8 Entrepreneurs and AI Self-Driving Cars
9 Autopilot Crash Lessons and AI Self-Driving Cars
10 U.N. Framework and AI Self-Driving Cars
11 Sports Cars and AI Self-Driving Cars
12 Railroad Crossings and AI Self-Driving Cars
13 Robots That Drive and AI Self-Driving Car
14 Smarts Over Speed and AI Self-Driving Cars
15 Havoc Ratings and AI Self-Driving Cars
16 Sex-on-Wheels and AI Self-Driving Cars

Companion Book By This Author

AI Self-Driving Cars Momentum

by Dr. Lance B. Eliot, MBA, PhD

Chapter Title

1 Eliot Framework for AI Self-Driving Cars
2 Solving Loneliness and AI Self-Driving Cars
3 Headless Issues and AI Self-Driving Cars
4 Roaming Empty and AI Self-Driving Cars
5 Millennials Exodus and AI Self-Driving Cars
6 Recession Worries and AI Self-Driving Cars
7 Remote Operation Issues and AI Self-Driving Cars
8 Boomerang Kids and AI Self-Driving Cars
9 Waymo Coming To L.A. and AI Self-Driving Cars
10 Getting To Scale and AI Self-Driving Cars
11 Looking Alike and AI Self-Driving Cars
12 NOVA Documentary On AI Self-Driving Cars
13 Birthrate Changes and AI Self-Driving Cars

This title is available via Amazon and other book sellers

Companion Book By This Author

AI Self-Driving Cars
Headway

by Dr. Lance B. Eliot, MBA, PhD

Chapter Title

1 Eliot Framework for AI Self-Driving Cars

2 Germs Spreading and AI Self-Driving Cars

3 Carbon Footprint and AI Self-Driving Cars

4 Protestors Use Of AI Self-Driving Cars

5 Rogue Behavior and AI Self-Driving Cars

6 Using Human Drivers Versus AI Self-Driving Cars

7 Tesla Hodge-Podge On AI Self-Driving Cars

8 Solo Occupancy and AI Self-Driving Cars

9 Einstein's Twins Paradox and AI Self-Driving Cars

10 Nation-State Takeover Of AI Self-Driving Cars

11 Quantum Computers and AI Self-Driving Cars

12 Religious Revival And AI Self-Driving Cars

This title is available via Amazon and other book sellers

Companion Book By This Author

AI Self-Driving Cars
Vicissitude

by Dr. Lance B. Eliot, MBA, PhD

Chapter Title

1 Eliot Framework for AI Self-Driving Cars

2 Leaving A Tip and AI Self-Driving Cars

3 Digital Nudging and AI Self-Driving Cars

4 Carpool Lanes and AI Self-Driving Cars

5 Sleep Solving and AI Self-Driving Cars

6 Nostradamus and AI Self-Driving Cars

7 Advanced Driving and AI Self-Driving Cars

8 Cybertruck Windows Shattered Mystery

9 Artificial Stupidity and AI Self-Driving Cars

10 Revenue Estimates Of AI Self-Driving Cars

11 Survivalists and AI Self-Driving Cars

This title is available via Amazon and other book sellers

Companion Book By This Author

AI Self-Driving Cars
Autonomy

by Dr. Lance B. Eliot, MBA, PhD

Chapter Title

1 Eliot Framework for AI Self-Driving Cars

2 Your Bucket List and AI Self-Driving Cars

3 Highway Stunts and AI Self-Driving Cars

4 Future Wonderment and AI Self-Driving Cars

5 AI On-The-Fly Learning and AI Self-Driving Cars

6 Level 4 and Level 5 of AI Self-Driving Cars

7 Explaining Key Acronyms of AI Self-Driving Cars

8 Walmart Edge Computing and AI Self-Driving Cars

9 Stonehenge Lessons and AI Self-Driving Cars

10 Levels of Autonomy Feud and AI Self-Driving Cars

11 Hide and Escape Via AI Self-Driving Cars

This title is available via Amazon and other book sellers

Companion Book By This Author

AI Driverless Cars Transmutation

by Dr. Lance B. Eliot, MBA, PhD

Chapter Title

1 Eliot Framework for AI Self-Driving Cars
2 Backup Drivers and AI Self-Driving Cars
3 Teaching Kids about AI Self-Driving Cars
4 Hand-off Problem and AI Self-Driving Cars
5 Racial Bias and AI Self-Driving Cars
6 AI Consciousness and AI Self-Driving Cars
7 Machine Learning Riddles and AI Self-Driving Cars
8 Spurring Financial Literacy via AI Self-Driving Cars
9 GM Cruise Minivan and AI Self-Driving Cars
10 Car Off Cliff Lessons and AI Self-Driving Cars
11 Daughter Prank and AI Self-Driving Cars

This title is available via Amazon and other book sellers

Companion Book By This Author

AI Driverless Cars Potentiality

by Dr. Lance B. Eliot, MBA, PhD

Chapter Title

1 Eliot Framework for AI Self-Driving Cars

2 Russian Values and AI Self-Driving Cars

3 Friendships Uplift and AI Self-Driving Cars

4 Dogs Driving and AI Self-Driving Cars

5 Hypodermic Needles and AI Self-Driving Cars

6 Sharing Self-Driving Tech Is Not Likely

7 Uber Driver "Kidnapper" Is Self-Driving Car Lesson

8 Gender Driving Biases In AI Self-Driving Cars

9 Slain Befriended Dolphins Are Self-Driving Car Lesson

10 Analysis Of AI In Government Report

11 Mobility Frenzy and AI Self-Driving Cars

This title is available via Amazon and other book sellers

Companion Book By This Author

AI Driverless Cars Realities

by Dr. Lance B. Eliot, MBA, PhD

Chapter Title

1 Eliot Framework for AI Self-Driving Cars

2 Non-Driving Robots and AI Self-Driving Cars

3 HealthTech and AI Self-Driving Cars

4 Rudest Drivers and AI Self-Driving Cars

5 Aliens On Earth and AI Self-Driving Cars

6 AI Human Rights and AI Self-Driving Cars

7 Pope's AI Ethics and AI Self-Driving Cars

8 Human Judgment and AI Self-Driving Cars

9 DoD AI Ethics and AI Self-Driving Cars

10 Group Dynamics and AI Self-Driving Cars

11 Medical Emergencies Inside AI Self-Driving Cars

This title is available via Amazon and other book sellers

Companion Book By This Author

AI Self-Driving Cars
Materiality

by Dr. Lance B. Eliot, MBA, PhD

Chapter Title

1 Eliot Framework for AI Self-Driving Cars

2 Baby Sea Lion and AI Self-Driving Cars

3 Traffic Lights and AI Self-Driving Cars

4 Roadway Edge Computing and AI Self-Driving Cars

5 Ground Penetrating Radar and AI Self-Driving Cars

6 Upstream Parable and AI Self-Driving Cars

7 Red-Light Auto-Stopping and Self-Driving Cars

8 Falseness of Superhuman AI Self-Driving Cars

9 Social Distancing and AI Self-Driving Cars

10 Apollo 13 Lessons and AI Self-Driving Cars

11 FutureLaw and AI Self-Driving Cars

This title is available via Amazon and other book sellers

Companion Book By This Author

AI Self-Driving Cars
Accordance

by Dr. Lance B. Eliot, MBA, PhD

Chapter Title

1 Eliot Framework for AI Self-Driving Cars

2 Regulatory Scapegoating and AI Self-Driving Cars

3 Trust Beliefs and AI Self-Driving Cars

4 Post-Pandemic Era and AI Self-Driving Cars

5 Debating The Future and AI Self-Driving Cars

6 Purposeless Driving and AI Self-Driving Cars

7 AI Dimwitted Trickery and AI Self-Driving Cars

8 Dangerous Roads and AI Self-Driving Cars

9 UFO Videos and AI Self-Driving Cars

10 AI Cannot Be An Inventor and AI Self-Driving Cars

11 AI Benefiting Humanity and AI Self-Driving Cars

This title is available via Amazon and other book sellers

Companion Book By This Author

AI Self-Driving Cars
Equanimity

by Dr. Lance B. Eliot, MBA, PhD

Chapter Title

1 Eliot Framework for AI Self-Driving Cars

2 AI Oligopolies and AI Self-Driving Cars

3 AI Intent and AI Self-Driving Cars

4 "Life On Wheels" Film and AI Self-Driving Cars

5 Murder Hornet Spread and AI Self-Driving Cars

6 Simons Sight Research and AI Self-Driving Cars

7 NASCAR Car Racing and AI Self-Driving Cars

8 Ballot Harvesting and AI Self-Driving Cars

9 Apollo 12 Lessons and AI Self-Driving Cars

10 Running Over Shooter and AI Self-Driving Cars

11 Grimes Soul Selling and AI Self-Driving Cars

12 Cyber-Hackers Make Money and AI Self-Driving Cars

This title is available via Amazon and other book sellers

Companion Book By This Author

AI Self-Driving Cars Divulgement

by Dr. Lance B. Eliot, MBA, PhD

Chapter Title

1 Eliot Framework for AI Self-Driving Cars

2 Discovering Intelligent Life and AI Self-Driving Cars

3 Pizza Deliveries Mystery and AI Self-Driving Cars

4 Provably Beneficial AI and AI Self-Driving Cars

5 City Streets Paintings and AI Self-Driving Cars

6 Cops Shooting At Vehicles and AI Self-Driving Cars

7 US Federal Testing Log and AI Self-Driving Cars

8 Drive-By Shootings and AI Self-Driving Cars

9 AI Ethics Knobs and AI Self-Driving Cars

10 Mighty Dust Storm and AI Self-Driving Cars

11 Amazon Buys Zoox and AI Self-Driving Cars

12 Tesla With LIDAR and AI Self-Driving Cars

13 Autopilot BK Whopper and AI Self-Driving Cars

14 Fireworks Celebrations and AI Self-Driving Cars

This title is available via Amazon and other book sellers

Companion Book By This Author

AI Self-Driving Cars
Consonance

by Dr. Lance B. Eliot, MBA, PhD

Chapter Title

1 Eliot Framework for AI Self-Driving Cars

2 Baby Yoda on Hoods Life and AI Self-Driving Cars

3 Ugliest Cars Looks and AI Self-Driving Cars

4 MacGyver Shrewdness and AI Self-Driving Cars

5 Strong vs Weak AI and AI Self-Driving Cars

6 Trolley Problem and AI Self-Driving Cars

7 Evasive Maneuvering and AI Self-Driving Cars

8 Movie Miscasting AI and AI Self-Driving Cars

9 Snakes In A Car and AI Self-Driving Cars

10 Cognitive Tests and AI Self-Driving Cars

11 Lightning Strikes and AI Self-Driving Cars

12 Neanderthal DNA and AI Self-Driving Cars

13 Plane Lands on Highway and AI Self-Driving Cars

14 Turing Test and AI Self-Driving Cars

This title is available via Amazon and other book sellers

Companion Book By This Author

Revelatory AI Self-Driving Cars

by Dr. Lance B. Eliot, MBA, PhD

Chapter Title

1 Eliot Framework for AI Self-Driving Cars
2 Congestion-Free Pipedream of Self-Driving Cars
3 Demolition Derby of Self-Driving Cars
4 AI Intelligence Explosion and Self-Driving Cars
5 AI Truthteller and Self-Driving Cars
6 Drive-In Theatres and Self-Driving Cars
7 AI Mind-Copying and Self-Driving Cars
8 Mental Wayfinding and Self-Driving Cars
9 Automated Machine Learning and Self-Driving Cars
10 Fast AI Ethics and Self-Driving Cars
11 I Think Therefore I Am and Self-Driving Cars
12 AI Politeness and Self-Driving Cars
13 Income by Sharing Self-Driving Cars
14 Mand on Hood and Self-Driving Cars
15 Puddles and Self-Driving Cars
16 Unhinged and Self-Driving Cars
17 Reversibility and Self-Driving Cars
18 Driving Nude and Self-Driving Cars
19 Towing of Self-Driving Cars
20 Consumer Reports and Full Self-Driving
21 Tire Blowouts and Self-Driving Cars
22 Wildfire Smoke and Self-Driving Cars
23 Crabwalk Mode and Self-Driving Cars
24 Dangerous Month and Self-Driving Cars
25 AI Apologies and Self-Driving Cars
26 Hawaii Testing and Self-Driving Cars
27 Too Many Objects and Self-Driving Cars
28 Halloween Issues and Self-Driving Cars
29 AI Chitchat and Self-Driving Cars
30 Game of Go and Self-Driving Cars

This title is available via Amazon and other book sellers

Companion Book By This Author

Edifying AI Self-Driving Cars

by Dr. Lance B. Eliot, MBA, PhD

Chapter Title
1 Eliot Framework for AI Self-Driving Cars
2 Steering Wheels and Self-Driving Cars
3 Hit-and-Run and Self-Driving Cars
4 Red Stop Button and Self-Driving Cars
5 Unaware Crashes and Self-Driving Cars
6 Paying Riders in Self-Driving Cars
7 Roadschooling Kids and Self-Driving Cars
8 Drug Mules and Self-Driving Cars
9 Zipper Merging and Self-Driving Cars
10 Daylight Savings and Self-Driving Cars
11 Near Misses and Self-Driving Cars
12 Tree Falls and Self-Driving Cars
13 Investments in Self-Driving Cars
14 Bothering Neighbors and Self-Driving Cars
15 Ice Cream Trucks and Self-Driving Cars
16 Parking Head-In and Self-Driving Cars
17 Barking Commands at Self-Driving Cars
18 How Am I Driving and Self-Driving Cars
19 No Parking In Red and Self-Driving Cars
20 Tailgating of Self-Driving Cars
21 Tullock Spikes and Self-Driving Cars
22 Vacation Homes and Self-Driving Cars
23 Car Buying Experiences and Self-Driving Cars
24 Asimov's Laws and Self-Driving Cars
25 Knowing Vs Telling and Self-Driving Cars
26 Snow Buried and Self-Driving Cars
27 Cyber Hack and Self-Driving Cars
28 Murder Cases and Self-Driving Cars
29 Pedestrian Misclassification and Self-Driving Cars
30 Scavenger Hunts and Self-Driving Cars

Companion Book By This Author

Apprising AI Driverless Cars

by Dr. Lance B. Eliot, MBA, PhD

Chapter Title

1 Eliot Framework for AI Self-Driving Cars
2 Move Over and Self-Driving Cars
3 Crossing Chicken and Self-Driving Cars
4 Code Breaches and Self-Driving Cars
5 Car Paint Colors and Self-Driving Cars
6 Bait Cars and Self-Driving Cars
7 Jinxes and Self-Driving Cars
8 Bouldering and Self-Driving Cars
9 Drivers Speeding and Self-Driving Cars
10 Snitch On Drivers and Self-Driving Cars
11 Reprogramming Pedestrians and Self-Driving Cars
12 Points Of Failure and Self-Driving Cars
13 Minecraft and Self-Driving Cars
14 Add-on Options and Self-Driving Cars
15 Car Pile-Ups and Self-Driving Cars
16 Crossing Guards and Self-Driving Cars
17 Driving Robots and Self-Driving Cars
18 Rain Driving and Self-Driving Cars
19 Stop Signs and Self-Driving Cars
20 Cloud and Autonomous Vehicles
21 Opposition to Self-Driving Cars
22 Neophyte Testimonials and Self-Driving Cars
23 Verbal Commands and Self-Driving Cars
24 Computer Chip Shortages and Self-Driving Cars
25 Chasing Dogs and Self-Driving Cars
26 Rolling House and Self-Driving Cars
27 Multi-Clouds and Autonomous Vehicles
28 Steep Hills and Self-Driving Cars
29 Bootstrapping and Self-Driving Cars
30 Teenage Drivers and Self-Driving Cars

This title is available via Amazon and other book sellers

ABOUT THE AUTHOR

Dr. Lance B. Eliot, Ph.D., MBA is a Stanford Fellow and a globally recognized AI expert and thought leader, an experienced executive and leader, a successful serial entrepreneur, and a noted scholar on AI, including that his Forbes and AI Trends columns have amassed over 4.5+ million views, his books on AI are frequently ranked in the Top 10 of all-time AI books, his articles are widely cited, and he has developed dozens of advanced AI systems.

He currently serves as the CEO of Techbruim, Inc. and has over twenty years of industry experience including serving as a corporate officer in billion-dollar sized firms and was a partner in a major consulting firm. He is also a successful entrepreneur having founded, ran, and sold several high-tech firms.

Dr. Eliot previously hosted the popular radio show *Technotrends* that was also available on American Airlines flights via their in-flight audio program, he has made appearances on CNN, has been a frequent speaker at industry conferences, and his podcasts have been downloaded over 100,000 times.

A former professor at the University of Southern California (USC), he founded and led an innovative research lab on Artificial Intelligence. He also previously served on the faculty of the University of California Los Angeles (UCLA) and was a visiting professor at other major universities. He was elected to the International Board of the Society for Information Management (SIM), a prestigious association of over 3,000 high-tech executives worldwide.

He has performed extensive community service, including serving as Senior Science Adviser to the Congressional Vice-Chair of the Congressional Committee on Science & Technology. He has served on the Board of the OC Science & Engineering Fair (OCSEF), where he is also has been a Grand Sweepstakes judge, and likewise served as a judge for the Intel International SEF (ISEF). He served as the Vice-Chair of the Association for Computing Machinery (ACM) Chapter, a prestigious association of computer scientists. Dr. Eliot has been a shark tank judge for the USC Mark Stevens Center for Innovation on start-up pitch competitions and served as a mentor for several incubators and accelerators in Silicon Valley and in Silicon Beach.

Dr. Eliot holds a Ph.D. from USC, MBA, and Bachelor's in Computer Science, and earned the CDP, CCP, CSP, CDE, and CISA certifications.

ADDENDUM

Apprising AI Driverless Cars

Practical Advances in Artificial Intelligence (AI) and Machine Learning

By
Dr. Lance B. Eliot, MBA, PhD

For supplemental materials of this book, visit:

www.ai-selfdriving-cars.guru

For special orders of this book, contact:

LBE Press Publishing

Email: LBE.Press.Publishing@gmail.com

Made in the USA
Monee, IL
05 November 2026

67886766R00223